HOW THE HEARTLAND WENT RED

PRINCETON STUDIES IN
AMERICAN POLITICS

Historical, International, and Comparative Perspectives

Paul Frymer, Suzanne Mettler, and Eric Schickler,
Series Editors

Ira Katznelson, Martin Shefter, and Theda Skocpol,
Founding Series Editors

A list of titles in this series appears in the back of the book.

How the Heartland Went Red

WHY LOCAL FORCES MATTER IN AN AGE OF NATIONALIZED POLITICS

STEPHANIE TERNULLO

PRINCETON UNIVERSITY PRESS

PRINCETON & OXFORD

Published by Princeton University Press
41 William Street, Princeton, New Jersey 08540
99 Banbury Road, Oxford OX2 6JX

press.princeton.edu

Library of Congress Cataloging-in-Publication Data

Names: Ternullo, Stephanie, 1993– author.
Title: How the heartland went red : why local forces matter in an age of
    nationalized politics / Stephanie Ternullo.
Description: Princeton : Princeton University Press, [2024] | Series: Princeton
    studies in American politics: historical, international, and comparative
    perspectives | Includes bibliographical references and index.
Identifiers: LCCN 2023047497 (print) | LCCN 2023047498 (ebook) |
    ISBN 9780691249698 (hardback) | ISBN 9780691249704 (paperback) |
    ISBN 9780691249780 (ebook)
Subjects: LCSH: Political culture—Middle West—History—21st century. |
    Republican Party (U.S. : 1854–) | Social change—Middle West—History—
    21st century. | Political parties—Middle West—History—21st century. |
    Party affiliation—Middle West—History—21st century. | Middle West—
    Politics and government—History—21st century.
Classification: LCC JA75.7 .T48 2024 (print) | LCC JA75.7 (ebook) |
    DDC 306.20977—dc23/eng/20231201
LC record available at https://lccn.loc.gov/2023047497
LC ebook record available at https://lccn.loc.gov/2023047498

British Library Cataloging-in-Publication Data is available

Editorial: Bridget Flannery-McCoy and Alena Chekanov
Production Editorial: Nathan Carr
Jacket/Cover Design: Katie Osborne
Production: Lauren Reese
Publicity: William Pagdatoon

Jacket/Cover Credit: Shutterstock

This book has been composed in Arno

10 9 8 7 6 5 4 3 2 1

For the two people who made this book possible:
Linda Ternullo and Oliver Turner

CONTENTS

ILLUSTRATIONS

Figures

Tables

ACKNOWLEDGMENTS

BEFORE I STARTED GRADUATE SCHOOL, I envisioned research and writing as solitary endeavors; had I read other scholars' acknowledgments, I would have known how wrong that image was. This book is the result of intellectual and emotional support from dozens of people. Before I address my advisors and colleagues, I would like to thank several people who took me under their wing and made this research possible. First, to M and J, the two women who housed me in Lutherton and Gravesend with only my lackluster cooking and an occasional bottle of wine as compensation. Second, to A, A, M, and J, who introduced me to Motorville. In a place where I knew no one, they made me feel at home.

Before I could enter the field and meet those people, I had to develop an idea and propose it to my committee: Lis Clemens, my chair, and Eric Oliver, John Levi Martin, and Robert Vargas. I don't know whether any professional experience has scared me as much as defending my dissertation proposal in front of these four amazing social scientists. I was terrified not only because Lis, Eric, John, and Robert were some of my toughest critics as I developed this project but because I cared so deeply about their feedback.

John was one of the earliest believers in this project, and his confidence in its potential contribution gave me the push I needed to set out for fieldwork so early on in my graduate school career, after less than two years in the program. Throughout my time at the University of Chicago, Robert showed me what success as a junior scholar looked like, in terms of both the ambition and intellectual contributions of his work and the kind of faculty member and mentor he is. He believes in big projects that change social science and public policy, and it's infectious to have someone like that in your corner. Eric played a unique role in shepherding this project to completion: as the only political scientist on my committee, he convinced me not only that qualitative research has a place in the study of American political behavior but that *my* research and *this* book could have a place in the discipline as well. I still don't quite believe him, but I wouldn't be writing these acknowledgments from within a political science department if it weren't for him.

I owe my dearest thanks to Lis, who has provided me with a model of mentorship and intellectual rigor that I will carry with me throughout my career. She always encouraged my research ambitions and challenged me to produce the best piece of work I could. I don't mean this in a trite way: Lis all but physically dragged this book toward greater theoretical rigor, analytical precision, and writing clarity. I don't know any faculty member who reads their advisees' work as carefully as Lis does, and at such a volume. She saw every version of this book—all three chapterizations—as well as various articles from these data. As all of Lis's advisees know, her feedback is detailed and comprehensive. She'll note a misspelled word and comment on a sentence or paragraph that is unclear, then send a full-page response summarizing her reaction to a piece of writing. I knew absolutely nothing about doing a PhD when I first applied (and if I'd known everything I know now, I might have skipped it entirely), but I knew I wanted to work with Lis Clemens. Somehow, that little bit of intuition brought me to just the right place.

I also owe an immense debt of gratitude to several of my colleagues and friends at the University of Chicago, in particular: Ariel Azar, Simon Shachter, Anna Berg, Nisarg Mehta, and Yuchen Yang. Ariel, Simon, and Anna were there every step of the way as I developed this project and then struggled to reimagine it amid the isolation of the Covid-19 pandemic. I also submitted draft after draft of this material to Anna, along with Nisarg and Yuchen, as part of our biweekly writing group. I am so grateful to have developed this book with such trustworthy feedback.

This book has also benefited from my postgraduate school life: the input of my new colleagues in the Harvard Government Department and the attendees at a book workshop I held in December 2022. I still feel so lucky to have found such a welcoming and vibrant intellectual home in the Government Department, and I am especially grateful to my new colleagues across the university who attended my book workshop or provided comments on the manuscript: Steve Ansolabehere, Daniel Carpenter, Ryan Enos, Peter Hall, Jennifer Hochschild, Michèle Lamont, Taeku Lee, Naijia Liu, Liz McKenna, David Showalter, Theda Skocpol, Jim Snyder, and Elizabeth Thom.

I cannot say enough about how productive my book workshop was, because of both my colleagues who attended and those who traveled to Harvard to participate: Bart Bonikowski, Japonica Brown-Saracino, Andrea Campbell, Jeremy Levine, Lilliana Mason, and Daniel Schlozman. If you've already read this book, you'll know that their work makes up a good chunk of my Zotero list. I cite them repeatedly because I admire and hope to build on their work, so having them all in one room engaging so thoughtfully with a project this close to my heart was an incredible professional experience.

I would also like to thank my editors, Bridget Flannery-McCoy and Alena Chekanov, for soliciting such excellent reviews for the manuscript, and Eric Schickler for providing such thoughtful feedback as one of the series editors. If all peer review processes were as collegial and constructive as this one, I am convinced we would produce much more rigorous social science.

Finally, there is my family. My parents, Linda and Salvatore Ternullo, are the reason I was able to complete this project. They have been unwaveringly supportive since I chose to pursue a career in academia. Throughout the tumultuous and sometimes precarious-feeling years of graduate school, my dad has always been my rock. Knowing he's there makes me feel safe to take risks, including pursuing a PhD in the first place. I am dedicating this book to my mom, Linda, and my husband, Oliver Turner. My mom taught me that learning from others requires empathy and humility: that I shouldn't listen to gather munition for a counterargument but to understand. I hope I was able to embody this lesson in every conversation during my fieldwork. I hold my deepest gratitude for the partner I have in my husband. Oli moved from London to Chicago to make our relationship work and support my career, which didn't really feel like a career at the time. He then moved again, unhesitatingly, from Chicago to Boston so I could take my dream job at Harvard. I'll never be able to thank him enough for his generosity in those moments. But I owe this book as much to his gentle encouragement and support during every day of writing a dissertation during multiple national and personal crises. Thank you.

HOW THE HEARTLAND WENT RED

Introduction

IT'S LATE ON A SUMMER afternoon in 2019, and I'm heading to a bar in Motorville City, Wisconsin, to meet Arthur, the former chair of Motorville's Democratic Party and a retired machinist.[1] Motorville is an overwhelmingly White city of about 25,000 people, founded on blue-collar work. The bar is housed in a former supply depot for the railroad, and the interior still contains remnants of its past purpose—wooden benches against the wall by the entrance and wide, wooden planks that make up the floors—but there is now a bar to the right of the doorway, and a bandstand beyond that. Arthur has asked me to meet him here because, as he says, politics in Motorville happens at the bar. While he nurses a beer, Arthur tells me about his love for Elizabeth Warren, his desire to do away with the "old White guys" in politics (despite being one himself), and his experiences growing up in Motorville and being involved in local politics. As he summarizes the city's political leanings: "The whole town is blue. After the election . . . I get to see who votes where and how they vote. This whole city is blue. Some of it stronger than others." Arthur is right: statistically, Democrats are favored in Motorville City—Joe Biden won the city with over 59 percent of the vote in 2020, and a Republican has not won a presidential contest in the county since before the New Deal.

Arthur is also correct when he tells me that politics in Motorville happens at the bar: later that same day, he and I gather again with a group of about twenty Democrats of all ages, seated around a long table in a dimly lit room at the back of a different bar along Motorville's Main Street. It's the monthly Democratic Party meeting, and a young organizer named Johnny, sent from the state Democratic Party, begins the gathering with a call to arms: "This meeting is about how we're gonna beat Donald Trump in 2020." The room whoops and cheers on cue. Over the course of the following hour Johnny doles out organizing roles to the group, articulating a multifaceted local, state, and national strategy on the long road from June 2019 to November 2020.

Motorville's Democratic Party is energized, although occasionally argumentative and somewhat disorganized. Meanwhile, the local Republican Party is, for all intents and purposes, nowhere to be found. In fact, an email to the county GOP renders a response from the Congressional District Republican Party. Even local politicians who might be interested in organized Republican Party support cannot find it in Motorville. As Ed, a city councillor, told me:

> When Scott Walker [a Republican] was governor, he came to town. I saw nowhere that he was coming to town, and he went to a little restaurant. They had assigned a room probably for thirty people or so, and there were probably twenty people in there. The governor is in town and hardly anyone acknowledged. . . . Whereas Tony Evers [a Democrat] comes to town and there are hundreds of people.

As he concludes, the Motorville Republicans are almost like "a secret club."

And that's because Motorville is a Democratic city. Even as the Republican Party has slowly marched toward dominance in most White, postindustrial cities like Motorville, Motorville residents have continued to vote majority-Democratic at all levels of office.

Motorville's exceptionalism becomes even clearer a few weeks later when I travel to Lutherton, Indiana. A small city in a rural part of the state, Lutherton shares many similarities with Motorville. And in July 2019, the county fair is in full swing. Beyond the dirt lot full of games and attractions stand booth after booth with crawling lines of patrons in T-shirts and jean shorts, waiting for their homemade baked goods, fried pickles, and taco salads from the biggest churches and service sororities in the county. Just past the individual tents, long, narrow buildings are lined with further stands for businesses, nonprofits, and the local Democrat and Republican Parties.

The Republicans have a booth set up near the entrance to one of these buildings. It's a small space, but the walls are plastered with brightly colored signs displaying the names of every Republican candidate running for local office that fall. Lauren, the chair of Lutherton County's GOP, is working the booth with three other elected officials tonight—all middle-aged White women with blond hair and easy smiles. On either side of the booth stand cardboard cutouts of the country's top Republicans—Trump on the left and Pence on the right. As I sit with Lauren and the others for the evening, I occasionally have to duck out of the way as residents stop to take photos in front of the Trump cutout. But the booth's main attraction sits at the tall table in front: paper fans bearing the label "I'm a fan of the Republican Party." On a hot summer evening, they're both funny and practical. Between the Trump/Pence figures, the paper fans, and Lauren's near-encyclopedic knowledge of everyone who passes by, the booth is a popular stopping-off point.

Later in the evening, I go searching for the Democrats' "booth." It is also located near the entrance of one of the major buildings—but at first, I almost miss it. When I eventually do find Carolyn, the party's secretary, she's seated on a folding chair in front of a card table with one other woman. Both appear to be in their sixties. Behind them sits a sign proclaiming "Sondra for Mayor," and another with the label "Democrat," but the other scant decorations are all red-white-and-blue—patriotic rather than partisan. On top of the table sits a small bowl offering Dum Dum lollipops to visitors, and next to that they have two clipboards to register voters. It's a quiet booth, especially compared to the energy that Lauren and company bring to GOP territory.

Republicans have increasingly dominated local and national elections in Lutherton since the 1960s: not a single Democratic candidate won their race in the 2019 municipal elections, and Donald Trump carried the county with over 75 percent of the vote in 2020. As we can see, the Republican Party also dominates when it comes to local social life. Lutherton is, without question, a Republican city.

But in Gravesend, Minnesota—a city much like Motorville and Lutherton—the Democrats and Republicans offer a relatively equal show of force. Each week the parties trade off writing an opinion column in the local paper, and both can count on a sizable group of energized activists to show up at local events with petitions, knock on doors, and attend the quadrennial caucuses for presidential primaries. And in late summer 2019, they both rent out the same pavilion in a local park for their annual picnic, hosted just weeks apart.

In mid-August, the pavilion is decked out in GOP fanfare. It is a cavernous space, with a tall, peaked ceiling and ten round tables filling the room, each with the same centerpiece: two small American flags crossed over each other. A much larger flag, about twenty feet tall, stands at the front of the room, right behind the cardboard cutout of Donald Trump. Various smaller GOP signs adorn the walls, carrying campaign materials for local Republican candidates as well as the Trump/Pence ticket. There are also signs advertising Republican slogans such as "If you love your freedom, thank your veterans" and "GOP" in large letters above the words "Greatest Opportunity Party." A long table in the back is laden with barbecue from a local restaurant and a podium is set up at the front to host local politicians from state representative up to U.S. congressional representative. By the time the speeches commence, the tables have nearly filled up—there are about forty or fifty people in the room, including the politicians and some of their staff.

The Republican congressional representative for Gravesend is the last to speak. He talks about local issues as well as Democrats' extremist abortion and gun control legislation in the House, and then he shifts his tone: "Have you all seen the recent polls?" he asks. "Elizabeth Warren is surging," he says. A murmur of recognition ripples through the crowd. "And I would love for her to be the nominee," he continues, "because she's a socialist Democratic candidate if I ever saw one." Someone snorts in the front row. "And we don't want a socialist, because it will put our health care at risk. America has the highest-quality health care in the world. Now, it might not have the best delivery, but it does have the best quality. And Democrats' health-care plans will ruin that for us. If we switch to single-payer, reimbursement rates for rural hospitals will fall even further." Your rural health care will struggle even more than it does now, he tells them. Then he concludes his speech: "Let's fight not to become Venezuela!" And the crowd bursts into applause.

Just a couple of weeks later, a similar-sized crowd gathers in the same room. Although the local Democrats—in Minnesota, the Democratic-Farmer-Labor Party, or DFL—have far less decor, they have a similar slate of speakers, from local- to state- and federal-level politicians. The DFL picnic is a potluck—someone scoffs when I tell them the GOP paid to order barbecue—and the back table is similarly full of food. Once we've all filled our plates and taken our seats, George—the informal emcee of most local DFL events—takes up the mic and introduces the speakers.

The last of these is the Democratic candidate for the U.S. House of Representatives. Although the content of his speech is different from his Republican counterpart's, the message is the same: Gravesend is under threat, and only one party can save them. He begins by talking about the closure of a local agro-business that will cost the district several hundred jobs. "Do you know why that happened?" he asks the crowd. "For three reasons: it happened because of the tax breaks given to big corporations. Do you know where the corporation is headquartered?" He pauses for effect. "China." The crowd grumbles in displeasure. "And it happened because of an endless trade war," he continues. "And finally, it happened because the corporation that owned the plant could just do that overnight because the workers had no unions to represent them." When he concludes, the crowd erupts in cheers. The relatively equal shows of force by both parties in Gravesend hint at the decades during which residents favored Democrats and Republicans about equally—Gravesend was a classic swing city. But since 2016, residents have been swinging to the right, although for different reasons than in Lutherton: just over 52 percent of the city's two-party vote went to Donald Trump in 2020, and Republicans swept statewide offices.

———

As these snapshots indicate, Motorville, Lutherton, and Gravesend each has a different set of politics: Motorville votes majority-Democratic; Lutherton votes majority-Republican; and Gravesend has sat on the line in most presidential races until 2016, when it began favoring Republicans. And yet, at one point in history—during the New Deal era of the 1930s and 1940s—all three places were part of the national Democratic coalition. Moreover, all three cities are nearly identical on several dimensions that are considered important for electoral outcomes: they have long been overwhelmingly White, blue-collar, small cities of 16,000–28,000 people, whose employment today is concentrated in manufacturing, transportation, public sector, and service sector jobs. I refer to these cities as part of the "American Heartland," because they are archetypes of the largely White, postindustrial cities in the Midwest that were considered singularly important in shaping the outcome of the 2020 presidential race.[2] In sum, while the usual explanations—demographic composition, region, and size—cannot account for why Motorville, Lutherton, and Gravesend vote differently, understanding politics in places like them is central to American electoral outcomes.

This raises several questions: How have historic political and economic transformations produced a fractured response among the places that were once part of a working-class political coalition during the New Deal, sending Motorville, Lutherton, and Gravesend on different political trajectories? And how does place *still* produce a persistent tendency toward Democratic partisanship among Motorvillians, despite pulls toward the right that have attracted most other White, postindustrial places, including Lutherton and Gravesend? And finally, how can place-based political differences persist despite the increasing nationalization of American politics? These are the puzzles at the center of this book. My contention is that, by answering these questions about the past, present, and future of these three cities, we can also learn something new about White, postindustrial politics and how local contexts are still shaping the trajectory of American national politics today.

Over the course of eighteen months, from May 2019 through the November 2020 presidential election, I interviewed just over 175 residents and community leaders across Motorville, Lutherton, and Gravesend. Before the onset of the Covid-19 pandemic, I conducted nearly six months of fieldwork and interviewed more than 90 "community leaders"—elected officials, labor leaders, heads of nonprofits, pastors, and party activists—about the challenges their cities are facing and how they work to resolve them. But the book's core arguments come from four waves of interviews with 86 White "residents" across Motorville, Lutherton, and Gravesend, beginning in June 2019 and concluding just before the 2020 presidential election. I refer to these interviewees as "residents" because they are not formally involved in local politics or governance.[3]

This book builds from these conversations to explain why Motorville, Lutherton, and Gravesend defy both commonsense and social scientific expectations. It offers three answers to the puzzles laid out above. The first is about how the past shapes the present. Places are bounded geographies that are defined by their structural demographic and economic characteristics; the cultural meanings residents share from living in those conditions; and the organizations that link the two.[4] As part 1 shows, the structural, organizational, and cultural features that define Motorville, Lutherton, and Gravesend today are products of each city's path-dependent evolution in response to state and national transformations: when residents and community leaders respond to external shocks they shape the organizational and cultural materials that are available in the future. Over time, such decisions not only make distinct places; they also create the conditions in which residents make sense of changes in national party politics.[5] While Motorville, Lutherton, and Gravesend were not *identical* places during the 1930s and 1940s, they shared sufficient characteristics for their residents to favor the New Deal Democratic Party. But as the cities adapted differently to extra-local disruptions, they became distinct places that made residents more or less open to shifting party coalitions, ultimately sending each place on a different political trajectory.

The second answer is about place and politics in the present: not just *that* place matters for politics but *how* it helps sustain residents' partisanship today. I use the term *place-based partisanship* to refer to the portion of one's partisan identity that is explained by where they live. I argue that place-based partisanship emerges as residents make sense of local structural conditions and national politics from within their organizational contexts, leading them to cohere around two cultural frameworks: (1) *diagnostic frames* that they use to define their social problems and identify political solutions; and (2) *narratives of community identity* that describe what kind of community they are and where they fit into party politics. Place is just one of many factors that inform Americans' partisanship, but my argument is that it is particularly important among *cross-pressured* voters: people whose political loyalties are sought by both parties, like the White, working- and middle-class voters I study here.[6] Within the constraints of individuals' social group memberships and national party maneuvering, place makes it more likely that residents will adopt certain social and political identities.

How does this happen in practice? As part 2 shows, Lutherton's churches, nonprofits, and volunteers constitute a private but collective problem-solving arrangement that makes *visible* efforts to address emergent social problems. Residents learn that problems related to economic precarity—including hunger and homelessness—are "community challenges," to be resolved locally. Over time, local and nongovernmental solutions become commonsense, and residents tend toward a particular kind of communitarian anti-statism. Their ties to the Republican Party are reinforced by routine social interactions that remind them they are part of a White, Christian community; and the Republican Party is the party for them. By way of contrast, in Motorville ties among unions and elected officials ensure that community leaders define their challenges as rooted in systemic economic decline—the drain of good jobs—and focus residents' attention on the government as a vehicle for shaping economic outcomes. Here, in a community "built on the back of labor," residents imagine themselves as part of a group of Americans disadvantaged by an unequal system and look to the state and the Democratic Party to solve their problems. Gravesend, alone among the three cities, lacks a stable organizational context that helps residents agree on how to solve their problems. Losses mount without solutions, and residents feel their community's survival is threatened. As the Republican Party wields a language of immigration and socialism as twin threats to the (White) small-town way of life, it resonates with Gravesend residents. None of these place-based processes create a monolithic set of politics—each city votes *majority* Democratic or Republican in local, state, and national elections, suggesting that many, but not all, residents identify with that party—but place does produce a tendency toward certain ways of defining each community, what their problems are, and which political party best represents them.[7] In short, place helps shape residents' partisan attachments and reinforce them over time. And in Motorville, it leads residents to reject the many pulls that have succeeded in turning other, similar places toward the Republican Party.

This brings me to the book's third and final argument, which is about the future of place in American politics: will national crises, elite polarization, and fragmented media eventually erode place-based partisanship? Political scientist Daniel Hopkins (2018) has shown that forces like these have *nationalized* politics, pulling Americans out of their local environments and making even local elections about partisan divisions. But part 3 will argue that these factors are not likely to erode place-based partisanship because they do not destabilize local organizational contexts or cultural frameworks.[8] Chapter 6 shows how residents of Motorville, Lutherton, and Gravesend continued to deploy existing diagnostic frames to make sense of the federal government's role in their lives amid the economic fallout of the Covid-19 pandemic, because the crisis did not undermine local organizational contexts. And even as individuals consuming partisan news did polarize on the public health response to Covid-19, chapter 7 will show that this issue polarization was temporary and did not undermine the narratives of community identity that residents used to locate themselves within partisan politics. In fact, throughout my time studying these cities, residents routinely evoked the talking points prevalent in national media at the time of our conversations but forgot them when the spotlight moved on to other issues; in other words, polarization on national issues was somewhat epiphenomenal to the place-based processes that sustain partisan tendencies in Motorville, Lutherton, and Gravesend.

Figure 1 summarizes this three-part argument, showing how the structural, organizational, and cultural dimensions of place are the product of past responses to external shocks (figure 1a), productive of partisan ties today (figure 1b), and resilient to certain kinds of national disruptions (figure 1c). Each panel corresponds to one of the book's three parts.

Taken together, this book offers two contributions. First, my findings suggest that existing accounts of the Heartland's reddening are both correct and incomplete: it is an outcome produced not just through a realignment of political parties and social groups amid a racialized backlash by White voters; rather, it emerged in interaction with local processes that have slowed down or sped up these voters' move toward the right. My contention is that, as the two political parties craft racial-, religious-, and class-based appeals to win over White, working- and middle-class voters, those appeals will resonate differently in different places.[9] As we will see in Motorville, place helps prevent racial resentment from pushing White voters out of (what they see as) a multiracial working-class Democratic coalition. In contrast, Gravesend voters are starting to view the Democrats as the party that wields the government for the benefit

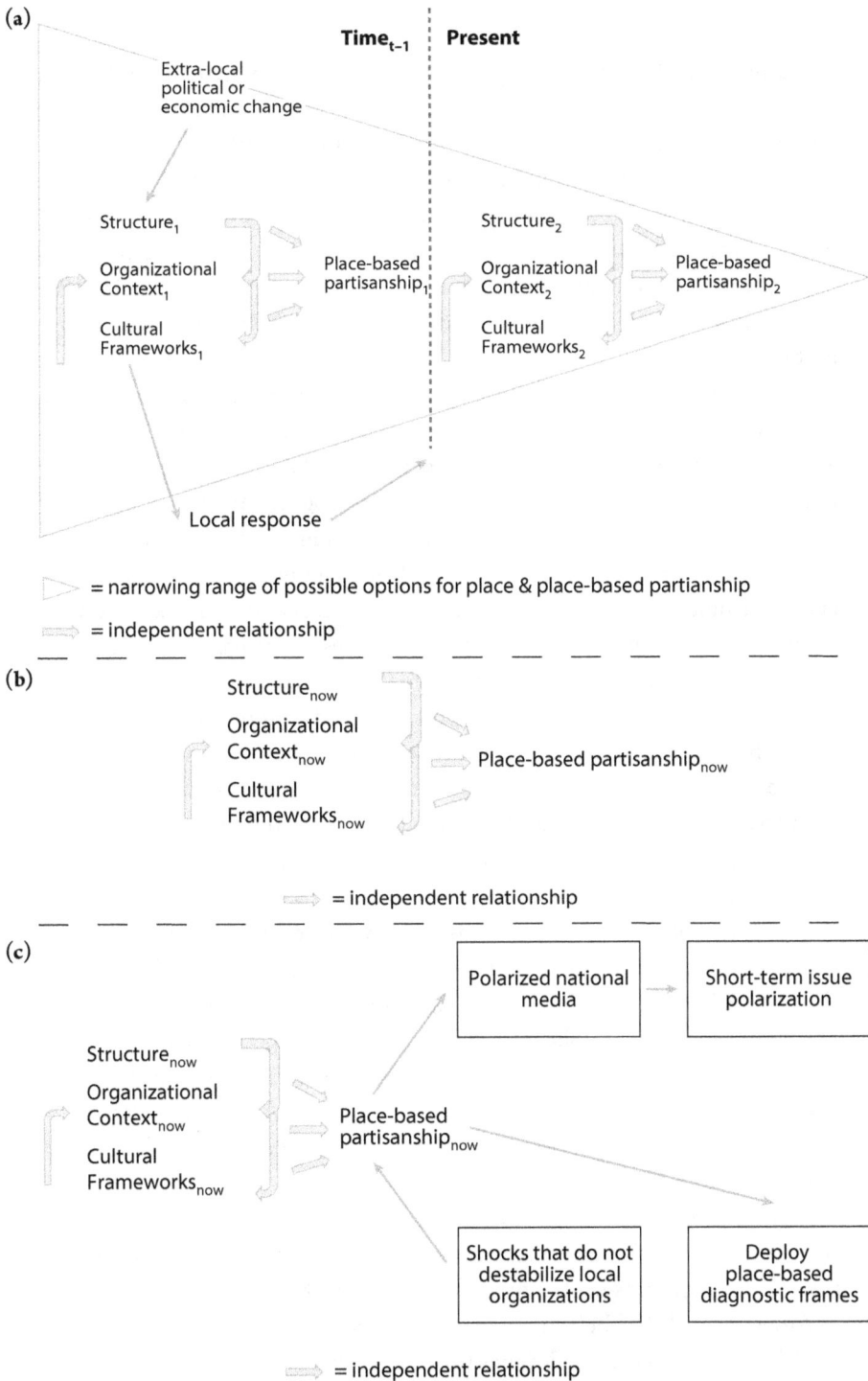

(a)

Time$_{t-1}$ | Present

Extra-local
political or
economic change

Structure$_1$

Organizational
Context$_1$

Place-based
partisanship$_1$

Cultural
Frameworks$_1$

Structure$_2$

Organizational
Context$_2$

Place-based
partisanship$_2$

Cultural
Frameworks$_2$

Local response

▷ = narrowing range of possible options for place & place-based partianship

⇨ = independent relationship

(b)

Structure$_{now}$

Organizational
Context$_{now}$

Place-based partisanship$_{now}$

Cultural
Frameworks$_{now}$

⇨ = independent relationship

(c)

Polarized national
media

Short-term issue
polarization

Structure$_{now}$

Organizational
Context$_{now}$

Place-based
partisanship$_{now}$

Cultural
Frameworks$_{now}$

Shocks that do not
destabilize local
organizations

Deploy
place-based
diagnostic frames

⇨ = independent relationship

FIGURE 1. The past, present, and future of place-based partisanship. **Figure 1a.**
How the past informs the present (Part I). **Figure 1b.** Place-based partisanship
in the present (Part II). **Figure 1c.** The (possible) future of place (Part III).

of immigrants, often at the expense of White voters like them. In Lutherton, race and religion both nudge residents into the Republican column, but here it is less about racial resentment than ethnoreligious identity, which leads Luthertonians to embrace Republicans as the party of White Christians.[10] These cases will show us that when we focus on macro- or micro-level accounts that privilege race, religion, *or* class as explanations of White, postindustrial politics, we miss the very sites in which voters are making sense of their social identities in a shifting political-economic terrain and figuring out which party best represents them.

Second, in showing *how* place shapes and sustains partisanship by guiding voters to the political party that best represents "people like them," I develop an argument that moves beyond White, postindustrial politics. In particular, my claim is that place will matter for partisanship among any Americans who *could* find representation in either of the parties—including Latinx, Asian, and new immigrant groups. In a world where people have a multiplicity of intersecting and overlapping group memberships, places help make certain identities more salient and then help residents link those identities to one party or the other.[11]

As such, this book's most ambitious goal is to revive and extend a contextual account of how partisan attachments form and endure. As the pioneers of survey-based voter studies noted in the 1940s and 1950s, Americans' relationship to their political party often persists for a lifetime.[12] Over the ensuing decades, researchers have developed an increasingly detailed portrait of the micro- and macro-level processes that shape and sustain partisan identities—how individuals develop social identities and how parties court social groups. But they have paid less attention to how everyday, contextual factors mediate between these processes. At the same time, researchers who have documented the links between contextual factors and other dimensions of political behavior—including public opinion, political participation, and intergroup hostility—have rarely extended these analyses to the study of partisan identity.[13] This book brings these two approaches together, arguing that place is among the contextual factors that inform partisan identity and that it is particularly relevant for cross-pressured voters.

Comparison across Motorville, Lutherton, and Gravesend will offer us insight into how social contexts return voters to their party, again and again, over time. This insight was central to the voter studies that helped found the field of American political behavior research, conducted by Paul Lazarsfeld, Bernard Berelson, and their colleagues from Columbia in the 1940s. According to them, partisanship endures in part because voters are part of social networks of similar people who interpret national politics for them and reinforce their political views.[14] This means that individuals' partisan attachments are rooted not just in social psychological processes but also in social-contextual ones.

This is the argument that I revive and advance in this book, adapting it for a twenty-first-century world in which voters are embedded in both local- and extra-local flows of information. The remainder of this chapter describes in greater detail how a study of these three cities will accomplish this, then situates my argument in the context of existing debates about the "reddening" of the American Heartland, and finally concludes by laying out the plan for the rest of the book.

Why Motorville, Lutherton, and Gravesend Can Tell Us Something New about Heartland Politics

Writing in 1969, Republican Party operative Kevin Phillips argued that Nixon's election signaled the beginning of a new "Republican Majority" that was "becoming much more lower-middle class and much less establishmentarian" (543). The GOP, he claimed, was the beneficiary of a political realignment around race, class, and geography, riding to victory on the backs of "a populist revolt of the American masses" in the South and West (550). Nearly forty years later, another political observer offered a similar argument, this time from a perspective that was critical of, rather than congratulatory toward, the Republican Party and their voters. In *What's the Matter with Kansas?* (2004) Thomas Frank argued that White working- and middle-class voters across the American Heartland had been swindled by Republican Party operatives who convinced them to vote against their economic interests in favor of cultural validation. And just a few years after Frank's writing, observers revived this same set of concerns about the Republican Party coalition in the run-up to the 2016 presidential election.[15]

The persistence of these questions alludes to their practical importance for American electoral outcomes. Although the United States is an increasingly urbanized, multiracial society, the politics of White voters in postindustrial towns and cities—particularly those in sparsely populated states—have an outsize impact on American elections because of the electoral college and the Senate.[16] Take, for example, Wyoming, the least populous state in the union, and California, the most populous state. In 2021, Wyoming had one U.S. senator for every 190,000 citizens and more than 80 percent of the population identified as White, Non-Hispanic on the U.S. Census. In California, where

Non-Hispanic Whites compose just under 35 percent of the population, each senator represents nearly 20 million citizens. In other words, Whites living in less-populous states are disproportionately important for national electoral outcomes, which means that it is also important to understand how they form partisan attachments amid the competing demands of both parties.

And as Phillips's and Frank's comments indicate, the question of whether these voters will vote with their class interests via the Democratic Party, or their racial (and religious, if they are Christian) interests via the Republican Party, has been a subject of concern among pundits and social scientists for decades. So why will this study of Motorville, Lutherton, and Gravesend be able to offer us new insight into this long-standing puzzle? My argument is that by examining political variation *within* White, postindustrial cities, we can better understand the role of race, class, and religion in the past and ongoing process of the Heartland's reddening. This logic informed the study's design: as a cross-city and over-time comparative study, grounded in in-depth interviews and contextualized with ethnographic observation, administrative data, and archival evidence.

But why these cities in particular? I arrived at Motorville, Lutherton, and Gravesend because I was interested in understanding how White, postindustrial politics today are rooted in national political and economic transformations since the New Deal. To do so, I needed cases with the *right kind of variation*: cities that have always been largely White and blue collar; that voted for FDR during the New Deal; but whose politics later diverged, such that only one still votes majority-Democratic today, one votes majority-Republican, and one is more of a "swing" city. I began by using historical census and voting data to identify all counties that could be considered part of the White, working-class, New Deal coalition and that have remained largely White and working-class to the present. This second constraint was important because I wanted to rule out demographic change as an explanation for political change: as political scientist Jonathan Rodden (2019) has shown, increasing racial heterogeneity is a key reason that many postindustrial cities and towns are still voting Democratic today. These criteria led me to 467 counties, shown in figure 2.

Next, I wanted to describe the different political trajectories that the New Deal counties took *after* the New Deal era. Although there is no clear date when New Deal politics "ended," I chose to focus on what happened after 1964, the year the Racial Realignment broke into national politics, as this was one of the first national ruptures in the New Deal coalition and posed a key challenge for White voters in particular.[17] I compiled the 467 New Deal counties' presidential vote shares from 1964 to 2016 and used a hierarchical clustering

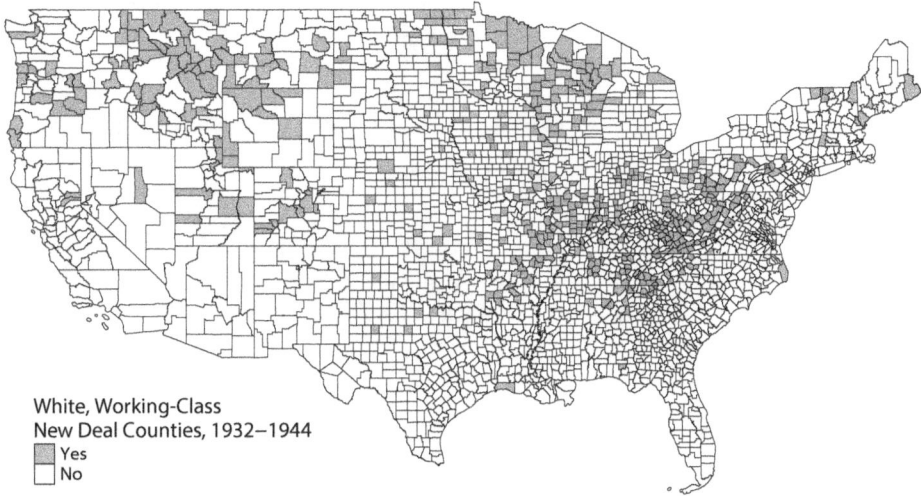

White, Working-Class
New Deal Counties, 1932–1944
☐ Yes
☐ No

FIGURE 2. Map of White, working-class New Deal counties. *Note:* Counties were coded 1 if they voted, on average, Democratic from 1932 to 1944; had third tercile employment (for all U.S. counties) in craftmen, operatives, or laborers occupations or in the manufacturing sector in the 1940 and 1950 census; had third tercile employment in construction, maintenance, transportation, or production occupations or the service sector from 2000 to 2016; and were more than 90 percent White in 1940 and remained more than 85 percent White and Non-Hispanic in 2016, according to the American Community Survey's five-year estimates.

algorithm to identify clusters of different voting behavior over that period.[18] I first found four clusters: two of the clusters, together containing 68 percent of the counties, began voting majority-Republican in 1968 after the Racial Realignment. This included Lutherton. The smallest cluster, representing 11 percent of the New Deal counties, began voting majority-Republican in 2000, after the political mobilization of the Christian Right. The mid-sized cluster, including 21 percent of the New Deal counties, remained reasonably competitive to Democrats through 2012/2016. Within this third group, I further identified one "swing" cluster that turned Republican in 2012/2016, a cluster that includes Gravesend; and one cluster that remained Democratic through the entire 1964–2016 period, a cluster that includes Motorville. This last cluster included just 4 percent of the original 467 New Deal counties.

Figure 3 summarizes the different political trajectories for the three clusters of which Motorville ("Stayed Democratic"), Lutherton ("Turned Republican, 1960s"), and Gravesend ("Lean Dem, Swing to Republican 2016") are a part.

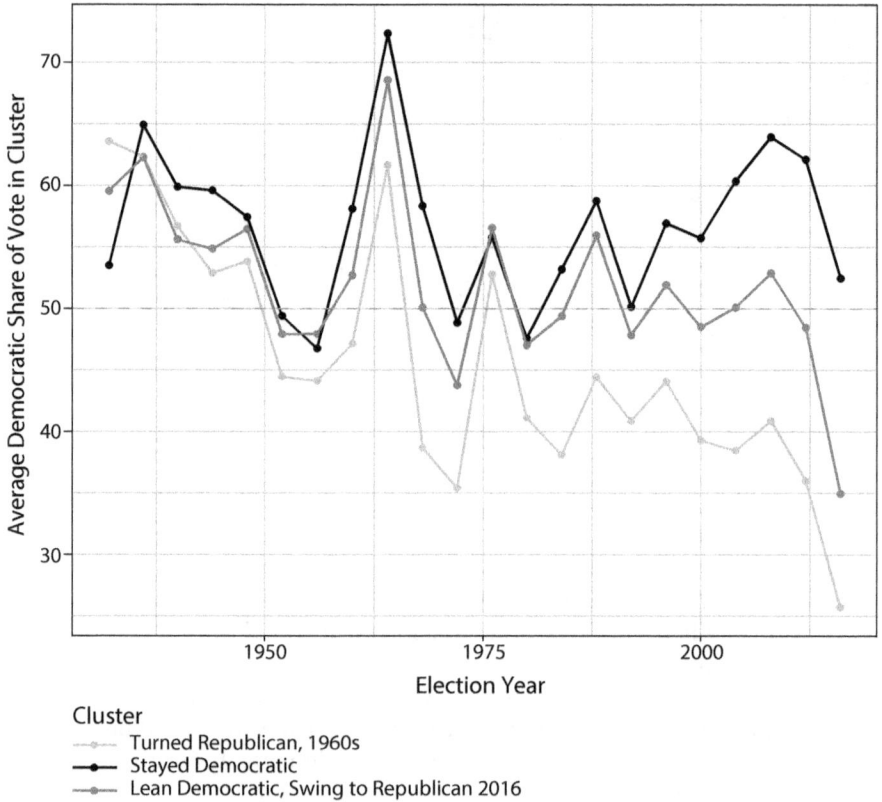

Cluster
- Turned Republican, 1960s
- Stayed Democratic
- Lean Democratic, Swing to Republican 2016

FIGURE 3. Presidential voting trajectories of former New Deal counties, 1932–2016. *Note:* The figure shows the average Democratic presidential vote share from 1932 to 2016 for all counties that were part of the same clusters as Motorville ("Stayed Democratic"); Lutherton ("Turned Republican, 1960s"); and Gravesend ("Lean Dem, Swing to Republican 2016").

The analyses that produced figure 3 provided exactly the kind of present-day variation, rooted in historical processes, that I wanted among my cases; but I still had over 200 counties from which to choose, and many more towns and cities within them. I further narrowed my focus to the Midwest, both to hold region constant and to study a region seen as critical to the outcome of the 2020 presidential election. Finally, I chose to focus on counties containing small cities of 10,000-30,000 residents. Amid growing rural-urban polarization, cities have a high probability of voting majority-Democratic, and rural areas have a high probability of voting majority-Republican. Smaller cities are somewhat more politically heterogeneous. As such, my argument is not limited to cities with fewer than 30,000 people; rather, I focused on cities of this size to identify cases where I could hold certain variables (demographics) constant, while allowing other variables (voting) to vary. At this point in the case selection process, I was somewhat agnostic about choosing my final cases, and I finally arrived at Motorville, Lutherton, and Gravesend with some amount of luck, as I detail further in the Methodological Appendix.

Based on these analyses, the overwhelming tendency among White, working-class, New Deal counties since the 1960s has been toward Republican voting; moreover, Lutherton and Gravesend each represent two distinct but relatively common pathways to that outcome. Motorville, in contrast, represents an exceptional case that bucks this trend: *a place where local processes have prevented White voters' defection from the Democratic Party*. I argue that by understanding this exceptional case we can also understand why the alternative outcome is more likely in other places, thus revealing how contemporary postindustrial politics has emerged from a point of interaction between national transformations and local contexts. And while this argument is about the political transformation of White, postindustrial cities across the country (per figure 2), it is particularly relevant for the "Heartland" region—states where U.S. manufacturing, unionization, and working-class political mobilization have historically been concentrated.[19]

The comparative cases are thus a key component of the study's research design, but it has two other important dimensions that will enable this book to shed new light on a long-standing puzzle: it is both longitudinal and qualitative. The spine of my argument comes from more than 400 interviews I conducted over the course of 18 months, including: four rounds of interviews with the same 86 residents between June 2019 and November 2020 (totaling more than 300); and 91 interviews with community leaders that took place largely during the summer and fall of 2019.[20] I also returned to each city in summer 2021 and reinterviewed a small subset of residents to see how they were faring under the Biden administration.

Before 2019 I had never heard of Motorville, Lutherton, or Gravesend. After choosing to go to those cities, my first informants were political party leaders and elected officials whom I contacted by email or social media. In Lutherton I stayed with the former Republican Party chair during my fieldwork, offering additional opportunities to chew over local politics at the end of each day. After these initial points of contact, I identified further local "opinion leaders"—local elites whose ideas are particularly influential—when I observed their activities at public events, when their names came up in interviews with other leaders, or when residents mentioned them as important to the community.[21]

To meet residents who were not involved in local politics, I used a variety of recruitment strategies: I posted flyers in popular places identified by community leaders and asked residents to advertise my study on local Facebook groups; I recruited strangers in person at public events, in bars, coffee shops, and the YMCA; and I asked my existing contacts to introduce me to their "least political" acquaintances. This combination of strategies proved useful because I heard from *both* the people who were interested in talking politics—they responded to my flyer or a Facebook post—and the people who typically prefer not to talk politics but were willing to do so because a friend vouched for me.[22] But even those who disliked talking politics typically participated in all four interviews over the course of a year and a half—in all, 80 percent of the people I first met in summer 2019 participated in four rounds of interviews with me, totaling about 4.5 hours of conversation each.[23]

You may wonder what kind of person was willing to speak with a stranger and an outsider about politics for so many months. Were they some bizarre subset of the public? Were they telling me the truth? Why would they trust a researcher from Chicago with their stories and political opinions? As I mentioned, some residents met with me initially out of a favor to a friend; some thought it would be nice to help a young student; for others, I wasn't that strange—a White woman raised in a small, overwhelmingly White town who attended a Catholic high school. And even though I remained an outsider to many—for example, that small town I grew up in was on the East Coast, synonymous with urbanity for many of my interviewees—I often didn't stay a stranger after hours of conversation, texts, and emails shared during a frightening national pandemic. In part because of this trust we built up over time, I do not think that people were lying to me, nor do I think they were shy about sharing their opinions. There are also several other reasons to support this conclusion. First and foremost, as I will discuss in chapter 7, there was a great deal of stability in the core concerns that residents shared with me over the course of our conversations. In other words, if they were lying, they were doing so with a remarkable degree of consistency. Second, people often began their responses by saying "I don't want to offend anyone, but . . ." and then went on to articulate an opinion that might offend many people. And finally, for many people, the "offensive" opinions they hold simply *aren't* offensive. People believe what they believe is right; and in a social context that supports this view, they are not shy about sharing those beliefs.

Although the kind of in-depth interviews I conducted are rarely used in studies of American political behavior, they are ideally suited for revealing patterns of meaning-making and the subjective interpretations that residents have about their social context.[24] But interviews cannot tell us the extent to which those perceptions are rooted in real features of residents' cities. In some ways, this doesn't matter for the political outcomes we're interested in here: just the fact that January 6 insurrectionists *thought* the 2020 presidential election was stolen led to an attempted coup d'état. But to understand *how* place shapes partisanship, I had to pin down the relationship between what is really happening in each place and the meaning that residents make from what's happening.[25]

To do this, I rely on a variety of other sources of data about Motorville, Lutherton, and Gravesend. During my in-person fieldwork, I took daily field-notes of my observations. Sometimes my notes consisted primarily of interview summaries; on other occasions, I attended City Council meetings, political party meetings, church services, or kaffeeklatsches. For three weeks in October/ November 2019 I cochaired the campaign of Lutherton's Democratic mayoral candidate. Along with a high school volunteer and the candidate, I canvassed, made phone calls, and attended public events. When this fieldwork was inter-rupted by the Covid-19 pandemic in March 2020 and I switched to phone and Skype interviews, I sought other sources of data about the cities to develop a clearer picture of the context I could no longer observe in-person.

First, I document the severity of social problems in each place and the organizational resources available to address those problems using county-level data on industrial output, public health and overdose rates, local govern-ment spending, local nonprofit revenues and assets, and church membership.[26] Second, I describe how the local information environment conveys both local and national issues to residents using two sources of data: the front and editorial pages from all three cities' local newspapers during the days preced-ing and following important national political events from 1932 to 2016;[27] public Facebook posts from local politicians—including, where available, from city councillors, county commissioners, all the way up to U.S. House of Representatives—from January to November 2020.[28]

These different sources of data were essential for developing the book's core arguments. As I analyzed the interview data, I saw that place mattered when I observed coherence within cities where I expected variation (particularly across lines of party affiliation and political knowledge) and when I observed differences between the cities where I expected coherence (particularly along demographic lines).[29] But to develop the argument about *how* places sustain partisanship, I triangulated among multiple sources of data to understand what it was about the local context that led to such unexpected patterns.[30]

The longitudinal interviews were a crucial piece of this process. For exam-ple, during my first interviews, I asked very open-ended questions that did not touch on social welfare or the appropriate role of the government. Even so, Lutherton residents often told me they preferred that churches rather than the federal government take care of social welfare provision—even if they didn't currently attend a church. This within-city coherence further stood out as surprising when I saw that Motorville and Gravesend residents rarely articulated similar beliefs unless they were actively involved in their own church or other civic associations. This suggested that churches were central to shaping residents' beliefs about the role of the state in Lutherton, and that church membership itself only explained part of this belief. After I identified these patterns through my analyses of the first-round interviews in winter 2019/2020, I developed more deductive questions to probe them during the second-round interviews: I asked residents across all three cities about how their community solves problems, how they learn about that problem-solving, and how they would solve similar problems on a national scale.[31] It became clear that church activity was much more visible to Lutherton residents, regardless of individual membership status, than it was in both Gravesend and Motorville. This began to make sense in light of interviews with local pastors, elected officials, and nonprofit leaders; administrative data on nonprofit and church revenue; and data I collected from local newspapers and Facebook posts. These data showed how central Lutherton's churches were to local problem-solving *and* how much local opinion leaders discussed and lauded their activities. From this process of triangulation, I developed one of the core arguments of chapters 2 and 3: relationships among churches and nonprofits shape the way local opinion leaders and residents talk about how to solve problems, leading residents to believe that issues related to poverty, such as hunger and homelessness, are community challenges that can be resolved without government intervention.

Social Groups, Partisanship, and Political Change

This research process was essential in helping me disentangle the two potential explanations for growing Republicanism in the Heartland: either that the Heartland's postindustrial cities are composed of certain social groups—White, working- and middle-class voters—who are increasingly affiliating with the Republican Party, or that places themselves "add something extra" to individuals' experience of politics, leading those cities toward the Republican Party.[32] This disentangling is important, because the point of departure for understanding Heartland politics is through the kinds of people who live there—in this case, White, working- and middle-class men and women, often Christians.

Decades of scholarship have shown how this group's turn toward the Republican Party began in the 1960s, after Nixon's successful appeal to the "Silent Majority" in the wake of the civil rights movement. It is a story rooted in group-based theories of American partisanship, which argue that political parties emerge to represent the prevailing divisions in society, and individuals join the party that represents their social group—or the people who share their position in the social structure. As pioneering political scientists in the "Michigan School" argued in the 1960s, partisanship represents the "perfect distillation" of voters' life histories and social positions (Campbell et al. 1960, 34). Although penned more than sixty years ago, this insight has proved foundational to research on American partisanship.

But the process of translation from social group membership—some objective categorical belonging—to partisan identity is not automatic: there are myriad lines of division in society that carve out different groups defined by ethnicity, race, religion, and gender, but rarely do all of these groups carry political meaning for their members.[33] And it's only in recent years that researchers have further specified both the *micro-* and *macro-level* processes that help connect social groups to political parties.[34] At the social psychological level (what I refer to as micro), an individual's objective group membership becomes a social identity when they incorporate that membership into their self-conceptualization and develop an attachment to the group; a social identity links to a partisan identity when voters see that a particular party embraces that social group.[35] As political psychologist Leonie Huddy (2013) has detailed, both of these processes—the move from group membership to social identity, and then from social identity to partisan identification—are contingent.[36] And they are contingent, in part, on political party maneuvering (what I refer to as the macro-level). Scholars have shown that political parties play a role in both steps of the translation process from social group membership to political identity: they can redefine group interests through strategic communication and efforts to incorporate social groups into their party coalition; and they can clarify to what extent certain groups "belong with" which political party.[37]

A groups-based account of party politics explains the Heartland's turn toward the right as a product of social groups' movement into and out of party coalitions in the decades since the New Deal. The New Deal was the height of "traditional" class politics in America, a brief period when the working classes were associated with the party on the left and the middle and upper classes with the party on the right.[38] But racism posed a barrier to true class-based politics, as southerners remained central to the Democratic coalition and fought to ensure Black exclusion from certain New Deal social programs.

Over the following decades, as chapter 1 will describe in greater detail, those White, working-class members of the New Deal coalition faced increasing contestation over their political loyalties. First, after the 1960s, Democrats' response to the civil rights movement and Republicans' nomination of Barry Goldwater propelled southern Whites into the Republican Party and Black Americans, those newly enfranchised voters in the South and those with lingering Republican sentiments in the North, toward the Democratic Party.[39] Then, over the following years, White Christian groups began mobilizing politically around several issues, including school segregation, school prayer, sex education, and—much later—abortion. By 1980, the Republican Party sought to capture these mobilized voters by endorsing a constitutional amendment to ban abortion and establishing itself as the party of White Christian conservatives.[40] Alongside these political shifts, unions' sociopolitical power began declining, threatening the importance of class as an organizing principle in Americans' lives. Race and religion increasingly seemed to be the most salient social identities for American voters.[41]

Thus, by the 1990s, three decades of political mobilization, social change, and economic restructuring had reshaped the political coalitions of both major parties. Consider what this meant for working- and middle-class White voters, many of whom were Christian, coming of age at different moments in this decades-long process. During the New Deal, their group memberships—both their race and class (and religion among Catholics)—pointed them toward the Democratic Party. But for similar kinds of people registering to vote after the Racial Realignment or the rise of the Religious Right, their racial, religious, and class identities pointed them in different partisan directions—in other words, they became *cross-pressured*.[42] Party maneuvering amid economic and social change (a macrostory) and how that process shaped political identify formation among different social groups (a micro-story) seemed to provide an apt lens for understanding the Heartland's reddening at the turn of the twenty-first century.

Place, Populism, and Political Change

But the 2016 presidential election reinvigorated questions about White, Heartland politics. To many observers, Donald Trump's election was the result of a swelling populist backlash, signaling new and troubling divisions around race, class, and place: working- and middle-class White voters across the American Heartland had become the foundation of the Republican Party, while urbanites, people of color, and educated professionals supported the Democratic Party.[43] One important explanation for this outcome was the changing political behavior among White voters, particularly those without a college degree: as they felt their social status under threat after the election of the first Black president and the changing racial demographics of the country, they moved toward populist candidates that reaffirmed their racial privilege—first the Tea Party and then Donald Trump.[44] This populist backlash accelerated the decades-long rightward shift among White voters described above; and crucially, it was just strong enough to tip key swing states like Michigan, Wisconsin, and Pennsylvania into the Republican column, carrying Donald Trump into the White House in 2016.[45]

But in these accounts, a place is just the aggregate of the kinds of people who live within it—in other words, they explain the rightward shift in White communities across the Heartland via the political behavior of individual voters living within them, not via any political effect of place itself.[46] In an alternative view, sociologists and political scientists have shown that place does have an effect on the current political stasis: places shape the way their residents interact with one another and interpret the world around them—including when it comes to politics.[47] And in the American Heartland, scholars tend to agree that the political meaning of place is defined by loss: at the same time as factories disappeared from these cities and union membership declined, the federal government also reformed the way it invested in citizens' lives, shifting the balance of social provision to local, private sources and forcing cities and nonprofits to compete for government funds.[48] As public and private resources fled from postindustrial and rural areas, so too did their best and brightest young residents, creating a negative spiral of economic and population decline.[49]

In sum, the people and places that make up the Heartland were left behind by this restructuring. And as Katherine Cramer (2016) has shown, in Wisconsin this created fruitful ground for rural dwellers to turn against the state as they began to imagine that the public resources draining from their towns were flowing instead toward urbanites. Cramer's argument is that a place-based identity as rural residents shapes a distinctive kind of populist anti-statism among the Wisconsinites she meets.

Cramer's argument is largely race-neutral, but as others like Arlie Hochschild (2016) have argued, individuals' race and class are key to understanding how place shapes politics. Hochschild finds that Whites in her Louisiana study support the anti-government Tea Party movement not just because of the many losses they've seen in their city but because they believe racialized minorities are cutting them in line for government assistance. This belief, what social scientists refer to as "racial resentment," has long undermined Whites' support for redistributive policies.[50] Hochschild shows that this can happen even in a place where residents would benefit from expanded government intervention to mitigate environmental pollution from local factories and increase health-care access.[51]

These studies reveal that place is a key piece of the explanation for growing populism in the American Heartland. But even these arguments are not quite sufficient for explaining the region's *partisan* shift: as Jennifer Silva (2019) argues, populist resentment toward government does not necessarily lead to Republicanism; it can also lead to political disengagement or even be encompassed within the Democratic Party.

Place-Based Partisanship

This means that even the most compelling explanations for the Heartland's reddening still cannot explain the puzzles at the center of this book: why the national changes described above produced a fractured response among the places that were once part of the White, working-class New Deal coalition, sending Motorville, Lutherton, and Gravesend along different political trajectories; *how* place still produces a persistent tendency toward Democratic partisanship among Motorvillians despite pulls toward the right that have attracted both Lutherton and Gravesend residents; and whether these place-based political differences can persist amid a growing tendency toward the nationalization of American politics.

So what can answer these puzzles? My contention is that what's missing from existing arguments is an understanding of *place-based partisanship*—the portion of Americans' partisan attachments explained by where they live—and that a comparison across Motorville, Lutherton, and Gravesend can show us not just *that* place matters for residents' partisan identities but also *how* it matters. I argue that residents make sense of both local structural conditions and national political-economic developments from within their organizational contexts, leading them to cohere around two cultural frameworks: (1) *diagnostic frames* for defining what their problems are and how to solve them politically; and (2) *narratives of community identity* that tell residents what kind of community they are and where they fit into the party system. Through this process, place helps produce and reproduce residents' partisan attachments.[52]

This is true not only among White voters in the American Heartland, or in small cities like Motorville, Lutherton, and Gravesend, but for anyone whose political loyalties are sought after by both political parties: today, as both parties vie for favor among a heterogeneous group of Latinx and Asian American voters on the basis of their possible identities as racialized minorities, Christians, or upwardly mobile immigrants from different nations, we should expect that place plays a role in shaping the salience of these identities and helping voters link them to party politics.[53]

How do places accomplish this? Building on work by Harvey Molotch, William Freudenburg, and Krista Paulsen (2000), I argue that places are defined by their structural conditions, local organizational contexts, and shared cultural frameworks. The structural conditions of a city—the kinds of people who live there and the objective material/economic conditions in which they operate—impose the most basic limitations on residents' diagnostic frames and community identities and, therefore, on their partisan attachments.[54] For example, it would be difficult to imagine that cities like Motorville, Lutherton, and Gravesend, which all experience varying degrees of postindustrial social problems like poverty and economic precarity, would understand themselves as communities of wealthy elites; but it is possible that each city has different ways of thinking about their postindustrial problems, which cannot be explained entirely by objective differences in demographic composition or material conditions. We will see that this is in fact the case.

And that's because of local organizational contexts—not just quantitative differences in organizational resources or even qualitative differences in the types of organizations across places but also how those organizations relate to one another and define their role within a city. These qualitative and relational dimensions of local organizational contexts are crucial for understanding place-based partisanship, because ostensibly similar organizations play different roles in different cities. For example, Gravesend still has many union members, but unlike Motorville the city no longer has a local labor movement that engages in community life and politics.

These differences are important because stable organizational contexts like those in Motorville and Lutherton lead residents—both organizational members and non-members alike—toward shared diagnostic frames and narratives of community identity. As we will see, shared diagnostic frames emerge over repeated experiences of collective problem-solving.[55] The local organizational context helps determine which community leaders get a seat at the problem-solving table *and* shapes the way those leaders think about what problem-solving strategies "work" within their city: they use past experiences of solving problems within local organizational constraints to diagnose and resolve similar problems in the future.[56] Community leaders then serve as local opinion leaders for residents, who come to share their place-based diagnostic frames and start to apply those frames to similar issues on both the local and national levels.[57]

Organizational contexts also inform narratives of community identity—the way residents learn about who they are as a community and where they fit into the party system. This happens both directly, via residents who are affiliated with local organizations, and indirectly, through friends (or friends of friends) with organizational ties or local news that discusses certain organizations more than others.[58] As sociologist Japonica Brown-Saracino has argued (2015, 2018), places are often the sites where people produce accounts of themselves and others in social interaction, creating place narratives—stories about what kind of a community this is—that shape residents' interpretation of their social identities. This kind of storytelling is important because it moves beyond the differentiating process (a way of framing a struggle in terms of us vs. them) and incorporates a "story of . . . becoming" that establishes "who we are" (Polletta 1998, 422) as a community.[59] And as the political parties craft appeals to different social groups, those appeals are more likely to resonate when they fit with the narratives residents already rely on to make sense of their lived experiences.[60] The result, as we will see in Motorville, Lutherton, and Gravesend, is that residents articulate place-specific interpretations of what the parties mean.

Diagnostic frames and narratives of community identity thus depend, in part, on a place's structural conditions and the local organizational context: as Mario Small observes (2004, 70), "residents do not merely see and experience the characteristics of their neighborhood 'as it is'; their perceptions are filtered through cultural categories that highlight some aspects of the neighborhood and ignore others." This is true in Motorville, Lutherton, and Gravesend as well. For example, the fact that church membership is so central to many Luthertonians' lives leads to social interactions where residents attempt to locate one another by asking which church they attend. The result is that residents are routinely reminded that they live in a churchgoing community. But over time, the idea that Lutherton *is* a churchgoing community becomes so taken for granted that, even if church membership began to dwindle, this social fact would continue to circulate in the way residents talk to each other, in what they tell newcomers about what kind of place Lutherton is, and in how they engage with the built environment. In other words, these cultural frameworks are partially independent from other place dimensions and play a distinct role in sustaining place-based partisanship.

For this reason, while it is possible to study place and place-effects at multiple scales, I focus here on *the local*—not just small, postindustrial cities like

Motorville, Lutherton, and Gravesend but cities and towns in general—because local contexts and the organizations they contain provide "the infrastructure of repeated interactional patterns" (Swidler 2001, 94) thereby circulating local cultural frameworks.[61] This is not to say that regions, states, and counties don't matter for residents' politics, but rather that places are nested—meaning that Motorville, Lutherton, and Gravesend are the cities they are because of their historic responses to disruptions from their external environments.[62]

Taken together, the structural, organizational, and cultural dimensions of place can lead similar people, living in different places, to arrive at different understandings of who they are, what their problems are, and which political party best represents them and their community. Moreover, because places are defined by this bundle of self-reinforcing factors, place-based partisanship is somewhat difficult to disrupt from within.[63] This means that changes in place-based partisanship are most likely to occur when external forces help destabilize local organizational contexts and over time residents no longer agree on shared diagnostic frames and community identities.[64] Gravesend offers an example of this: as we will see, organizational instability produces a kind of despair about their community's future. As the Republican Party increasingly appeals to threatened towns like theirs, Gravesend is becoming increasingly Republican.

Much of this argument about how place helps shape and sustain identities is not new. Since the early 2000s, a growing group of sociologists has argued for greater analytic attention to how place matters for social action and interaction. Like those studies, this book draws on a comparison of "like" places (e.g., not rural vs. urban or midwestern vs. coastal), which, as Japonica Brown-Saracino (2018) writes, is a powerful methodological tool to reveal how "similar places make us different" (18).[65] What *is* new here is that I extend place studies to the world of partisan politics. In doing so, I will show how the relationship between place and political identity formation is contingent on political constraints—the parties' efforts to incorporate particular social groups and not others.

A Contextual Account of Partisan Identity in a National Era

Although my argument builds squarely on a growing research tradition within sociology, the idea of reintroducing context to the conversation about partisan identity formation within political science faces two challenges. The first is that Lazarsfeld and colleagues (1948), the mid-century scholars who offered the first account of how social contexts shape partisanship, were writing at a time that we might think was much more "local": before social media and digital communications made politics an increasingly national affair; when local newspapers thrived; and before globalization undermined the local industries that sustained many U.S. cities in the postwar era. This means that residents of Motorville, Lutherton, and Gravesend are not just situated within their *local* contexts; they are also operating in a *national* context in which their political information comes from cable news, Twitter, and the *New York Times*, their social networks may stretch across the country, and their employers may be headquartered in other states, making global decisions about supply chains and employment.

Even as I develop arguments about place, it will be clear that the residents I spoke to do not exist in an isolated context. The influence of "the national" on the local—whether that is partisan news sources, political party realignment, or deindustrialization—is evident throughout the book. Chapters 1, 5, 6, and 7 highlight national forces that have caused change in place-based partisanship (chapters 1 and 5) and those that have not (chapters 6 and 7). Taken together, they suggest that the national factors most likely to disrupt place-based partisanship are those that undermine local organizational contexts and cultural frameworks. Residents' consumption of partisan media, for example, does create temporary issue polarization and may be consequential for other political outcomes, but it does not disrupt the processes that sustain place-based partisanship.

The importance of "the national" hints at the second challenge to reviving an argument about how context helps sustain partisan attachments: because partisanship seems to explain so much of Americans' political behavior, it can be difficult to pin down anything that explains partisanship.[66] By arguing that place supports partisanship, I am not ruling out the idea that partisanship itself may shape certain aspects of place (as well as other political beliefs my interviewees articulate); nor am I arguing that place is the *only* factor (nor even the most important factor) in explaining partisanship.[67] Instead, I am arguing that place *also* has an explanatory role in sustaining partisan attachments and that this is particularly true for cross-pressured voters. Among these individuals, place helps make certain social identities more salient than others and helps link those identities to certain interpretations of party politics.

Plan for the Book

The remainder of the book addresses each of the puzzles posed by Motorville, Lutherton, and Gravesend in turn. In part 1, "The Past Informs the Present," I examine how historical interactions between local and extra-local processes have shaped the trajectory of the Heartland's reddening, producing different organizational contexts within each city (chapter 1), which today shape who the community leaders are in each city and how they work to resolve social problems (chapter 2). Chapter 1 draws on archival evidence from each city to show how they reacted differently to historic political and economic transformations, drawing on their existing resources to do so. After every juncture of disruption and reaction, each place emerged as an increasingly distinct bundle of structural, organizational, and cultural materials—with a distinct set of politics. In chapter 2, we see how these historical processes have reverberated through to the present, producing the places I observed during my time in each city. Motorville, Lutherton, and Gravesend still share certain structural conditions and challenges common to White, postindustrial cities, but they have different organizational resources to address them. I argue that there are two dimensions of local organizational contexts that are consequential for residents' partisanship today: content and stability. Although the content of organizational life differs across Motorville and Lutherton, organizational contexts in both cities are stable relative to Gravesend, which means they provide a source of continuity to civic life and shape who community leaders are and how they diagnose and attempt to resolve social problems.

Part 2, "Place-Based Partisanship in the Present," turns to the cultural dimensions of place. We will shift our view from community leaders to residents to advance a central contention of the book: how place operates in the present to sustain residents' partisanship, keeping Motorvillians in the Democratic fold while reinforcing Lutherton's Republican partisanship and drawing Gravesenders to the right as well. In chapters 3 and 4, I focus on Motorville and Lutherton to show that the stable organizational contexts described in chapter 2 lead residents of each place to cohere around shared diagnostic frames and narratives of community identity. In chapter 3 I argue that structural differences between Motorville and Lutherton do not explain residents' different *diagnostic frames* for solving social problems; instead, it is the routine experience of problem-solving within local organizational contexts that leads Motorvillians to understand themselves as a community that would benefit from state intervention while Lutherton residents understand themselves as a community that takes care of itself. Chapter 4 then shows how everyday social interactions in Motorville and Lutherton lead residents to distinct *narratives of community identity*. Lutherton residents think of themselves as a community of churchgoers, a place where Christianity is central to residents' identities and the community takes care of itself with no need for state intervention. And because they view the Republican Party as the party that stands for Christianity and local control, it is the party for them and their community. Motorvillians, in contrast, think of their community as struggling under the weight of challenges beyond their control—a community of "have-nots"—in an unequal society that requires state intervention to balance the scales. And to them, party politics express class divisions, with the Democrats working to bring in the state and support organized labor to level the playing field.

In chapter 5, I turn to Gravesend and its recent swing to the right. I argue that local organizational decline—described in chapters 1 and 2—is essential to understanding the swell of right-wing populism here and in other Heartland cities: in the midst of devastating economic and population decline, *and without coherent local leadership to fill the vacuum*, Gravesenders increasingly feel their community's survival is threatened. Residents are often left sad and angry, and as the Republican Party increasingly argues that they are the party to defend White America from the twin threats of immigration and socialism, those appeals resonate with Gravesenders.

Parts 1 and 2 thus advance two central arguments of the book, showing: *first*, how the reddening of the American Heartland, as a historical and ongoing process, is shaped by interactions between local and national processes; and *second*, that those processes have also created distinct places, defined along structural, organizational, and cultural dimensions, which today help sustain place-based partisanship. We will also see the importance of place throughout these chapters: as the overwhelming majority of White, working-class New Deal counties peeled off from the Democratic coalition, either because of racial and religious identities—like Lutherton—or because of a more recent populist backlash—like Gravesend—place has helped hold Motorville back from both pulls to the right.

Part 3, "The (Possible) Future of Place," then turns to examine challenges to the persistence of place as a consequential factor in American politics, addressing the final puzzle that we started with: will place still matter for politics in the future? Focusing on residents' experience of the Covid-19 pandemic and elite polarization on novel issues during the 2020 presidential election, I find that even national tumult did not dislodge the cultural frameworks that sustain partisan differences across Motorville, Lutherton, and Gravesend. Chapter 6 illustrates how local diagnostic frames were reproduced as residents continued to draw on local reference points when they considered how the state should intervene to mitigate the economic crisis. And chapter 7 shows that even when individuals' partisanship and media consumption drove polarization on novel issues, this was short-lived compared to the enduring narratives of community identity that told residents who they were and where they belonged in party politics.

PART I

The Past Informs the Present

1

The Uneven Geography of Heartland Politics

THE LOCAL RAMIFICATIONS OF POLITICAL TRANSFORMATION FROM THE NEW DEAL TO TRUMP

ON MY FIRST EVENING in Motorville the late spring air still carries a winter chill. From the passenger seat of Elaine's car, I watch as we pass by the railyards and skirt the towering industrial park that lines the riverfront. Elaine was born and raised in Motorville, and she's volunteered to show me her hometown tonight in what, to her, is its truest form: the bar scene. Each time we approach a bar, over the course of several hours, Elaine describes the typical clientele: there is a generic "working-class" bar, but there are also bars catering to workers coming off the night shift, shippers, jocks, pool players, and hipsters. It is a "hard-drinking and hard-working" city, as Elaine—who no longer drinks—likes to say.

In the midst of our travels, we crisscross Main Street and Elaine gestures out the window: "This is all redone. Just from like three years ago. This did not look like this." Although I cannot see exactly what she's referring to in the dark, Elaine is the first of several Motorvillians who proudly tell me about all the changes on Main Street: the wide lane is split by a row of new trees, and the sides of the street are lined with tall, wrought-iron streetlamps that have banners attached to them advertising Motorville's business district and its proximity to outdoor activities. The nineteenth-century buildings with brick facades appear in relatively good repair, and several boast fairly new businesses, including two independent coffee shops. But the progress appears to be somewhat stilted, as Elaine indicates: "Some of these, these are all closed," she says, pointing at a few empty storefronts. "They come and go . . . it's a high tax rate in Motorville."

Over the next few hours, Elaine continues to punctuate our journey with a mental map of her own history and Motorville's. As she does so, she regularly compares Motorville to other places she's lived, reflecting on the years she spent away from home. "So were you ready to come back when you came back?" I ask. "No," she says in a joking tone, "I was never ready to come back here." I laugh along, but then realize that she is serious, as she continues: "'Cause it's a very depressed economy. It's hard to make a living here."

Just a few weeks later, I arrive in Lutherton, where Wayne—a former county commissioner—is offering a similar tour of the area. We're making our way along the roads that wind through the countryside outside of the city in Wayne's large black pickup. As we drive, Wayne continually returns to the same theme: "This is a heavy Lutheran—German Lutheran area," he tells me. "You drive through Lutherton [City] and you're gonna see a lot of Lutheran churches. You drive through the country, and I can show you a lot of Lutheran churches." And he sticks to his word. A few hours later, as we come up a hill, he teases: "Guess what kind of church it's gonna be up here on my right?" "Lutheran?" I ask. "Ding, ding, ding!" he says.

Back in the residential lanes of Lutherton, the city's layout is similar to Motorville's. The nineteenth-century business district is also crossed by a larger, busier road that carries you to CVS, Wal-Mart, and other major retailers. But Main Street itself houses the small businesses: a gift shop, bike store, and small clothing boutique, as well as a handful of local restaurants, new and old. The crown jewel, perhaps, is Peterson's, the family diner on the corner of Main Street with a large wooden sign above the store reading, "If it ain't fried, it ain't food." But if Peterson's is a Main Street institution, Café 153 and The Depot—two new restaurants within a block of the diner—are signs of an ongoing downtown revitalization process that mirrors Motorville's. There is also a new "pocket park" nestled between buildings and fresh coats of paint on one-hundred-year-old facades. But much like Motorville, revitalization is not an unmitigated success: a long-standing family-run hardware store closed just before I arrived in town, leaving its storefront vacant.

Gravesend, in contrast, has had the most success with its downtown. As I walk along Main Street on my first morning in town, I see that familiar nineteenth-century brick buildings line the street, but they are in excellent condition, and I cannot see a single empty storefront along the way. There are boutiques, jewelry stores, antique stores, a flower and gift shop, an insurance

agency, and two or three bars and restaurants. A glossy blue storefront advertises an insurance firm which, as someone tells me the next day, is relatively
new. There is also a coworking space and several arts-related spaces: a gallery,
a local theater in a historic building, and an arts center. The arts center has a
rainbow-colored "All Are Welcome Here" sign in the window.

Round planters sit next to benches and hanging flowerpots adorn the
wrought-iron streetlamps, very similar to Motorville's—I learn later that
the flowers faced some local opposition because many residents did not think
they were worth the cost. But now they draw people down Main Street, where
it opens onto a bluff, just above a park with a gazebo and built-in seating ar-
ranged in a semicircle. A large sign advertises concerts in the park here each
Thursday of the summer. Main Street in Gravesend is, in short, charming.

But despite Gravesend's success with Main Street revitalization, residents
are more likely to describe it as a city in decline than one that is thriving. As
Anthony, who grew up in Gravesend and now serves on the County Board,
summarizes the city's challenges: "Aging population, changing demographics,
available jobs." Echoing Elaine from Motorville, he says of the people who
have left: "but what's here to come back to?" Anthony's concerns are all related: because of a lack of jobs, kids have nothing in the city to return to, and
the overall population ages.

———

In many ways, Motorville, Lutherton, and Gravesend are all variations on a theme:
like so many other Heartland cities, all three were White settler communities
whose early industries were often related to agriculture and natural resources.[1]
By the mid-twentieth century, they were small but growing industrialized cities
full of manufacturing jobs for their largely White, blue-collar workforce. But by
the end of the 1980s, globalization and corporate restructuring had decimated
industrial employment.[2] As my first glimpses of each city indicate, the scars of
the past are etched across the physical landscape to varying degrees today, available to residents as they tell stories about who they are as a community.

But while they have always been similar, Motorville, Lutherton, and
Gravesend were never identical. As we will see, the organizational and cultural
differences that today distinguish Motorville, Lutherton, and Gravesend have
their roots in late nineteenth- and early twentieth-century patterns of immigration and labor organizing: that Lutherton's early White settlers included a large portion of German immigrants who attended conservative,

German-speaking Lutheran churches and later institutionalized segregation and other anti-Black practices; that Motorville had a late nineteenth-century tradition of militant labor organizing to call upon during the New Deal as labor began to reengage in politics; and that Gravesend's radical labor movement quickly fractured into apolitical organizing, focused primarily within the walls of the town's largest employer, Rivervalley.[3]

But during the 1930s and 1940s, these subtle organizational differences between the cities did not lead to different political outcomes: Motorville, Lutherton, and Gravesend were all part of the working-class, New Deal coalition that brought FDR to power. It wasn't until many decades later that the cities diverged politically. Today, only Motorville remains a Democratic stronghold. The oft-told account of post–New Deal politics points to three major changes that, together, killed the New Deal coalition and turned places like Motorville, Lutherton, and Gravesend from blue to red. First, after the Democrats' consolidation of a pro-labor, pro-working-class constituency in the 1930s and 1940s, the realignment of the parties around race during the civil rights era divided the White, working class, as many of them—particularly from the South—defected to the Republican Party.[4] Then, in the 1970s and 1980s, White evangelical Christians mobilized politically within the Republican Party, further undermining Democrats' appeal to those same New Deal constituencies.[5] And finally, amid these changes, deindustrialization and union decline dramatically altered what it meant to be part of the American working class, as both a social and political group.[6]

Daniel Schlozman (2015) has shown that these national political transformations are the result of compromises meted out between social movement groups and political party leaders, which led to both the political incorporation of mobilized groups and changes in the parties' issue positions.[7] Nothing in this chapter, nor in the remainder of this book, contests this national account. Instead, this chapter will show how these macro-historical processes were emplaced: place rendered changes in national party coalitions *legible* to voters. But New Deal cities and their politics were also changing as community leaders made choices about how to respond to state- and national-level transformations. These responses were historically layered: past decisions set the cities on different pathways that constrained future actions; the cities became increasingly distinct places; and those places provided the context in which residents made sense of future political-economic developments.[8] For example, different state labor laws and histories of local organizing led unionists in Motorville, Lutherton, and Gravesend to respond differently to economic crises during deindustrialization. In Lutherton, workers rejected an opportunity for labor mobilization in the 1970s but residents still attended evangelical churches, whose activities were featured regularly in local news. As a result, by the time of the Moral Majority's march into politics, Lutherton was a place where Christianized politics made sense. The accumulation of these local responses to external disruption produced a distinctive set of places—defined along structural, organizational, and cultural dimensions—each with distinctive politics.

The remainder of this chapter will draw on two sources of data to build this argument. First, I use county-level electoral returns, economic data, and organizational data to situate Motorville, Lutherton, and Gravesend within the macro-historical context of political realignments since the New Deal. Second, I draw on front- and editorial-page newspaper articles from each city during the days preceding and following key national events from 1932 to 2016.[9]

From these data, we will see that each city's structural characteristics—the kinds of people who lived there and the cities' objective economic conditions—were just one piece of the story in how their place-politics evolved. And as we will see throughout the remainder of the book, this is also true of their contemporary politics. Structural conditions do matter, but to explain why Motorville residents have bucked the trend of Heartland politics, we need to understand how they are making sense of those structural conditions from within distinct organizational and cultural contexts.

The New Deal in Motorville, Lutherton, and Gravesend

The New Deal was a watershed moment in American politics when the United States came as close as it ever would to having a leftist, working-class political party akin to its European, social democratic peers.[10] But even then, the emergence of class politics was conditioned by race. It was a coalition of working-class Whites, southern Democrats, and northern urbanites who carried FDR to the White House in 1932. As an increasing number of Black voters joined them over the years, party elites avoided racial politics at the national level and made various concessions to the South on racial policy to protect this unwieldy coalition for decades.[11]

But despite the New Deal's limitations, its working-class—or at least, White, working-class—appeal produced a shift in the geographic bases of the Democratic Party, as industrial towns and cities with growing labor activism—particularly outside the South—became the foundations of the new coalition.[12]

As figure 2 shows, these cities were scattered across the country but concentrated in the former manufacturing centers of the Midwest and to some extent the Mountain West.

During the presidential elections between 1932 to 1944, Democratic candidates won 64 percent of Motorville County's votes, on average; 57 percent of the votes in Lutherton County; and 54 percent in Gravesend County. In Lutherton, which offered Donald Trump more than three quarters of its votes in 2020, the local newspaper in 1932 heralded not only Roosevelt's "sweeping" victory in 1932 but also a Democratic "landslide" in local races throughout the county.

In their Democratic enthusiasm, Motorville, Lutherton, and Gravesend were much like the other New Deal places shown in figure 2: at the county level, all three were over 99 percent White in 1930, and outside of agriculture, the largest industrial sectors during the 1940s and 1950s were manufacturing in Lutherton and Gravesend and transportation in Motorville. At that time, Motorville was larger than Lutherton and Gravesend and its economy was more industrialized and less agriculturally dependent.

But all three cities had large, blue-collar workforces that provided fertile ground for unionization. Schlozman's (2015) national account of social movements and party politics marks the New Deal era as the beginning of a decades-long symbiotic relationship between the Democratic Party and organized labor. The Congress of Industrial Organizations (CIO) under John Lewis led the charge into electoral politics in 1936, rallying workers to FDR's cause, while FDR and other New Dealers aided the rise of unionization with passage of the Wagner Act in 1935. The Wagner Act gave workers the right to organize and made it illegal for employers to refuse to bargain collectively with workers' chosen representatives. It also established the National Labor Relations Board (NLRB) to adjudicate disputes, leading to a rapid rise in private sector unionization. During this heyday of the American labor movement, unions were both an economic and political force.[13]

These national trends, however, bely substantial regional, state, and local variation: both unionization and labor militancy have historically been concentrated in industrial cities in the North and Midwest, but even there, union strength has typically varied across cities as union organizers struggle to gain representation plant by plant.[14] As such, while unions were part of New Deal politics in Motorville, Lutherton, and Gravesend, they played different roles in each place.

Long before the New Deal, Motorville contained a politically engaged labor movement and a relatively active socialist community.[15] Already in the late nineteenth century, there were at least thirty-five union locals in Motorville and two Knights of Labor assemblies, one of which published a newspaper helping to spread the Knights' version of "labor radicalism."[16] Motorville workers were routinely striking for higher wages and better working conditions, occasionally leading to violent clashes with local police.[17] Similar actions were erupting in other cities surrounding Motorville, as European immigrants migrating to work in America's growing industrial sector brought socialist and communist thinking to the nascent labor movement.[18]

These unionists were attempting to build a coordinated labor movement in Motorville that fostered residents' working-class identities.[19] Their efforts persisted even as the local Knights of Labor assemblies foundered in the 1890s and craft unions affiliated with the American Federation of Labor (AFL) formed a Trades and Labor Assembly. The AFL's emergence tempered the radical political potential of the labor movement nationally, but Motorville's labor movement remained deeply political.[20] As the first elected president of the Motorville AFL's Trades and Labor Assembly explained the organization's raison d'être in 1895: "The various labor organizations of Motorville are now sufficiently strong in numbers to secure political recognition, and while not out for the purpose of booming any candidate, would much prefer to see one elected who is friendly to the labor interests than one who is not." The assembly subsequently voted to stay out of local elections, but they continued to convey a clear political message to Motorville workers: they were not just economic actors geared toward "bread and butter" concerns but also political actors.[21]

Although Motorville workers continued their political engagement into the twentieth century, the labor movement struggled in the years following World War I, as it did across the United States, amid high unemployment, coordination among anti-union employers, and a lack of protection from the federal government.[22] As one Motorville labor leader would later recall, it was FDR's presidency and a groundswell of new labor activism that allowed unionists to revive Motorville's local labor movement.[23] By the end of the 1940s, the city saw a growing number of strikes and the newspaper recounted labor's active engagement in local politics. Although FDR's pro-labor policies certainly played a role in this outcome, it also happened because Motorville already contained the materials for such a revival: a strong base of previous or current labor leaders who wanted to fight for workers not just on economic grounds but also in the political sphere.

The early 1930s were also a time of militant labor mobilization in Gravesend, but by the end of the decade their engagement in community and political life had already begun to dwindle, in part due to changes within the national labor movement. After industrial unions within the AFL were expelled in 1936 and formed the independent CIO, the two organizations competed with one other and with independent labor organizations to win over new members. Gravesend had contained a vibrant independent labor movement since 1933— the United Gravesend Workers Association (UGWA). The UGWA had a strong, though not uncontested, foothold among workers in the city's two largest plants, and as leaders later discussed in oral histories, they saw themselves as part of a community-wide labor movement.

Part of the UGWA's success was due to the Wagner Act: when Gravesend's largest employer, a metal manufacturing plant called Rivervalley Foundries, sought to set up an employees' association that undermined the UGWA's organizing efforts in 1937, the NLRB stepped in to "disestablish" the employees' association. But within a few short years, the UGWA crumbled under competitive pressures from the AFL and CIO. In 1939 the UGWA worked with Gravesend employees at four different plants to coordinate sit-ins and strikes for over a week. After violent clashes with the police, resulting in several arrests, the Gravesend mayor—a Farmer-Labor politician in council with the CIO—negotiated a settlement between the four employers and their workers that protected their right to unionize. But the settlement was not an outright victory for the UGWA: it required workers to vote in a union affiliated with a *national* organization—that is, not the UGWA. Workers at Rivervalley joined the Steelworkers Organizing Committee, a CIO union, while those at the second largest employer joined the AFL.

Labor activism in Gravesend did not stop after the 1939 settlement, but without the UGWA, the most politically engaged and radicalized elements of the labor movement ceased to exist. In the meantime, coordinated opposition to organized labor persisted—in fact, the *Gravesend Ledger* was considered a staunchly anti-labor outlet, so much so that a pro-labor publication emerged in the mid-1930s to offer a "local newspaper that would present facts that the conservative press consistently refuses to publish," as they wrote by way of introduction in their first issue. While neither side achieved an outright victory during the battles of the 1930s, they did reach a cautious détente: unions remained active in Gravesend's largest employers, but their increased organizational ties to the CIO and AFL seem to have circumscribed their realm of activity, focusing labor leaders on collective bargaining rather than building a working-class political movement.[24]

Although a deeply political labor movement never materialized in Lutherton, the 1930s were also a period of labor movement growth in the city. At that time, AFL-affiliated unions in Lutherton formed a central labor council, which claimed to have seven local affiliates, 1,000 members, and plans to recruit 500 more members within the next few months. For a labor market that employed approximately 9,000 people in 1940, this was no small feat. Although the unions were part of the AFL, the formation of the council suggests that workers were interested in more than just collective bargaining: as the *Lutherton Gazette* wrote at the time, they wanted to educate both the "organized and unorganized" as to the benefits of unionization for all workers. During the late 1930s and 1940s, the labor council met twice a month, organized Labor Day parades and dances, and had speakers from the Indiana State Federation of Labor join them to talk about labor-related bills moving through the state legislature.

Thus, the 1930s marked a time of union resurgence in Motorville and the inauguration of an organized labor movement in Lutherton and Gravesend.[25] In all three places, the Wagner Act provided organized labor with the toehold it needed to grow—or regrow. This positive feedback loop was taking place across industrialized cities in the American Heartland, helping to sustain the map shown in figure 2. But while all three cities appeared to have quantitatively strong labor movements, they were qualitatively different: Motorville's was the most militant, the most willing to strike, and the most engaged in local politics.

The Civil Rights Movement and a New Politics of Race

During the New Deal era, this variation across the cities' organizational contexts did not lead them to different national politics. But the New Deal coalition was only able to persist through the 1930s and 1940s by carefully subsuming a racial tension between White southerners and growing numbers of northern, Black voters that made up the party. During the 1950s and 1960s, this tension slowly bubbled to the surface, as northern Democratic congressional representatives increasingly embraced a pro–civil rights message at odds with the demands of their southern colleagues.[26] But it was the 1964 presidential election that finally, and dramatically, cracked the coalition on a national scale, as LBJ campaigned on a platform supporting civil rights, while his Republican opponent, Barry Goldwater, opposed federal intervention to enforce integration. The campaign left no doubt that the Republican Party was now the home of racial conservatives.[27]

The ensuing realignment around race is often understood as a regional phenomenon, nudging southern Whites into the Republican Party over several decades and propelling newly enfranchised Black voters in the South to join the legions of already Democratic Black voters in the North.[28] But all White, industrialized cities were involved implicitly in the story of national political change: the new racial cleavage threatened the class bases of the New Deal system, as it drove White voters toward a Republican Party that now represented their racial interests.

Amid these national transformations, Motorville, Lutherton, and Gravesend all rebuked Goldwater's segregationist platform, awarding LBJ over 55 percent of their vote in 1964. But the local ramifications of the Racial Realignment began to show by 1968: Nixon won a narrow victory in Lutherton that year because George Wallace, the governor of Alabama and a staunch segregationist, garnered more than 10 percent of the vote. Both Motorville and Gravesend voted for Hubert Humphrey. Over the following years, Lutherton's politics only became increasingly red.

Why did the Racial Realignment provoke a turn toward Republican voting in Lutherton but not in Motorville or Gravesend? Local newspaper accounts suggest the answer is rooted in historical ideas about race and the role of the federal government in Lutherton. Despite the overwhelming importance of the civil rights movement to American party politics, it was only a sporadic feature on the front and editorial pages of all three local newspapers during the 1950s and 1960s. In fact, the *Gravesend Ledger* was the only one of the three to mention the Montgomery Bus Boycott on its front page. But as the Birmingham Campaign developed in the spring of 1964, both the *Motorville Post* and the *Gravesend Ledger* routinely gave prime space to its activities: during the days leading up to and following these major events in the campaign, the *Gravesend Ledger* ran 50 front-page articles about them, the *Motorville Post* ran 41, and the *Lutherton Gazette* a scant 18.

The *Lutherton Gazette's* relative silence on the civil rights movement echoes an informal conversation I had with a retired Black resident named George, who grew up in a neighboring city and worked in Lutherton for many years during his adulthood. As he told me, the whole area had "slept through" the civil rights movement—there was hardly any political activity. This was not because Lutherton did not need radical social change. Like many northern states, Indiana, Minnesota, and Wisconsin all had histories of segregation, employment discrimination, and White supremacist violence. Indiana had even, during the 1850s, adopted a constitutional amendment barring Black immigration into the state. But conditions also varied between cities within states.[29] The same is true of Motorville, Lutherton, and Gravesend. Of the three, Lutherton has the most profound history of institutionalized racism: as a handful of residents recalled during our conversations, often with a shake of their heads, one of the smaller towns in Lutherton County was a sundown town. A sign warning Black visitors to leave town before sunset stood along the roadside well into the 1960s. At the time, Lutherton County was more than 99 percent White, perhaps due in part to this threat of racial violence. The few Black residents who did reside within Lutherton City limits lived in a segregated neighborhood—one that many older White and Black residents can still identify—and could not participate in many elements of public life.

It was also during the civil rights movement that the *Lutherton Gazette* began running syndicated opinion columns from William F. Buckley Jr., perhaps the central figure in the intellectual development of the American conservative movement in the 1950s and 1960s. During the civil rights movement, this included pieces challenging the Supreme Court's decisions on civil rights issues and supporting Barry Goldwater's segregationist campaign. Many of Buckley's complaints about the civil rights movement took a "states' rights" angle, arguing that the federal government was overstepping its appropriate authority in ruling on issues of segregation.[30] Although we may understand these complaints as poorly coded racist appeals to White voters, this rhetoric also echoed arguments from several local editorial pieces run in the *Lutherton Gazette* since the early 1950s, in which the editors decried the "trend to centralization" in the United States, arguing as they did in a December 1955 piece that the country has long faced the same debate: "between those who want a strong central government and those who would build up local and state powers as a bulwark against centralization. The local-state champions have been losing out in recent years." In making this argument, Lutherton's editor was not just echoing the national Republican Party: by 1955 Republican president Eisenhower had made the interstate highway system a legislative priority, and it seemed that both parties had come to agree on the much-expanded role for the federal government that began with the New Deal.[31]

And yet, editorials of this kind were relatively common in both Lutherton and Gravesend but exceedingly rare in Motorville. This means that Buckley's "states' rights" argument against the civil rights movement may have resonated with Lutherton residents (who otherwise heard relatively little about the civil rights movement) on two fronts: not only their racial conservatism but their preference for local control.[32]

Although Motorvillians and Gravesenders had access to a greater quantity of civil rights news, this coverage did not always cover the movement favorably: both local papers ran nationally syndicated columns that opposed the movement. Moreover, Motorville had been the site of occasional flare-ups of racial violence during the 1920s as Black workers migrated north in search of work and found the White union members hostile and, occasionally, violent. In other words, it is unlikely that any of these overwhelmingly White cities was a bastion of racial progressivism in the 1960s. But only the *Lutherton Gazette* and *Gravesend Ledger* ran *local* editorials voicing opposition to the civil rights movement, and only Lutherton voters reacted to the movement by ceasing to vote for the national Democratic Party.

In sum, residents of Motorville, Lutherton, and Gravesend lived in different informational and institutional environments, which shaped how they learned about the civil rights movement and what its ramifications would be for their own lives. For White Lutherton residents, the civil rights movement was perhaps a far-off development, but one that threatened the White supremacist order of their city. The states' rights arguments routinely trumpeted by segregationists also would have resonated in a place where residents were used to hearing this kind of logic. The result was Lutherton's sharp turn to the right in 1968.

In making this turn, Lutherton was not alone: 49 percent of the White, New Deal counties were part of the "Turned Republican" cluster shown in figure 3. Another 19% turned even further Republican in 1968. This included places all across the country, of varying sizes: suburbs like Butler County, Kansas, and Archer County, Texas, as well as small cities like Vincennes, Indiana, and Sidney, Ohio. But even as these places moved into the Republican column, the other 32 percent of the original White, New Deal counties—including Motorville and Gravesend—remained in the Democratic fold with varying degrees of enthusiasm.

The Moral Majority and a New Politics of Religion

The same geographic unevenness occurred after the rise of the Religious Right. During the 1960s, religious groups mobilized for several reasons—including school segregation, sexual morality, and the separation between church and state. Although these disparate mobilizations did not amount to a united political movement at that time, they laid the groundwork for the rise of the Religious Right in the late 1970s, when evangelical Christians joined the Catholic-dominated anti-abortion movement and, under the auspices of Jerry Falwell's Moral Majority, began to seek incorporation into the Republican Party.[33] When, in 1980, the Republican Party officially endorsed a constitutional amendment to ban abortion, they sent a strong signal that they were now the party of Christian conservatives. Over the following election cycles, they succeeded in winning over the votes of this group, ultimately creating a new political cleavage between devout, traditionalist Christians and less-devout or non-Christians.[34]

But even before the 1973 Supreme Court decision, various Christian groups—primarily Catholics—had been concerned about abortion as a moral issue.[35] Given this denominational variation in the trajectory of national abortion politics, we might expect that places like Motorville and Gravesend, where Catholics made up 23 and 12 percent of the respective populations in 1980, witnessed anti-abortion movements first, followed later by Lutherton, where Catholics made up just 4 percent of the population in 1980 but evangelical Protestants made up 36 percent.[36] This is, to some extent, what happened: although anti-abortion activists appeared to have made little public headway in Motorville, they made early inroads within Gravesend's Republican Party via local Catholic churches but foundered within a broader community that was largely mainline Protestant. In contrast, anti-abortion activism arrived later in Lutherton but eventually managed to transform Lutherton politics.

In the days following the Supreme Court's January 1973 decision in *Roe v. Wade*, the *Motorville Post* and *Gravesend Ledger* were the only papers to note the event on the front page. But despite the city's large Catholic population, the *Motorville Post* ran a piece with a headline citing a doctor from a Wisconsin abortion clinic who "hailed" the decision. In contrast, the *Gravesend Ledger* carried both an editorial piece and a letter to the editor decrying the immorality of abortion in the week after *Roe*. Over the next two years, local Catholic women hosted gatherings in Gravesend for the Minnesota Citizens Concerned for Life, a statewide anti-abortion organization. But the local Republican Party, as evidenced by coverage of their 1978 caucus, remained somewhat divided on the issue. Over the years, this began to change—in part, as retired Republican activists recalled to me in summer 2019, because of their dogged efforts to bring the issue to the forefront of the party. But even as local conservative activists coalesced around a pro-life stance, this did not radically alter broader politics in Gravesend: apart from the 1980 presidential election, Gravesend's support for Republican Party presidential candidates remained lukewarm for decades. This is because, while Catholics were a sizable minority of the population, most Gravesend residents attended mainline Protestant churches (a full 66 percent of residents were mainline adherents in 1980). Even as a large evangelical church opened its doors in Gravesend in the 1990s and created a vocal Christian conservative minority by the time of my fieldwork, they did not transform place-politics.

In contrast, Lutherton's politics were indeed transformed. But in the 1970s, this outcome would not have been obvious: without a large Catholic population in Lutherton, the anti-abortion movement was slower to materialize than it was in Gravesend. It wasn't until 1988 that Lutherton held its first "Vigil for Life" in a local park to mark the fifteen-year anniversary of the Roe decision. It was Catholics who organized the first two annual gatherings, but by the early 1990s some of the most prominent and well-resourced evangelical churches in the city got involved, including the Baptist church and several evangelical Lutheran churches. For much of this time, the city's abortion politics were not yet monolithic: as the *Lutherton Gazette* recorded in 1991, the county's state representative who went on to win federal office in the district opposed abortion on "moral grounds" but did not think it should be legislated.

But by the early 2000s, Lutherton's support for Republican candidates at all levels of government appeared complete. As a former Republican Party chair recounted in summer 2019, he credits Bill Clinton with Republicans' sweep of all Lutherton County's elected offices in 2000: the churchgoing community could no longer stand Democrats' immoral politics. In many ways, Lutherton residents followed the path of White southerners—defecting first from voting for the Democratic Party in presidential elections, then slowly moving into alignment with the Republican Party at all levels of government.[37]

Thus, while Gravesend saw the earliest political mobilizations around abortion, pro-life politics remained limited to Catholics and a contingent of Republican activists. Several local and national factors played a role in this: Christian denominational variation, labor organization, and each city's earlier reaction to the Racial Realignment. By the 1980s, Lutherton was—as we will see—already devoid of an active labor movement, but it was still full of evangelical churches. This denominational variation mattered not just for the timing of Lutherton's pro-life movement but for its size: even though Lutherton had about two-thirds the church adherence per capita as Gravesend from 1970 to 2010, evangelical church adherents are more likely to attend church services than are mainline Protestants and Catholics.[38] Moreover, Democratic partisans in Lutherton had already experienced one chip in their loyalties to the national Democratic Party after the Racial Realignment, making it easier to continue to vote for Republicans and ultimately affiliate with that party. In contrast, during the same decade, Catholic and mainline Protestant Gravesenders were still embroiled in labor disputes and the drama of Rivervalley's decline, as we will see, and had yet to experience any serious disaffection from the Democratic Party. In short, the historic layering of past changes in local organizations and cultural frameworks meant that Lutherton had become, by the 1980s, the ideal place for local evangelical churches to merge anti-abortion politics with Republican Party politics.

Lutherton's growing Republicanism was not unusual at this time: in the 2000 presidential election, another 11 percent of the original New Deal counties, also relatively evangelical, began voting majority-Republican.[39] All told, just over 20 percent of the original White, New Deal counties remained competitive for Democrats after the 2000 presidential election—some, like Gravesend, were part of the "Lean Dem" cluster shown in figure 3; others leaned Republican but swung Democratic in 2004; and just 4%, Motorville among them, "Stayed Democratic."

Deindustrialization and the Decline of Organized Labor

But by 2016, only 4 percent of the original New Deal counties remained Democratic. Gravesend, like so many other counties, finally turned to the right during the 2016 and 2020 election seasons: up and down the ballot, residents voted majority-Republican. Alongside Gravesend, Republicans in 2012 and 2016 began winning other places that were part of the "Lean Dem" cluster, including: Fayette County, Pennsylvania, part of the state's coal region, and Belmont County, Ohio, which is in Appalachia and had already slipped Republican in 2012. But unlike so many of its peers, Motorville remained majority-Democratic in 2016 and 2020, continuing to elect Democrats in local, statewide, and national races. If neither of the political realignments of late twentieth-century American politics swept up Gravesend, what happened in recent years that has? And how has Motorville, alone among the three cities, resisted the rightward pull? Part 2 will answer these questions in full, but the remainder of this chapter will set the stage for those arguments, showing what happened to organized labor, the key link between the working classes and the Democratic Party, during the period of deindustrialization in Motorville, Lutherton, and Gravesend. We will see how residents' previous experiences within local organizations shaped their responses to structural shifts during deindustrialization, which then went on to shape the cities' organizational futures. Although both Motorville and Gravesend emerged into the twenty-first century with some semblance of a labor movement intact, a combination of depoliticization within Gravesend's unions and setbacks to the broader economy left the city with a more anemic movement. Although that was insufficient to turn residents toward the Republican Party in the early 2000s, it had become more meaningful by 2016, as we will see in chapter 5.

In the 1970s and 1980s, globalization led to the outsourcing of supply chains, spurring on a decline in manufacturing employment in the industrial Heartland

and a growth of precarious labor.[40] Total manufacturing employment in the United States did not begin to decline until the 1980s, but already by the 1950s and 1960s, the share of workers employed in the manufacturing sector was dwindling.[41] This of course presented challenges to the U.S. labor movement, particularly in the Heartland, but as Barry Eidlin (2018) and Marc Dixon (2020) have recently shown, these structural economic challenges were not deterministic: internal labor movement struggles, increasingly aggressive anti-union tactics by businesses from the 1950s to the 1970s, and the erosion of labor protections all chipped away at private sector unionization. Already in 1947, Congress passed the Taft-Hartley amendments to the Wagner Act, which allowed states to pass so-called "right-to-work" laws outlawing the union shop. Where they passed, the laws reduced union organizing and, ultimately, union membership.[42] The amendments forced the AFL-CIO in many states into a defensive position, working to fend off or even reverse right-to-work laws rather than advance the labor movement.[43] The result was not just national union decline—union membership fell from a peak of 35 percent of nonagricultural workers in 1954 to 20.9 percent in 1980—but an uneven geography of decline.[44]

These changes of course had ramifications in Motorville, Lutherton, and Gravesend: each economy was impacted somewhat differently by global economic forces, but just as importantly, each city responded to macroeconomic disruptions in ways that reshaped the trajectory of their local labor movement. Deindustrialization reached Motorville first. Founded as a rail and river-based transport hub, Motorville's freight traffic had historically been a mix of agricultural products and coal. As industrialized nations shifted away from coal and toward hydrocarbons as a source of fuel in the 1940s–1960s, Motorville's freight business dwindled. With population and employment falling away, Motorville's leaders in the 1960s were already working on a plan of economic diversification—moving away from its industrial roots toward urban renewal that would promote tourism. The city formed an Economic Development Association, on which the leader of the Motorville Labor Council sat for several years. It is challenging to compare industrial employment data over time given changes in how industries have been classified, but even with that caveat in mind, it's clear that Motorville saw large losses in its largest employment sector: transportation and utilities made up over 25 percent of Motorville's employment in 1940 and just under 15 percent in 1980.

Although these were challenging years for Motorville, the losses did not entirely devastate the local economy. Core industries remained: nine of the county's twelve largest employers from the manufacturing, transportation, and construction sectors in the 1950s remained in business through 2010, although two merged together, many got smaller, and most changed ownership during that period.[45] Moreover, three of these employers still have unionized workforces—some of the same locals that were the most militant in the early twentieth century.[46]

With this economic stability, Motorville's labor movement was also able to remain actively engaged in both economic and political battles through the 1950s, 1960s, and 1970s. In fact, in 1964, just after the city hired a consulting company to address its economic challenges, voters overwhelmingly elected a "man who has largely been associated with the labor union movement," according to the *Motorville Post*, who then worked to ensure public contracts went to union labor. At the same time, Motorville's unions continued to engage in semi-regular strikes. Following national trends in work stoppages, local newspaper accounts indicate that Motorville's strike activity peaked in the 1950s, then saw a lull in the 1960s, only to skyrocket again in the 1970s, a period of widespread labor militancy.[47] This surge was driven in part by public sector unions, after Wisconsin became the first state to grant public employees the right to bargain collectively in 1959.[48]

Margaret is a retired teacher and labor movement leader who was active in Motorville's local teachers' union, affiliated with the American Federation of Teachers (AFT). As she recalls, those years were tumultuous: although it was illegal for teachers to strike in Wisconsin, Motorville teachers went on strike six times between 1967 and 1977. The Motorville school board took an oppositional stance to the AFT, leading to several dramatic moments, as Margaret recounts: "[During the last strike] I was served with summons to report to court. . . . The bargaining team moved every day for about two and a half weeks. . . . And my mom lived with me. . . . And she sat in the dark for two weeks so they wouldn't try to serve her the summons." The animosity fizzled out after this, but only because the state passed a law forcing public sector employees into binding arbitration, rendering strikes moot.[49] But the AFT's experiences underscored, for labor leaders like Margaret, the importance of local political engagement: having school board members on their side could have changed the outcome of their contract negotiations.

In sum, even as Motorville's economy was changing, the local labor movement remained somewhat intact. This outcome was not guaranteed, as Margaret's comments show: organized labor fought for its survival and made itself relevant to rank-and-file members, and it was helped along by a favorable state policy context.

By the mid-1980s, when Motorville's city planners were already hoping that their economy had weathered the worst of its storms, Lutherton and

Gravesend were watching their economies crumble.[50] In 1970, fully 45 percent of Lutherton's residents were employed in manufacturing. This had dropped to 30 percent by 1990. During the 1970s and 1980s three of Lutherton's largest employers closed or relocated. The biggest blow came from the relocation of an auto parts manufacturer called McMaster Auto, which employed approximately nine hundred workers in Lutherton throughout the 1950s, 1960s, and 1970s. The workers were part of the national United Auto Workers (UAW) and participated in at least two strikes during the 1950s and 1960s. When McMaster abruptly relocated after a contentious contract negotiation with the union in the 1970s, the opinion pages of the *Lutherton Gazette* shared the rumor that they were relocating to the South in search of "cheaper labor." Although the company's official statements did not corroborate this, the *Gazette* contained a brief back-and-forth between local residents who either supported or blamed the UAW for the devastating outcome. When a new manufacturer took over McMaster's vacated plant that same year, they employed about one-third of the workforce. The UAW attempted to unionize the plant twice— probably speaking to many of the same workers who had just recently been part of their union—and failed both times. Instead, perhaps learning from McMaster's departure, workers favored an employees' association—one not connected to the AFL-CIO or any broader labor movement. Some of the differences between Motorville and Lutherton are due to state-level politics: Indiana never offered as favorable a climate for labor politics as did Wisconsin. But by the time of McMaster's departure, the Indiana labor movement had overcome internal divisions, successfully repealed the state's right-to-work law, and won collective bargaining rights for teachers just two years after Minnesota.[51] And yet, Lutherton workers opted out of the union.

This marked a turning point in both the quantity of union workers in Lutherton and the nature of the local labor movement. In 1978, just three years after McMaster left, Lutherton's Labor Council was absorbed into a regional labor body, which later also disbanded. The political and community arm of Lutherton organized labor was dying, not by chance but in part by choice. Contrast this to Motorville, where—despite changes in the economic bases of the city— local labor leaders remained actively involved in politics and community life.

Conditions continued to deteriorate in Lutherton: just a few years after McMaster left, two other major employers closed their Lutherton operations. But then, in the late 1980s, Lutherton's decline halted abruptly. Pete Risher witnessed this turnaround firsthand. He's the director of the Lutherton

County Economic Development Association, and as he says, when he took on the role in 1986: "unemployment was double digits. The tax base was declining. There were absolutely fewer jobs for students graduating from high school." The turnaround came just two years later, when he managed to "land" one of the biggest suppliers of tractor parts in the country, AgTrac, and convince them to build a factory in town. By 2000, manufacturing employment had risen again, to make up 34 percent of Lutherton's employment. Today, as Lutherton's largest private sector employer, AgTrac's success has helped Pete market the city as "business friendly" to other manufacturers. They are not now, nor have they ever been, a union shop.

Pete's successes were on such a scale that, today, nearly everyone I met in Lutherton characterizes the city's economy as "booming." When I mentioned Lutherton County Economic Development Association's annual investment target to the head of the Gravesend Development Association, he gaped at me. It was not just the size of the target that was shocking: part of Gravesend's five-year development plan is to simply begin setting investment targets. These conversations reflect real differences in how deindustrialization has played out in Gravesend, relative to Motorville and Lutherton, as figure 4 shows. The figure summarizes the extent to which each county's economy had shifted from industrialized labor to service sector work by the twenty-first century. Each panel shows the share of the county's total GDP produced by the three most unionized private sector industries from 2001 to 2019, in the solid black line, and the share produced by the service sector, in the dashed gray line. The most unionized industries during this period, according to data from Barry Hirsch and David Macpherson (2019), were manufacturing, transportation and utilities, and construction.

As we can see, the figure highlights Lutherton's economic rebound—among the three counties, unionized industrial output was largest in Lutherton, and a far larger share than the United States as a whole. For most of this period, manufacturing, transportation, and construction made up just about 20 percent of total U.S. GDP. But the figure also emphasizes the differences between Gravesend, on the one hand, and Lutherton and Motorville, on the other: both Lutherton and Motorville's economies are still based in manufacturing, transportation, and construction while Gravesend's is much more evenly divided between those unionized industries and service sector work.

But this was not always the case. Gravesend reached a height of manufacturing employment in 1970—29 percent of total employment—a figure that

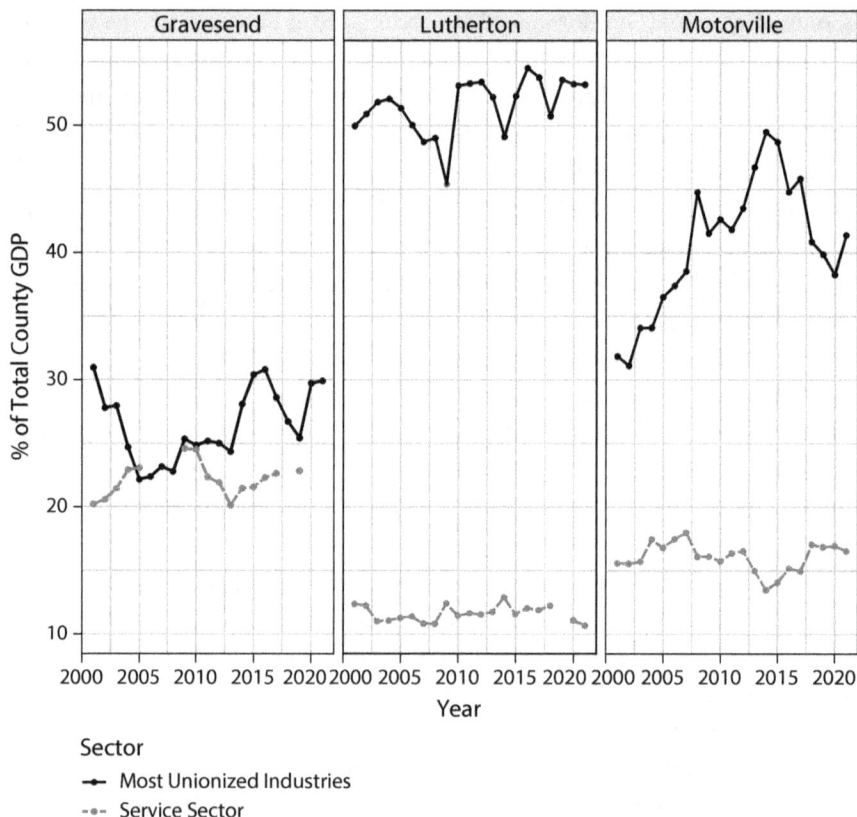

FIGURE 4. County GDP by unionized industries vs. service sector, 2001–19.
Note: Data are from the Bureau of Economic Analysis (BEA). They show
the share of total county GDP produced by the service sector and the most
unionized private sector industries, according to 2012 NAICS industrial codes.
According to Hirsch and McPherson's (2019) unionization-by-industry data for
2001–19, the most unionized private sector industries were—on average—
transportation and utilities, construction, and manufacturing. The BEA data are
missing several years of service sector output for Motorville and Gravesend.

had fallen to 18–20 percent in the years leading up to the 2016 presidential
election. Gravesend's *relative* decline in manufacturing employment during
this time was actually smaller than Lutherton's, but it left a far smaller share of
people working in manufacturing overall.

Moreover, decline in Gravesend took a particularly dramatic path from which
the city has never fully recovered. Even though organized labor in Gravesend
became less politically active after the 1930s, the city remained a "union town"

for many decades, as several older residents told me in summer 2019. This is because Rivervalley Foundries remained Gravesend's largest employer for most of the twentieth century, with over one thousand employees until the 1980s. As a result, much of the city's workforce was unionized and—as they showed on four occasions between 1940 and 1980—willing to strike for better wages and working conditions. And while Rivervalley steelworkers were the majority of local unionists, they were not alone: the *Gravesend Ledger* reported five strikes during the 1950s (a fraction of Motorville's seventeen), often including both Rivervalley and other union shops. The strikes made an enduring impact on Gravesend. In 1956, after the final one, the *Gravesend Ledger* ran an editorial encouraging the town to adopt a labor-management-citizens council that could help them "head off labor disputes before they progress to the economic wars we call strikes," which the author worried would "drain the life blood from the city" and give Gravesend "a poor reputation in the business world."

This was one of several editorials that the *Ledger* ran during the decade voicing opposition to strikes—an unsurprising stance, given that the paper was understood by some to be "anti-union," as described earlier. But while Gravesenders were likely divided over what this period of labor unrest meant for their city, the fact that it was significant seems indisputable: in my conversations it wasn't unusual for residents today, especially retirees, to refer to the strikes in the 1950s as emblematic of the kind of city Gravesend once was.

But for the most part, when residents spoke to me of organized labor, they did so with the recognition that it was part of a bygone era. This is because in 1979 Rivervalley filed for bankruptcy and sold the plant, sending shockwaves through the local labor movement. I learned about this history in late summer 2019 when I spoke with Charlie, the retired president of the steelworkers' union whose two-decades-long presidency encompassed most of the plant's ups and downs since 1979. As we sat around a conference table in Gravesend's union hall, we examined a ten-foot chart with handwritten dates on one side and dollar amounts on the other. It was the union's log of every annual wage increase they'd gained between 1941 and 1982. The effect of the 1979 bankruptcy filing is clear. Up until that Friday—"Black Friday," as Charlie calls it—Rivervalley had been paying their workers $10.69 base wage, plus a piece rate. By the following Monday, they had slashed wages to $6 an hour. As Charlie tells me: "I was making $14.32 cents an hour on a Friday, came in on Monday morning, I'm making six dollars an hour."

While a three-week strike succeeded in raising wages to $8 an hour, this was a pyrrhic victory: by the late 1990s, when Charlie retired, the foundry workers were up to just $11 or $12 an hour, just over where they'd been before the 1979 bankruptcy declaration. And in the interceding decades, Rivervalley declared bankruptcy and switched hands multiple times before the end of the millennium, routinely throwing employees into unemployment. Each time they reopened, they employed fewer workers. This period of uncertainty concluded in dramatic fashion when—in the late 1990s—the plant burned down. While no lives were lost, all jobs were: the owners decided not to rebuild. "We were on vacation when it happened," Rich, who worked at the plant, told me of his wife's and his reaction. "And we just looked at each other and said, I guess we better stop spending money!" While residents today often point to the fire as the end of their city's viability, the pressures of globalization had been slowly eroding its economic foundation for decades.

Although Gravesend's economy experienced a particularly dramatic downturn in the 1990s, a smaller foundry eventually opened in town and the city has ultimately made up the jobs it lost. Moreover, the United Steelworkers (USW) was able to reunionize workers in the former Rivervalley plant each time it changed ownership, and the new foundry in town is still a union shop. Although the current USW president, Alex, feels that organizing is much harder today than it was decades ago, workers in Gravesend repeatedly made different choices than workers in Lutherton, despite the fact that Lutherton has proved much more economically resilient in an era of deindustrialization. But the broader Gravesend labor movement also made different organizing choices than did their counterparts in Motorville: during the 1950s–1970s when Wisconsin and Minnesota were both expanding rights for organized labor, particularly in the public sector, Gravesend's labor movement failed to rebuild the political coalition they had consolidated during the 1930s. After the 1950s, I found little evidence of movement-building across Gravesend's locals. As is the case with the national labor movement, structural factors were not determinative of local organizational outcomes: state-level politics and local organizing histories also played a role in how each city's workers responded to economic crises.

This has important consequences for the kind of place that Gravesend is today: while the city has been struggling much more than both Motorville and Lutherton with the spiral of economic and population decline plaguing other postindustrial cities, it still has *quantitatively* strong union membership but, relative to Motorville, its unions play little role in the city's public sphere.[52]

In sum, Motorville, Lutherton, and Gravesend were never identical places, but they shared enough structural similarities in the 1930s and 1940s—occupational and racial characteristics as well as economic conditions—that we could not have predicted that each would respond so differently to the political-economic developments of the late twentieth century. But as those developments unfolded, community leaders and residents made choices that changed the local organizational and cultural context, making it *more likely* future actors would respond to political and economic shocks in certain ways. This historical layering of local response to extra-local disruption ultimately carved out distinctive cities from within regional similarities.[53]

For example, the Wagner Act did help produce an organized labor movement in all three cities by the 1940s. But by the end of the 1970s, decisions about how to organize—some of them structured by local economic conditions and state policies toward organized labor—left each city with a very different kind of labor movement. As a result, when the Moral Majority entered into a coalition with the national Republican Party, as Schlozman (2015) describes, this had different impacts on each city according to the kinds of places they had become: only in Lutherton, which had strong evangelical roots and had already made choices that decimated the local labor movement *and* moved residents away from the Democratic Party, did this national coalition transform local politics.

These are just three cases, drawing on archival evidence, of how these processes of local response to extra-local disruption created distinctive places and distinctive sets of politics; but this chapter also indicates potential explanations for the different political trajectories of the other White, working-class New Deal cities since the 1960s. To underscore this point, table 1 summarizes the political, economic, and religious changes that took place in each of the clusters of which Motorville, Lutherton, and Gravesend are a part.

As we can see, while all three clusters started during the New Deal with relatively equal portions of the workforce employed in working-class occupations as laborers, craftmen, and operatives, the counties that stayed Democratic until 2016 had a much larger portion of that workforce employed in the industries that were most unionized, including manufacturing, construction, and transportation and utilities. We can also see that the counties that turned toward the Republicans under Nixon, including Lutherton, had both the least employment in unionized industries and the most evangelical adherents per capita.

This table is not meant to suggest that aggregate counts of organizational adherents or industrial employment are sufficient indicators of how place

TABLE 1. Changes in Occupational, Racial, and Religious Characteristics among New Deal Counties

	Turned Republican, 1960s	Lean Dem, Swing to Republican 2016	Stayed Democratic
% Employed as laborers, 1940	20	19	14
% Employed as craftmen, 1940	8.8	9.7	12.1
% Employed as operatives, 1940	16	18	24
% Employed in most unionized industries, 1940	26	29	39
Change in unionized industry employment, 1980–90	−2.8	−2.8	−4.9
% Employed in maintenance, 2016	4.3	4.1	3.4
% Employed in construction, 2016	6.6	6.0	5.6
% Employed in production, 2016	9.8	9.8	6.1
% Employed in transportation, 2016	8.3	8.6	6.2
% White, 1940	98	99	99
% White, Non-Hispanic, 2016	92	92	90
Evangelicalism per capita, 1952	17.5	8.9	2.7
Change in evangelicalism per capita, 1952–2000	1.4	2.1	2.1

Note: The measure of employment in unionized industries includes employment in manufacturing, construction, and transportation/communications/utilities from the 1940 industry codes; and construction, manufacturing, transportation, and communications/utilities from the 1980 and 1990 industry codes. These are the private sector industries that were most unionized during the time period for which we have unionization-by-industry data (see Hirsch and Macpherson 2019). Although the sharpest national declines in manufacturing took place after 2000, the census changed industry codes in 2000, making over-time comparisons difficult. The 1980–90 change thus provides a snapshot of a longer process of deindustrialization. The measure of evangelicalism is based on the Association of Religion Data Archives (ARDA) combined 1980–2010 file of religious adherents and RELTRAD coding for denominational groupings (Steensland et al. 2000).

shapes politics—in fact, as we have seen, Lutherton has the most employment in unionized industries of all three cities, and still has several apolitical unions, but its labor movement is the least active. Instead, when we consider table 1 alongside historical evidence from this chapter and contemporary accounts of how local organizational arrangements operate in each city today, it suggests that Motorville's *particular kind of politically engaged labor movement* is what has helped it buck the regional trend toward the Right. This offers some indication of what it would have taken to keep the other 96 percent of New Deal counties in the Democratic fold amid political realignments and deindustrialization.

In sum, Motorville, Lutherton, and Gravesend are three cases that hint at a broader pattern of local response to state and national transformations, which shaped the trajectory of the Heartland's reddening. Chapter 2 will take us to the present day of each city, as we examine how these historic place-processes have produced the cities as they are today, defined by distinct organizational contexts. And as we will see throughout the rest of the book, it is the legacy of these processes that continues to hold Motorville residents back from the rightward pulls that have carried Lutherton, Gravesend, and almost all of the other New Deal counties into the Republican column.

2

Local Organizations and the Shape of Problem-Solving in Motorville, Lutherton, and Gravesend

THE FIRST TIME I MEET with Mike, the head of the Political Action Team for the building trades local in Motorville, it's an early summer evening in 2019. As we sit sipping beer at a local brewery, he recounts how the union changed his life: because of union wages, Mike—a single father and veteran—will be able to take his kids on their first vacation this summer. Now, he's dedicated to giving back to the union. And a big part of that, as he explains, is getting involved in local politics. It can be hard to convince his coworkers that this is important: "We work hard. I mean, all week I'm putting in eleven-, twelve-hour days," he tells me. "But then, like I go to a council meeting and show up in my work clothes. Nobody wants to do that. They want to go home. They want to have a beer." I already knew that showing up at City Council meetings was part of Mike's political repertoire, as I had met him during a protest he spearheaded at a meeting the week before. To corral members to these events, he works diligently to remind them of what the union has done for them and how they need to protect it politically. As he tells me:

> And then when we do endorse [a politician], it's 100 percent. None of this bullshit where we're just going to give you money for your campaign. No, we're going to have our guys out there door knocking for you. We're going to have our guys at the Q and As for you, we're going to have our guys at City Hall for you.

Mike is part of one of the most active unions in Motorville, but what he describes indicates the contemporary instantiation of Motorville's long history of union organizing: organized labor is still fighting economic battles on political terrain, working to elect candidates who support pro-labor policies. And in so doing, they reinforce long-standing links, both symbolic and material, between the political and economic spheres in Motorville.

Contrast this to Lutherton, where unions are apolitical and the public sphere is instead dominated by churches and nonprofits. Lauren, the chair of the Lutherton County Republican Party, tells me this the first time we meet, munching grilled cheese sandwiches at a restaurant on Main Street: "If you drive around, there's probably just about a church on every corner." She pauses after she says this and points out the window: "Seriously, there's a church right there around the corner, the Catholic church. . . . Religion is very important to people in Lutherton."

But churches are more than just a sign of Luthertonians' religiosity, as Lauren indicates later in the conversation. She's mentioned that Donald Trump is so popular in part because of how he talks about Christianity, and I ask her if local candidates talk about the same things. She considers this, and then responds: "I don't know. When you're running on a local level, I don't think you have to talk about that . . . but if people know that you are affiliated with a specific church, that's going to help you." When I ask her to explain what she could mean by a "specific church" she responds:

> LAUREN: . . . I'll use Mayor Lubock as an example. Mayor Lubock grew up in Lutherton. He went to Immaculate School. That's the local parochial school just down the street too.
>
> ST: Is that also where you went?
>
> LAUREN: Yes.
>
> ST: All right.
>
> LAUREN: So we went to school together. So that's the thing, Mayor Lubock and I both got to say we attended Immaculate Lutheran School for eight years, and in turn, made a connection with every single person who has ever sent their child to Immaculate School or belongs to Immaculate Church [one of the biggest congregations in town]. Lubock, he attends church at Immaculate Lutheran Church, the church affiliated with the school. Huge congregation. Huge. Connections that never end. Just personal connections, financial connections. And I'm not going to lie, when I look for a candidate, that's something I consider, like where you go to church.

Lauren is far from the only person who points to churches as a kind of linchpin in Lutherton's public life—not to tell me that churches are preaching politics from the pulpit, although they sometimes do—but to tell me that they are the center of community life, stitching people together through their "connections that never end." And as I later learned, some of the most important connections they facilitate are among other congregations, volunteers, and nonprofits, which create a kind of private, collective problem-solving network outside of local government.

When it comes to churches and unions, Gravesend shares similarities with both Motorville and Lutherton: both organizations have had large memberships for decades, as we saw in chapter 1. But today, as Connie, the head of Gravesend's Tourism Board, tells me, they are no longer central to how the city gets things done. Instead, she explains, it's public-private partnerships that have helped revitalize Gravesend's idyllic Main Street and served as a model for all her work in the city:

> That's what you see with our community, because there's a lot of different partnerships, and I think you see a lot of passion. Rather than some communities, [where] they have maybe one big huge corporation and they go to them for everything. And that's the beauty of having maybe more of a diverse community with businesses and so forth, because you can partner with them, and everybody gets something.

To Connie, what many Gravesenders view as one of the community's greatest weaknesses—its lack of one large corporation since Rivervalley's demise—is also an opportunity for strength. But in its absence, she and other community leaders must find ways of scraping together resources each time they confront a new challenge or want to get something done for the city.

————

What Mike, Lauren, and Connie are describing are distinct organizational contexts, or public and private entities and their relationships with one another, that structure contemporary problem-solving in each city. Unions are tied to local government and elected officials in Motorville—an arrangement that links the political with the economic—while churches facilitate a network of volunteers and nonprofits in Lutherton—an arrangement that promotes nongovernmental action. But despite these differences, both Motorville and Lutherton contain organizations that have long provided continuity and structure to collective problem-solving. In Gravesend, this is not the case. Here, the city lacks a stable set of organizations to turn to in times of need, such that community leaders often pull together ad hoc partnerships among government, nonprofits, and local businesses to address challenges.

We can see how each of these organizational contexts is a legacy of the historic place-processes described in chapter 1: Lutherton's core of large, well-resourced churches has long been part of local social life and civic action, while Gravesend's church ecology has changed over the years and Motorville's has simply dwindled; Motorville's unions have been involved in local politics since the nineteenth century, while Gravesend's typically employer-focused unions have taken serious hits since the 1980s, and Lutherton's workers opted out of the political labor movement in the 1970s.

In short, these organizational contexts are products of historic place evolution, and today they help reproduce place and place-based partisanship.[1] As we will see in chapters 3 and 4, when these contexts are stable, they lead residents to cohere around two cultural frameworks that reinforce their partisan attachments: (1) *diagnostic frames* for defining what their problems are and how to solve them politically; and (2) *narratives of community identity* that tell residents what kind of community they are and where they fit into the party system.

This chapter will focus on *why* these organizational differences matter so keenly to place-based partisanship today: because local governments rarely get things done by themselves. Instead, they work in partnership with private entities, including local nonprofits, corporations, and foundations, to deliver social services to residents.[2] The importance of public-private partnerships to successful local governance stems from the Great Society era, when LBJ departed from urban renewal practices that demolished entire communities and began investing federal dollars in local, neighborhood-based nonprofits. This arrangement was then reified during the Reagan era, when the federal government worked to devolve social service provision to the local level. The reforms also forced local governments and nonprofit agencies to compete for funds once granted to them, such that cities could no longer depend to the same extent on federal resources.[3]

At the same time as public investment was retreating and transforming, local economies in industrially dependent places were facing a crunch, as we saw in chapter 1: by the 1980s and 1990s, even family-owned businesses were no longer safe from the wave of mergers, cutbacks, and layoffs sweeping across the United States as corporations sought ever-higher profits by moving jobs across the globe. As sociologist Jessica Simes (2021) has recently shown, this dual process of public and private disinvestment in small, postindustrial cities mirrors what happened to inner-city neighborhoods in the early years of deindustrialization—often producing the same kinds of social problems.[4] Places like Motorville, Lutherton, and Gravesend now face a rise in both poverty and precarious employment; a brain drain of educated youth that threatens the tax base and ages communities; aging housing that is poor quality and expensive to maintain, particularly for residents who are not making the same real wages their parents did; and a rise in drug addiction.[5]

But even as postindustrial cities face similar challenges, their ability to address them now varies according to their local organizational context, which determines which organizations get a seat at the table and how they coordinate among multiple other organizations within and outside of government.[6] As Josh Pacewicz (2016) has shown, cities "win" economically when local organizations learn to become "partners"—just as Connie described—to better compete with other cities for scarce resources. Partnerships between local government, nonprofits, businesses, and foundations are thus increasingly the norm in how cities govern themselves. The same is true to an extent of Motorville, Lutherton, and Gravesend.

But this chapter will depart from previous accounts of how local organizations get things done for their cities in two ways. First, I argue that new partnerships are embedded in long-standing organizational contexts: today's community leaders, partners or not, are products of distinct, local contexts characterized by ties to different kinds of organizations. This means that union leaders are more likely to participate in economic development decisions in Motorville while church leaders do the same in Lutherton. Second, Motorville, Lutherton, and Gravesend show us that local organizational contexts are consequential for residents' experience of social problems—and ultimately for their partisanship—not just because of differences in their content but because of differences in their relative stability. Organizational contexts in Motorville and Lutherton are characterized by long-standing relationships and experiences of collective action, which means they provide a regularity to problem-solving and social interaction that is lacking in Gravesend. And as we will see in chapters 3 and 4, this organizational stability is what sustains the cultural frameworks that prevent Motorville from drifting toward the right.

This chapter describes the distinct organizational contexts in each city. I show how unions' political activism creates ties to local government in Motorville, and how Lutherton's churches facilitate a private, collective problem-solving network outside of local government. And in Gravesend we can glimpse a kind of counterfactual—perhaps even the more typical pathway—of a city in which unions, churches, and local industry once played a prominent role but now no longer do.

This chapter also picks up on a common thread that we will follow throughout the book: local structural conditions—the kinds of people who live in a place and its objective economic conditions—are not sufficient indicators of how place shapes politics. While postindustrial cities are navigating similar resource-constrained environments, the comparison across Motorville, Lutherton, and Gravesend shows that distinct organizational contexts shape how cities address their problems. And to understand how local and national politics mutually constitute one another, this kind of local variation is central to the story.

Shared Postindustrial Social Problems

Motorville, Lutherton, and Gravesend all experienced severe declines in industrial employment at the end of the twentieth century, but those declines have had different consequences for each city's well-being today (per figure 4). Stagnating wages, population decline, and difficulty retaining educated young people (leading to aging populations) are all challenges common to postindustrial cities, but each of these manifests differently in Motorville, Lutherton, and Gravesend.

Figure 5 summarizes these indicators of postindustrial challenges for each county, based on census data from 1980 through 2020. To contextualize the counties' trajectories, it shows county median age, household income, and the portion of residents with a college education as a fraction of the national figures. County population is shown as a proportion of the 1980 population.

Figure 5 makes clear that Motorville and Lutherton each had some successes in fending off the worst threats of the postindustrial era, while Gravesend struggled across the board. All three counties saw their incomes fall, relative to the rest of the country, during this period. This is somewhat unsurprising given that real wage growth was concentrated among high-earning, college-educated workers.[7] Despite this, it is clear that Motorville's incomes fared the best, particularly after 1990: all told, Motorville saw real income growth of more than 12.5 percent from 1980 to 2020. And while Motorville became more than 10 percent older than the rest of the country, it nearly maintained its population, losing just about 2 percent of residents.

In contrast, Luthertonians' incomes were relatively stagnant over the same period, with just over 4 percent in real income growth. But Lutherton aged at the slowest rate of all three counties and it was the only one that saw any population growth—an astounding 21 percent. Moreover, by the time I first visited in summer 2019, Lutherton's community leaders were raving about the local

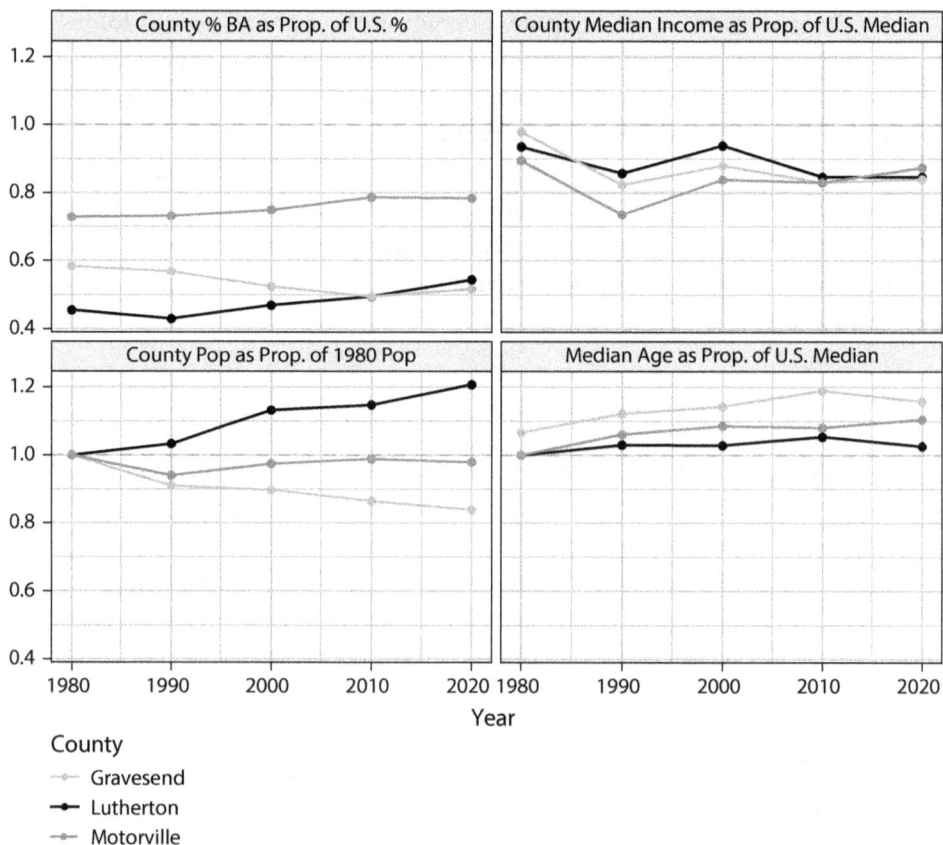

FIGURE 5. Postindustrial economic and population change in Motorville, Lutherton, and Gravesend. *Note:* Data are from census decennial counts for 1980–2000 and ACS 5-year estimate for 2010 and 2020.

economy, and for seemingly good reason: unemployment hovered around 2 percent, a historic low. As former mayor Ron Lubock explained it to me at the time:

> The economy is booming here. Our biggest thing is workforce. Everybody else can't find enough people. There's probably two to three thousand jobs right now unfilled right here. . . . Our economic department has created a Facebook page in Ohio, Illinois—and we just recruited a kid from South Dakota to come work at one of our factories as an engineer.

To Lubock and several of Lutherton's community leaders, finding people to fill the available jobs is the central challenge for the city. But Facebook ads barely make a dent in Lutherton's employment needs. Instead, it is immigration from Mexico and Central America that sustains Lutherton's economy. Between 2000 and 2017, Lutherton's White, non-Hispanic population declined by over ten percentage points, and its immigrant population grew by over four percentage points.

In comparison with Motorville and Gravesend, Lutherton's employment and population trajectory is even more startling. Although Gravesend has seen some immigration, the figures pale in comparison with Lutherton's. And in contrast to both Motorville and Lutherton, Gravesend suffered on all three metrics of postindustrial decline: real incomes stagnated while the population aged and shrank. The county lost 16 percent of its residents between 1980 and 2020, and it was the only county to see a slight decline in real income (just about 1 percent). It also seems that Gravesend suffered the worst brain drain. All three counties saw growth in their college-educated populations between 1980 and 2020, but Gravesend was the only county in which the education rate grew slower than that in the country as a whole. Motorville has had the highest education rate since a small college opened in the county in the 1960s and its graduates began settling in the city, but college education in Lutherton has been growing at a faster rate.

And yet, even as Motorville and Lutherton have escaped the negative demographic and economic spiral that plagues other postindustrial cities, including Gravesend, all three cities face similar challenges endemic to a postindustrial economy: poverty, expensive and decaying housing stock, and the opioid epidemic have touched all three cities, although to varying degrees. Figure 6 shows how several postindustrial social problems have manifested across Motorville, Lutherton, and Gravesend. It depicts the portion of children eligible for free or reduced lunch in schools, the number of drug overdose deaths per 100,000 people, and the opioid prescriptions dispensed per 100 people—all as a portion of the national average. The dashed gray line represents the point at which the county equals the national average. This allows us to compare how each county is experiencing these challenges relative to the country as a whole.

As we can see, between 2016 and 2020, Lutherton was the only place where the portion of children eligible for free or reduced lunch (a common metric of poverty) ever exceeded the national average. In Motorville, the eligibility rate declined steadily and ended 2020 at almost 75 percent of the national average. We can also see that the opioid epidemic is particularly acute in Lutherton, with both overdose deaths and opioid prescription rates well above the national average, and well above both Motorville and Gravesend. In fact,

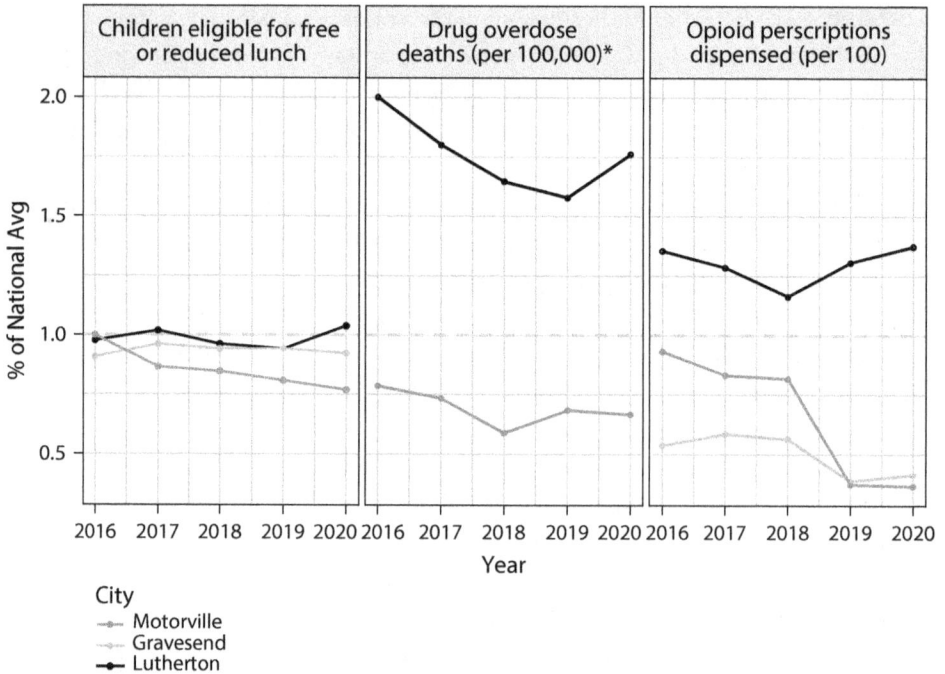

| Children eligible for free or reduced lunch | Drug overdose deaths (per 100,000)* | Opioid perscriptions dispensed (per 100) |

FIGURE 6. Postindustrial social problems in Motorville, Lutherton, and Gravesend. *Note:* Data on eligibility for free and reduced lunch and drug overdose deaths are from the Robert Wood Johnson Foundation's 2020 County Health Rankings, www.countyhealthrankings.org. Data on the rate of opioid prescriptions dispensed are from the CDC: https://www.cdc.gov/drugoverdose/data /statedeaths.html. In all five years, Gravesend County had too few drug overdose deaths to present data (fewer than five).

overdose deaths are so low in Gravesend ($<$ 5 people per 100,000) that they cannot be reported.

In sum, while postindustrial social problems present themselves differently in Motorville, Lutherton, and Gravesend, all three cities struggle with similar challenges related to economic precarity, the result of decades of public and private disinvestment. But as the remainder of this chapter will show, community leaders work to address those challenges within different organizational contexts.

Motorville: Organized Labor as a Political Movement

Harry is a young labor leader in Motorville, who, when I first met him in June 2019, explained the city to me by saying: "This town was built on the back of labor." I heard similar comments from other community leaders, both inside and outside of the labor movement, when I first arrived in Motorville. The fact that many people still think of Motorville as a "union town" is symbolically important, as we will see in chapter 4, but it was not immediately clear to me what organizational activities this term referred to during an era of declining union power. Then, just a few days later, Motorville's Mayor Hayte laid it out for me:

> Now, Motorville is a labor city. It is deep in this city's history. And so there is still a great deal of organization, particularly among the construction trades, a lot of professions, especially teachers, public safety unions, those are still very strong. They still have some political muscle. I mean, they were in our council chambers two days ago. But it's not nearly what it was. Labor bosses, even in the 1980s, could at a word get a mayor elected, and that's no longer true. In fact, I lost my first election for mayor with full union support.

Mayor Hayte's description of Motorville's political history—although perhaps idealized—reflects both the story laid out in chapter 1 and the Wisconsin labor movement's more recent challenges. Although Wisconsin politicians have historically supported unionization, this changed under the governorship of Republican Scott Walker, who made union-busting a priority during his tenure from 2011 to 2019.[8]

But despite these challenges, Mayor Hayte suggests that unidirectional decline is not the entire story in Motorville: although "labor candidates" do not always win and labor's political strength is no longer what it once was, several unions in Motorville still understand economic outcomes as a fundamentally political process. As such, they still work to elect local officials in return for their support on pro-labor policies. But for this politicking to matter, elected officials like Mayor Hayte must care about union support. And in Motorville, they do.

The result of these relationships is a symbolic link between the economic and the political, but also a real one: Motorville's leaders agree that politicians should fight to bring good, union jobs back to the community, and this is—to an extent—what politicians do. Below, I describe how this is accomplished amid Wisconsin's ongoing threats to the labor movement.

————

Organized labor is a long-standing player in Motorvillian politics. Although it is now somewhat battered, there are signs of revitalization, fueled by leadership, organization, and membership strength—all legacies from Motorville's past. Today, people like Margaret—who told me about the teachers' strikes— as well as other retired teachers and labor leaders, continue to participate in both the Wisconsin state AFL-CIO and Motorville's local labor movement. That labor movement now exists primarily within the local labor council, the Motorville Labor Council (MLC). Labor councils were historically responsible for organizing political cooperation among different locals in a geographic area, but most councils have been "weak or moribund" for many years now.[9] Neither Gravesend nor Lutherton has one any longer.

But according to the MLC's current president, Harry, the organization has two roles: working toward "the benefit of labor as a whole" and acting as the "political wing" of its constituent locals. A draft membership roster he shared with me in 2019 shows the MLC representing 21 locals, encompassing more than 1,700 workers. This represents just over 12 percent of the employed population in Motorville in 2019, likely an undercount of actual union density, as not all unions are part of the MLC.[10] In sum, the MLC's reach extends to a sizable portion of Motorville's workforce, although this reach is likely far smaller than it once was. Moreover, as Harry explains, meeting attendance can be "spotty," reducing the MLC's influence on its members and on local politics. In recent years, the MLC has continued to endorse candidates for local office—they are the "labor candidates" that Mayor Hayte describes—but they've offered little by way of material support during campaigns besides a bit of door-knocking. And yet, the very existence of the MLC means that there is such a thing as a "labor movement" that endorses "labor candidates" and offers a space wherein labor leaders can discuss their community and plan collective action. Even during a relatively anemic MLC meeting that I attended in October 2019 (there were only twelve attendees representing five locals; two in the public sector and three in the building trades), those representatives heard about the status of both the ongoing General Motors strike and a strike that had just concluded in a neighboring county. They also learned about the statewide AFL-CIO's training sessions for campaigning in the upcoming presidential election. Such meetings ensure that the organizational leaders—people like Mike who train the rank-and-file union members—are routinely reminded that union membership is a political proposition with significance far beyond their local union or even their city.

These elements of movement infrastructure helped Motorville respond in the wake of Wisconsin's passage of Act 10 in 2011 and right-to-work in 2015, both under Scott Walker. Act 10 revoked collective bargaining rights for public sector unions and required 50 percent of employees to vote to recertify their union each year. Amid these onerous requirements, only 47 percent of Wisconsin's school districts passed the 50 percent threshold to vote in a union in 2017.[11] Despite this, the Motorville AFT not only continues to be voted in but usually maintains 70–80 percent membership, according to their current president. Union leaders today attribute the AFT's success to long-time labor leaders' quick thinking and mobilization in the wake of Act 10. Even so, like all public sector unions in Wisconsin, those in Motorville were hurt under Scott Walker's governorship—the legislation ultimately decimated the local municipal workers' union, AFCSME.

In addition to protecting their membership, Motorville's unions saw Act 10 for what it was—a political attack on their economic future—that necessitated a political response. As the *Motorville Post* recalls, the legislation propelled Motorvillians into the streets and down to Madison to protest. The experience also reinvigorated labor's efforts to engage in local politics. As Mayor Hayte describes it, a handful of "personalities," led by the building trades, began organizing their locals and courting state and national PAC money to contribute to labor candidates. As he explains: "So now, whereas the 2015 mayor and council races had almost no union involvement at all, the 2019 mayor and council races had thousands and thousands of dollars of union PAC money funding them and dozens and dozens of union volunteers knocking on doors."

In sum, unions in Motorville tend to be political organizations that have long viewed politics as central to shaping their economic fortunes—as chapter 1 showed—and continue to do so today. And while deindustrialization followed by Act 10 and right-to-work laws have diminished their membership strength, local movement infrastructure and individuals' experience of political mobilization ensure that unions continue to be political bodies rather than merely economic ones. This is, of course, not true of all unions—just a handful of the MLC's constituent locals send representatives to monthly meetings, for example—but those who do are sufficient in force to sustain these minimum features of a politically engaged labor movement.

But labor's involvement in local politics doesn't necessarily mean that local politicians will seek their support. And yet, in Motorville, they do. In part, this is because, in small-city politics, the resources unions provide candidates are the only game in town. Unions are the sole organization that elected officials can recall turning to for endorsements or support during their campaigns. In nonpartisan City Council races, even the political parties don't get involved.

For these reasons, Motorville's elected officials believe that a pro-labor stance is almost a prerequisite for election. Brian, a Democratic city councillor, describes local politics in this way:

> Everybody who wants to get elected needs to say pro-business and pro-union. . . . [I]f you have a card that you're going to hand out, it'd better have

the union bug on it [meaning it was printed by a union printer]. If it doesn't have the union bug on it, people aren't going to like it. It's a symbol.

Other officials agree: getting the endorsement of the local labor council, the MLC, is among candidates' first stop on the campaign trail. Losing that endorsement, another councillor tells me, is not a nail in your coffin. But, he says, you probably want to win it. This idea persists despite evidence of labor's mixed results in electing their chosen candidates, as Mayor Hayte alluded to. In 2019, four out of ten city councillors were also labor leaders, three of whom regularly attend MLC meetings, and the mayor and one further councillor had been labor candidates. Even so, several labor candidates have lost in recent years, including two during the 2021 municipal elections. But while the stories that elected officials tell about unions' role in their electoral success may be more myth than reality, the resources that unions provide are real. And some combination of officials' *belief* in unions' power and their *actual* power ensures that local government is generally sympathetic to labor issues. As a result, even the non-labor council members, Brian explains, are generally "understanding" of labor's issues.

Thus, while Motorvillian labor no longer holds the keys to the kingdom, they have enough political clout to pressure officials to support pro-labor policies. And this garners them some material benefits: Motorville's mayors regularly sign Project Labor Agreements (PLAs) before beginning new construction projects, which means the city bargains collectively with the unions before hiring a contractor, and that contractor has to abide by the terms of the agreement. And when faced with specific challenges, the City Council generally votes in line with labor. Mark, a former city councillor, was elected just before Act 10 was passed, and he recalls the drama-filled weeks of action on the City Council in the wake of its approval. As part of his campaign, he pledged to ratify new contracts with public sector unions so that they would be effectively protected from Act 10's effects on their bargaining power for the duration of those contracts. Once elected, he led the City Council in extending those contracts for two years, effectively delaying the effects of Act 10 on several local unions. He explains the decision as commonsense:

Motorville is like a Blue Dog Democrat type town. So the working-class labor people, union type people. And so the unions very much wanted somebody that was gonna be in there, that was going to support the labor side completely. So I supported whatever they want—not like blindly following them, but more, I agree with that.

It was thus not by coincidence that Motorville had a city councillor prepared to fight the state to protect unions—he had been voted into office to do just that. It was also not by coincidence that the council rapidly agreed to the contract extension. As was the case during my fieldwork, there was substantial overlap between local labor leaders and city councillors at the time of Act 10's passage in 2011.

There are other regular opportunities for the council to take these kinds of actions that provide material benefits to organized labor, and during my fieldwork, they almost always did. The one exception led to the protest during which I met Mike, quoted in the introduction to this chapter: he and other labor leaders were angry that the city had hired a non-labor-friendly contractor to build a portion of a new public building, and they made their concerns public—local news cameras captured their silent vigil in the atrium of Motorville City Hall.

In other words, Motorville labor holds elected officials accountable to their promises. And when the government helps bring union jobs and union wages to Motorville, this proves labor leaders right: if they engage in politics, their economic fortunes improve.

Partners in Labor Politics

These relationships between local government and organized labor in Motorville feel somewhat anachronistic—more appropriate to the post–World War II period, when municipal elections were targets of labor activism.[12] As Josh Pacewicz (2016) has shown, since the 1980s, waning union power and changes in federal policy have disincentivized such contention in local politics; and yet, labor's efforts to fight economic battles on political terrain remain central to understanding what makes Motorville so Democratic today.

This is not to say that Motorville has been shielded from the organizational changes characteristic of contemporary urban governance: government officials collaborate with local businesses and the Development Agency to market their county and town to new businesses, and a young, energetic cadre of educated professionals have worked together through both formal and informal mechanisms to think about creative ways to "modernize" the town by putting together festivals and working on downtown redevelopment. Elliot, for example, has lived in Motorville all his life and spent several years on the boards of local business and economic development organizations. He describes Motorville as a "smallish town with good midwestern values" that is just now "kind of emerging." The city's "old guard" is in decline, and now:

> We've got a lot of new people opening businesses and younger people, and they're really into partnership. They realize that working together is better than working against each other because everybody was so siloed before. Now we see a lot of new partnerships and people working together and doing things together; cross-promoting.

Elliot's efforts—and those of the other Motorvillians who are also civically engaged—mirror many of the strategies for problem-solving that Pacewicz documents in similar postindustrial cities. But these new leaders remain embedded in older organizational contexts: Mayor Hayte himself is one of this "younger generation." But he was elected not because of his ties to other partners but because of his ties to a revitalized labor movement. Even as he pushes forward with ideas to renew Motorville's downtown, make the city more walkable, and prepare it for a warmer future as climate change marches on, Mayor Hayte also votes with organized labor.

In other words, the national processes that incentivize a particular mode of local problem-solving have collided with a long-standing organizational context in Motorville, reshaping but not erasing it.

Lutherton: The Church-Nonprofit-Volunteer Nexus

In Lutherton, by contrast, unions are absent from the public sphere. But this is not because there are no unions: in fact, a former membership chair of the Lutherton teachers' union estimates they have a 90 percent membership rate, higher than in Motorville. And as chapter 1 described, one of the largest private sector employers in town has had an employees' association since the 1970s. But both unions are decidedly apolitical; as we saw, Lutherton workers rejected the UAW, delinking themselves from the AFL-CIO and its political movement. Similarly, the teachers' union is an affiliate of the National Education Association (NEA) rather than the AFT; as such, it is not part of the AFL-CIO and has historically been less politically active than the AFT. As a result, Mallory, a local NEA member, thinks of the union as an insurance policy rather than a political body. And while the NEA did send a small contingent of teachers to the Indiana statehouse to rally for better wages in 2019, not a single political operative I spoke to in Lutherton—including from the Democratic Party—can recall unions being active players in local politics. Even during my time volunteering with the Democratic mayoral candidate, unions were nowhere to be found. As then-mayor Lubock told me in the late spring of 2019: "We're not a union community, and that's really been beneficial [for attracting business]."

———

But Lutherton is, as Lauren indicated, full of large, well-known, and well-resourced churches. Churches' role in community life is multifaceted: they are more than just religious institutions; they also form a crucial connection in a network of private organizations that work together to solve social problems. And as in Motorville, this organizational context is not reducible to individual-level organizational affiliations, although these are important: nearly 60 percent of Lutherton County residents are church members, while the comparable figure is about nine percentage points lower in Motorville. Gravesend's church adherence is more than 10 percentage points higher than Lutherton's and has been for decades.[13]

While these quantitative differences do matter for local political outcomes, equally important are qualitative differences in the meaning of church membership across the three cities and how churches in Lutherton facilitate connections among their congregations, volunteers, and local nonprofits. Many people I spoke to in Lutherton view church membership as much more than attending services every Sunday. Emma, for example, is a stay-at-home mom who describes the deep roots she has with her church:

> Our church is . . . we're forming a youth group. I had a big youth group when I was going through church. And still great friends with some of those kids today. And then, you know . . . there was just nothing. . . . [So a couple of years ago, a girlfriend and I] said, we either need to start looking at other churches or we just need to hope and pray that something happens here. . . . And so, I talked about how it was easy to look at the bigger churches that have it all put together. Because there are some in this town. And think, I could just go there and it's all right there on a silver platter for me. But then the history of our church, and being basically born and raised in our church and . . . and so, we just decided to put the work in.

The quality of ties to their churches and the high membership rate in Lutherton are not coincidental, as Emma's comments show. Most churchgoers I spoke to expect the kind of reciprocal relationship between their families and their churches that Emma describes: they are willing to "put the work in," but they want to be part of congregations that offer vibrant youth groups and Vacation Bible Schools for their children. Seventeen of thirty residents I spoke to in Lutherton describe volunteering with their church, being involved in leadership roles, youth groups, or Sunday school. In contrast, even among the Motorvillians I met who do attend church regularly, active involvement beyond Sunday service is rare.

These differences in individual church involvement are also consequential for civic life in the city. First, churches in Lutherton teach a pool of volunteers that civic engagement is an important part of social citizenship and train them to offer those skills elsewhere.[14] Most people I met in Lutherton—particularly churchgoers—believe that helping the community is central to the church's mission. In the same conversation in which he lists numerous church programs to address food insecurity and homelessness in Lutherton, Fred reflects on his own congregation and sighs: "I don't think we do enough. I honestly don't." To Fred, churches should be helping those in need, and even in a place like Lutherton where churches routinely take up that task, he believes their efforts are insufficient. As a result, these residents think about how their activities, both inside and outside of church, are serving their city. As Veronica summarizes, being a good citizen "means doing my part as far as helping . . . being involved with a church and using your resources that you can help." The high level of civic engagement among the people I met in Lutherton, many of whom attend evangelical churches, is somewhat surprising given the fact that evangelicalism is typically less associated with non-religious volunteerism than mainline Protestantism or Catholicism—but in Lutherton, churches are community actors.[15]

Second, a vibrant church community pools together private financial and volunteer resources.[16] This is reflected in the distribution of public and private resources in Lutherton and Motorville: relative to Motorville County, Lutherton County collects only 85 percent of the tax revenue per capita and receives only 4 percent of the per capita funding from the state, but Lutherton's service-based nonprofits have three times as many assets per capita as Motorville's.[17] Lutherton's private resources have thus become substitutes for public resources amid fiscal restraint by both state and local governments.

And finally, because church leaders are seen as *community leaders* with connections to nonprofits and other churches, they are able to use their resources to facilitate collective problem-solving as new issues emerge. One way they do so is through informal ties between pastors and among pastors and congregants: with some congregations of one thousand members or more in a county of about forty thousand, certain pastors have direct relationships with a large portion of residents. Pastor Brown, for example, preaches at Immaculate, one of Lutherton's largest churches. As he explains: "We have lots of members . . . who are actively involved in leadership positions in these other groups, whether there's Drug Awareness Advocates, or one of our gals is the director of the Clothing Co-op, another one works with the homeless shelter." As a result, he often learns about local challenges and organizations working to resolve them through casual conversations with his parishioners. These are the "connections that never end" to which Lauren referred.

But there are also formal mechanisms for facilitating interfaith collaboration and church-based problem-solving: each month, Lutherton's pastors meet at the Lutherton County Consortium of Churches (LCCC). According to Pastor Brown, the LCCC offers a monthly venue where county pastors can come together to "focus on a specific organization that's doing something helpful in the life of the community. . . . We look at things that are broader than our own parish and that probably affect all of us one way or the other, and we can all kind of cooperate with." It was through these gatherings that Immaculate Church heard more and more about the lack of affordable childcare services in Lutherton a few years ago—a challenge that Motorville and Gravesend share—and decided to open a childcare center. Among the litany of services churches fund or directly provide are support for the unhoused, food pantries, hot meals, recovery programs, and ad hoc benevolence funds when people come knocking.

Partners in Church and Nonprofit Governance

Local government, for its part, agrees that this private but collective approach is the best way to meet local social needs. Mayor Redner, for example, is a long-time civic leader and young politician, much like Mayor Hayte. When Mayor Redner ran for office in 2019 he was elected along with a wave of new, young faces to the City Council and County Commission—defeating the candidate on whose campaign I had volunteered. As with Mayor Hayte, Mayor Redner's way of thinking about how to solve problems in his city is shaped by the local organizations in which he has participated for many years. This means, when I ask him about local challenges in summer 2019, Mayor Redner runs through a list of the many nonprofit and church-based organizations that provide social services in Lutherton and concludes: "As a city, we're lending support to those organizations, but we're not doing the work." I follow up, asking: "Do you feel you should be doing something?" He answers quickly: "We need to be doing more." But as he goes on to explain, by "more," he does not mean taking over the provision of services but rather supporting the existing system of nongovernmental provision: "I don't know the exact answer to what 'need to be doing more' means, but we do need to be still supporting them more so than we are. . . . It's just a matter of bridging the gaps between some of these organizations." In Lutherton, even those in government see nongovernmental solutions as the way to meet many residents' needs. Mayor Redner envisions an expanded role for the city as a kind of public-private partnership in which the public entity takes a back seat.

In contrast, Motorvillian officials hardly ever mention nonprofits and churches taking on similar roles in local problem-solving. This is in part because of objective differences between the two cities: as described above, Motorville lacks the private resources contained within Lutherton's churches and nonprofits. The pastors I met in Motorville explain that their congregations are combining to save money on clergy and physical buildings, as membership declines and they lose the members who used to consider tithing central to church membership. While these churches still prioritize social service work, they do not always have the financial and human capital to carry it out. And this is not just because of a difference in the quantity of evangelical and mainline Protestant churches in Lutherton and Motorville. It is also about whether residents are willing to put churches at the center of their own and the city's life. And in Motorville, they are not. As an evangelical pastor there told me, his small church sees barely twenty parishioners each Sunday, and he has been unable to grow the congregation despite several years of trying.

In sum, it is the quantitative, qualitative, and relational aspects of Lutherton's churches that define the city's organizational context. As in Motorville, my argument here is not that churches are the only organizations that matter for Lutherton politics; it is the very fact of their cooperation with local government, other nonprofits, and business leaders that makes them so central to political outcomes. Churches play the key role of facilitator in solving emergent problems by coordinating among churchgoing volunteers, local elected officials, and nonprofits. As we will see in chapter 3, over repeated iterations of this process, Lutherton residents begin to look to their community rather than the government to solve problems. This is a central component of why place-based partisanship varies in Lutherton and Motorville, but the preceding sections have also

revealed similarities between the two cities: both have stable organizational contexts, characterized by long-standing ties between organizational leaders.

Gravesend: Decline and Instability

This is where Motorville and Lutherton differ most from Gravesend. Despite
sharing many organizational characteristics—Gravesend has a rich history
of labor organizing and an even higher rate of church adherence than
Lutherton—neither unions nor churches in Gravesend are integrated into
coalitions of community leaders, as they are in Motorville and Lutherton.
Gravesend unions do not work to politically engage the rank and file nor do
they engage in local politics, and churches are not part of a long-standing network of social service provision.

But Gravesend is not just a negative case relative to Motorville and Lutherton. It also offers evidence as to what happens when the organizations that
once shaped social and civic life in the Heartland decline, leaving cities to
confront social problems with a different set of resources—or few resources
at all. In Gravesend, the instability of the local organizational context means that
residents do not cohere around diagnostic frames to the same extent as they
do in Motorville and Lutherton.

Why Gravesend Is Not Motorville

Like Motorville, Gravesend was in many ways "built by union" but with a meaningful difference: it was also a company town, as chapter 1 described. This
meant that each time Rivervalley changed ownership, the local labor movement suffered. And today, the USW's current president, Alex, explains that he
has had trouble voting the union in at new plants due to a lack of enthusiasm
among the "younger generation."

But as we also saw, after a few years of political mobilization in the 1930s,
Gravesend labor largely ceased to engage in local politics, unlike their counterparts in Motorville. Charlie, the retired USW president, can recall hosting
phone banks from the old union center, but that ended when the building
flooded two decades ago. It was also then that the Gravesend Labor Council
died, taking with it the only political element of Gravesend's labor movement.
But Charlie describes this incident with greater concern over the loss of the
building than the loss of the organization: "It was a nice place. It's too bad we
couldn't have moved it out here," he laments. As he recalls, the organization

only existed to inform the state AFL-CIO about local goings-on rather than to intervene in local politics.

The result is that today's politicians do not have a beaten path to the unions' front door. Derek, a Democrat who recently ran for statewide elected office in Gravesend, describes his experience with local labor organizations in this way:

> You know, I went in to see them right away, as soon as I announced. Because unions are such a big part of my family history. . . . I got the impression that most of the candidates in the past that have run as Democrats have not gone in to see them. And I was so surprised and shocked by that. So they were very happy to see a candidate who embraced organized labor.

Although Alex has begun endorsing state- and federal-level candidates for office, Derek still encountered surprise at the union hall. Unlike in Motorville, where many candidates view their pathway to local electoral success as running through the labor movement, Gravesend lacks both an institutionalized tie between unions and local politics and dense personal ties between the Democratic Party and the unions. During my time in Motorville, Democratic leaders and labor leaders routinely pointed me to one another as crucial sources of information if I wanted to understand local politics. In contrast, Derek was the only politician I met in Gravesend who similarly sent me to organized labor; and even then, Charlie and Alex did not remember him.

Organized labor in Gravesend has historically focused their energy on collective bargaining rather than local politics. And those choices have durable legacies today. Now, even as Alex has begun bringing the USW into politics, he has engaged only at the state level, rather than city or county level. In part, this is because Gravesend has a city manager system, meaning that the most local level of engagement—municipal elections—appears to promise fewer rewards than it does in Motorville.[18]

Why Gravesend Is Not Lutherton

Gravesend thus differs from Motorville in important ways, as it does from Lutherton: Gravesend lacks a dependable network of churches to fund and facilitate the provision of public goods. This is despite the fact that church adherence is higher in Gravesend than in Lutherton. But as several residents explain, the quality of Gravesenders' church membership has changed. As Pastor Taylor—whose own membership is relatively steady—explained, local churches are competing for congregants, especially with the rise of the large evangelical churches that have drawn in congregants looking for a less traditional church service. Engaged, civic-minded churchgoers like Emma from Lutherton—especially those who donate large sums of money—are a scarce resource.

Despite these looming difficulties, Gravesend churches are indeed involved in many of the same social service projects as Lutherton churches: they rotate responsibilities for a local soup kitchen; they contribute to food pantries; and over the past two years they have worked together to fund the school district's Backpack Program. Now, each Friday across all of Gravesend's elementary schools, social workers slip resealable bags of food into the backpacks of needy children.

Pastor Taylor describes how the Backpack Program spread quickly from a small group within his congregation to the rest of the city: "I invited the other pastors and then the other leaders, the lay leaders, the congregational members, they were invited to talk about it with their friends who go to those other churches. It happened within three weeks." From their first year serving students in one elementary school, the program has grown to encompass most of the churches in town, serving 550 children across all five elementary schools and the middle school. While the program has been enormously successful, this level of engagement and problem-solving is relatively new to Gravesend: churches have long rotated the hosting of a weekly soup kitchen, but apart from that, their collaboration has been minimal.

This means that Gravesenders have not had the same experiences of problem-solving with and through their churches that residents of Lutherton have shared. Moreover, because of this lack of institutionalized collaboration, community leaders worry about the program's longevity. Marge, a former United Way director, explains that while she thinks Gravesend's churches "can be" great partners, and she applauds their work on the backpack program, she would be cautious to rely on them too heavily: if one particularly dedicated congregant or pastor should leave, she fears the entire system could crumble.

Even so, Gravesend churches have worked together to create an extensive system of food provision in their city. This would not have been possible without many of the factors common to Lutherton and Gravesend: a relatively robust membership that contributes their time and money. The difference is that, in Gravesend, this arrangement is relatively new and weakly institutionalized; as a result, community leaders like Marge do not think of churches as key partners to lean on when new social problems emerge.

Why Gravesend Is Neither Lutherton nor Motorville

Even without unions and churches sitting at the center of a stable set of organizational ties in Gravesend, it's possible that some other organization plays this role. But as Connie described, this is not the case. Instead, as many of the organizations that used to structure public life—including Rivervalley, its unions, and countless local churches—have begun to decline or have disappeared altogether, Gravesenders now scrape together ad hoc coalitions from whatever organizational resources are available to get things done in the city. Each time Connie or others want to accomplish something, they must "go around to different businesses," "form a committee," and seek support wherever they can, as she explains.

And as we saw in chapter 1, these activities have been immensely successful at revitalizing Gravesend's Main Street and giving the city a kind of facelift. Connie, rightfully so, is proud of these accomplishments. But her belief in the success of these partnerships is not shared among many of the residents I met. Instead, they often compared themselves unfavorably to a neighboring city, Greenwood. Not only has Greenwood retained its largest employer of several decades but that employer has a philanthropic wing that, according to Gravesenders, funds everything from social welfare organizations to local festivals. Such a vivid image of the counterfactual right next door—what Gravesend could have been had Rivervalley survived and thrived—only serves to remind residents of what they lost.

This is because Gravesend differs from Motorville and Lutherton along not only organizational dimensions but structural ones: they are struggling with a negative spiral of population and economic decline, per figure 5. These differences explain part, but not all, of each city's contemporary organizational context. In Motorville, for example, the longevity of the city's largest employers and a relatively stable population base are key pieces of what enables the local labor movement to remain so politically engaged. But, as we have seen, structure is not deterministic: the city's history of labor activism and unions' close ties to elected officials also help unions remain a force in local politics today. In Gravesend, by way of contrast, Rivervalley's decline did cause the local labor movement to suffer, but labor leaders also disengaged from politics.

In this context of objective economic decline, organizational deterioration, and a lack of coherent community leadership as to the path forward for Gravesend, residents still talk about what it was like back in the heyday of the Rivervalley plant. Even as a smaller foundry has come into the city and other local businesses have grown to replace the jobs lost in the fire, it is not the same to Gravesenders who can remember those golden years. In part, this is because of the town's population decline: as Vanessa, a local Democratic Party activist, tells me, there is "an overall sense of loss in rural communities like Gravesend . . . we've lost about 20 percent of our population since 1970. So, the last fifty years, to lose 20 percent of your population . . . I mean that, I think, is a bit frightening. Or it's, you feel the sense of loss, like the way things used to be."

Community leaders' efforts, however successful, have not made a dent in residents' sense of loss and decay because the city lacks a stable organizational context that visibly and routinely provides answers for how to diagnose and solve social problems. It is not structurally *impossible* for Gravesend to achieve this kind of stability—most of their major employers are unionized and they do have high rates of church attendance, after all—but it requires a degree of organizational activity and cooperation that the city has not seen for decades.

———

Motorville, Lutherton, and Gravesend each offer one version of what Heartland cities in the postindustrial era look like: governmental and nongovernmental organizations partner together to win scarce resources for their cities and resolve the mounting problems of a postindustrial society. But public-private partnerships take on a different hue in each city because of their preexisting organizational contexts and variation in their experiences of postindustrial decline. The result is that, today, different kinds of nongovernmental organizations retain seats at the table in each city.

In Motorville, we see a governance structure that was lost in many cities during the post-Keynesian era: one in which political conflict centers around government as the entity responsible for the city's health and for providing "good union jobs." In Lutherton, by contrast, residents' dedication to church life creates a private pool of financial and human capital outside of local government, which churches direct toward addressing emergent social problems through networks of other churches and nonprofits.

But despite their differences, both Motorville and Lutherton have relatively stable organizational contexts. Gravesend alone lacks this stability, as the organizations that were once central to the city's governance—Rivervalley, unions, and churches—have declined. Even as organized labor and church membership in Gravesend retain some strength, they are not part of city governance in the way that they are in Motorville and Lutherton. To some extent, they haven't been since the 1930s.

This chapter has laid out the key organizational differences across Motorville, Lutherton, and Gravesend—defined in part by quantitative differences in membership strength and financial resources but also by what organizations do and how they interact with one another. I have argued that we can better understand the historic and ongoing process of the Heartland's reddening by being attentive to place. We have now seen how interactions between national, state, and local processes shaped the past trajectory of Heartland politics, producing different organizational outcomes from within similar structural possibilities (chapter 1), which today shape the way community leaders think about, and are able to respond to, similar postindustrial social problems (chapter 2). We will now turn to part 2, which will focus our analytic lens on the present: how the distinct structural and organizational dimensions of each city lead residents to develop shared cultural frameworks that sustain their partisanship.

PART II

Place-Based Partisanship in the Present

3

How Local Contexts Produce (Anti)-Statism in Motorville and Lutherton

EVERYONE WHO KNOWS PAM sings her praises. As the director of Lutherton's Downtown Redevelopment Group (DRG), she presides over Main Street revitalization, often in collaboration with Pete from the Economic Development Association, Lutherton's mayor, and a small army of volunteers. I meet Pam for the first time at her office in the Lutherton City building, which sits at the end of Lutherton's Main Street. Pam is full of enthusiasm for her town as she tells me how revitalization has advanced under her watch. As she explains, the biggest obstacles to restoring Main Street to its former glory are Lutherton's workforce shortage and the opioid crisis, two issues she sees as mutually reinforcing: "I think the biggest thing that as a community we're facing is the drug problem. I think that is going on in a lot of towns. It's the opioid crisis. And that's creating an issue with workforce, I would say." She then pauses, before continuing:

> Well, I think we have a drug problem, and so that's an issue on its own. And then workforce is another issue, and I don't know if they're directly correlated, but we have a really low unemployment rate here. It's about 2 percent. And so, for me, when I'm trying to recruit a business to come downtown, they say to me, "Am I going to have trouble getting help?" "Yes, absolutely." And then when you get help, is it going to be someone who's on drugs and you get them trained and they do it for six weeks and then they quit?

Pam goes on, explaining how the opioid crisis has taken root in Lutherton: "I think everybody here knows somebody who's being affected by it," she begins, echoing a common refrain in both Motorville and Lutherton.

Pam is concerned about addiction as a problem unto itself but also as a problem for business. The solution, she goes on to say, is greater coordination among the many faith-based and other nonprofit organizations that are already working to care for people suffering from addiction. This would help them and their families and, as a happy by-product, help the local economy. In the way she both defines Lutherton's social problems and thinks about a viable solution, she is very much like the other community leaders I spoke to in Lutherton.

But her take is vastly different from what I heard in Motorville. Where Lutherton's elected officials and civic leaders tout the low unemployment rate as a sign of economic vibrancy, even amid ongoing concerns about housing insecurity and addiction, their counterparts in Motorville beat a different drum. As Wendy, a Motorville county commissioner, tells me in summer 2019, opioid addiction is so widespread that it "affects anybody" in town—much like in Lutherton. As such, it is a top concern for the county. But, Wendy continues, "[the county is] extremely strapped and so we don't have the resources. And Wisconsin doesn't provide inpatient treatment. And the people that have mental health issues, there's no place for them to go, which is—it's really a struggle." As community leaders petition the state for more resources, they also focus on the root cause of addiction. So the solution to the city's myriad challenges? "It's jobs," Wendy says. "Yes, the jobs with the benefits, the decent-paying jobs with benefits."

———

Wendy's and Pam's accounts are indicative of broader patterns in their respective cities. In Motorville, ties between unions and elected officials ensure that community leaders and residents define Motorville's problems as systemic—related to long-term trends of deindustrialization and deunionization that have exacerbated economic inequalities—and center public attention on government as a key vehicle in shaping local economic health. Other problems, such as the opioid crisis, are construed as symptoms of the city's systemic woes. Within this framework, residents look to state, and occasionally federal, government to help address their social problems. In contrast, people in Lutherton define social problems related to poverty as *community* challenges rather than systemic ones. And in a city full of well-resourced churches, the community can take action to address these challenges. But even when problems are not resolved by objective measures, residents tend to deem community efforts successful—often because of their *visibility*, in contrast to the hidden ways that the federal government supports middle-class families. As a result,

Lutherton residents rarely look beyond their city boundaries for assistance. They are a community that takes care of itself.

But as we saw in chapter 2, what unites Motorville and Lutherton and distinguishes them from Gravesend is the stability of their local organizational contexts. As such, the remainder of this chapter and the next will focus just on Motorville and Lutherton, showing how the structural and organizational contexts we saw emerge in chapters 1 and 2 sustain the *diagnostic frames* (this chapter) and *narratives of community identity* (chapter 4) that reinforce residents' partisanship today. In Motorville and Lutherton, residents' experiences of solving postindustrial social problems within local organizational contexts lead them to cohere around shared diagnostic frames for defining their problems and determining whether they are suitable for public or private intervention. In other words, these experiences shape residents' beliefs about the appropriate role of government.

In many ways, this outcome conforms to what we already know about how citizens come to make demands on the government: they learn how government should act by observing how it does act.[1] But because these arguments generally rely on cross-national comparisons, they tend to focus on what makes the United States distinctive from similar advanced industrialized nations: the United States has historically provided welfare through a combination of means-tested programs that impose deservingness criteria on the poorest of recipients alongside hidden government support in the form of tax credits for lower-middle- and middle-class families. As Suzanne Mettler (2011) argues, these particular institutional configurations have enabled Americans' high degree of anti-statism and individualism, because even people who do benefit from public resources may be unaware of this benefit or distinguish themselves from the "real" welfare recipients who rely on means-tested programs.[2] And for White Americans like those I spoke to in Motorville and Lutherton, this distinction is symbolically important because of the way the media has racialized welfare recipients as Black. As a result, racial resentment toward racialized others further limits Whites' support for state intervention of various kinds, even when they would benefit (or already are benefiting) from those policies.[3] And in a place like Lutherton, with a long history of institutionalized racism, we might expect this to be a particularly important factor in shaping residents' orientation toward the state.

But in what follows I will argue that individualism and racial resentment are important, yet insufficient, explanations as to why Lutherton residents prefer community-based solutions to local social problems and why Motorvillians call on the government to resolve similar problems. And that's because researchers' focus on national institutional contexts has obscured the importance of local variation in social provision that, as the last chapter described, increasingly defines how the American government takes care of its people.

Perhaps unsurprisingly, this variation is a crucial source of meaning-making as residents think about what they want their local, state, and federal governments to do. But there is not always a direct link between what is actually happening in each place—for example, the community has not resolved hunger or homelessness in Lutherton—and what residents believe about what is happening—that Lutherton takes care of itself.

In this chapter we will shift the analytic lens toward residents to observe how diagnostic frames, describing who the community is and what its problems are, circulate through both direct and indirect means. First, community leaders work to solve social problems within the organizational contexts described in chapter 2, and residents who observe that problem-solving learn what *kinds of solutions* resolve the *kinds of problems* their city faces; that is, they earn local diagnostic frames.[4] Then, other residents come to share those diagnostic frames when they learn about them from local opinion leaders, friends, local news, and even Facebook—because local information flows are structured in part by the organizational context. Over repeated instances of problem-solving, diagnostic frames become both shared and taken for granted.[5] This means they are only partly dependent on the underlying organizations.

This argument indicates that we need to move beyond accounts of local organizations as sites of democratic training or political socialization. Such an approach suggests that we focus on straightforward quantitative indicators of organizational density as predictors of residents' trust in each other and in government.[6] In contrast, by drawing attention to how organizations define their roles in the community and participate in collective problem-solving, this chapter shows how distinct organizational contexts can lead residents (both organizational members and non-members alike) toward the state or away from it.

Shared Postindustrial Social Problems

As we saw in chapter 2, Motorville and Lutherton have each fared somewhat better than Gravesend in terms of population and economic decline since the 1980s, but both cities still face several postindustrial social problems related to poverty, housing, and addiction (see figure 6). And residents are well aware of these issues. It was rare, for example, that I had to pose direct questions about opioids in either city; instead, the residents I spoke to tended to bring them up immediately when I asked about local challenges. As Sybil from Motorville tells me: "We have an extremely high issue or big problem with opioids, drugs, heroin, meth. A lot of drinking." Sybil's stepson is in recovery, as is Sam's son and Elliot's friend whom he never knew had a problem until she started getting clean. Just as in Motorville, a handful of people I spoke with in Lutherton had direct experiences of losing loved ones to addiction, recovering from addiction themselves, or seeing others struggle with recovery. Many more have found needles in parks and other public spaces.

But even those who did not have direct experiences of the opioid crisis still tended to identify it as a pressing issue in their city because they learned about it through discussions with friends, family, and neighbors or at church; via the local paper or TV news; or on Facebook. In fact, residents of both cities rely on social media just as much as legacy media to learn local information. This is because their social media networks are much like their face-to-face ones[7]—that is, overwhelmingly local. In fact, precisely half of the people I spoke to in Motorville and Lutherton estimate that 75 percent of their Facebook friends live within their county. Although we cannot take these self-reports as indicative of their actual networks, they do give us a sense of what residents usually see when they go on Facebook—and that is posts from local friends, often about local matters. For example, Mallory from Lutherton tells me about the opioid crisis: "I do see often, like on Facebook, people will post pictures of finding needles in public places." Local politicians—city and county councillors, state representatives, and representatives to Congress—also contribute to these information flows. In fact, most of their posts refer to local matters, such as community events, charities, small businesses, and Main Street development.[8]

For the most part, these information channels circulate news and gossip in much the same way in both Motorville and Lutherton, but in Lutherton residents further reported learning about local social problems through their own churches and volunteer work—or that of their acquaintances.[9] Katherine, for example, volunteers for a church in Lutherton that provides meals to those struggling with substance abuse, and she is also familiar with a new ministry working to serve the city's unhoused population because her sister volunteers there. The fact that social networks in Lutherton are embedded in church networks shapes the kinds of conversations residents have with one another.

The result of these local information ecosystems is that residents are aware of both the challenges facing their cities *and* what their local organizations are doing—or not doing—to resolve them. And because different organizations are doing different things, shaping the way local opinion leaders talk about social problems, residents of Motorville and Lutherton draw largely different lessons about how to resolve similar kinds of postindustrial social problems. As we will see, a purely structural explanation for statism in Motorville and anti-statism in Lutherton—in other words, that different experiences of deindustrialization have left the cities with different problems—is insufficient. Structural conditions do matter for how residents make sense of their problems, but so too do organizational contexts and local diagnostic frames.[10]

Lutherton: Local Opinion Leaders at the Nexus of Churches and Nonprofits

In Lutherton, the organizational context is defined by relationships among churches and nonprofits, and the private, collective problem-solving approach they take. Lutherton's churches are more than just the sum of their parts: they bring together an active and engaged set of volunteers and a pool of private financial resources, which are then available to nonprofits and other churches to solve problems. In this chapter, we will see how the durability of this organizational context supports specific diagnostic frames among Lutherton residents; as new social problems emerge, residents look to churches to solve them, and churches make *visible* efforts (alongside nonprofits and city government) to address the challenges. Residents deem these efforts successful and repeat this process each time they encounter a new challenge. As a result, residents come to take for granted that social problems can and should find community-based solutions—and they come to view the federal government as superfluous.

We can observe the start of this process in the way residents view churches' role in Lutherton. Kyle, for example, is a young Independent in his second year of college who describes Lutherton's churches in the following way: "I mean, [churches] give people their religion, of course, and they go to them for that. But, in the community. . . . A lot of the churches, like if there's a need in the community and they need help, the churches are the first places that people contact." Kyle recognizes that churches are, of course, religious institutions first and foremost. But in Lutherton, they're also the place to go "if there's a need." And he is not alone in thinking this way. Regardless of their own church membership or denominational affiliation, Lutherton residents told me again and again that they would turn to local churches if they encountered a problem in the city.

This understanding of churches' role in Lutherton comes from both every-day ways of sharing information in a city full of civically engaged churches and well-publicized moments of problem-solving. For example, even as the Covid-19 pandemic took hold and the presidential election unfolded between January and November 2020, the sixth most popular kind of Facebook post by Lutherton's politicians was the type that discussed social service activities by local organizations.[11] And this is not a new feature of Lutherton's informational eco-system: 29 percent of the front-page articles I collected from the *Lutherton Gazette* (on days surrounding important national events from 1932 to 2016) mention local churches. The corresponding figure for the *Motorville Post* is 2 percent.

As a result, Luthertonians routinely learn that in their city, churches are central to local problem-solving. This view is also reinforced each time a new social problem emerges and churches step in to try to resolve that problem. I observed one portion of this cycle during my fieldwork. At the time, Lutherton was still reeling from events that had taken place a few years prior, when an unhoused man was found frozen to death in his car. The tragedy was a shock that led several residents to coalesce around a new organization dedicated to resolving homelessness: Service & Action Ministries (SAM). SAM, as its founder, Karla, describes it, provides a place where

> . . . churches can give their benevolence money and we work with individu-als and do some screening, do some follow-up and after-care, and just some responsible stewardship of money and a little bit more than what the nor-mal church is able to do, because they just don't have the training and the time that we do.

In contrast to the ad hoc services that churches on their own can provide to those in need, SAM is intensely focused on serving as a centralized clearing-house that, as one volunteer describes it, does "charity wisely."

Within a short period of time, SAM grew from a small group of volunteers serving meals each Wednesday evening to constructing a permanent shelter in Lutherton and serving this centralizing function for the city's pool of private resources. SAM's rapid growth was made possible by Lutherton's organizational context: many residents I spoke to knew that homelessness was a local chal-lenge because of their churches' involvement in an earlier shelter operation, and SAM developed further support by speaking in front of the LCCC and other churches. Informal networks linking pastors and nonprofits also helped: Pastor Brown, a minister at one of Lutherton's largest churches whom we met in chapter 2, explains that while he'd heard of SAM through the LCCC, he really got acquainted when one of his parishioners married a woman who was actively involved in their Wednesday evening ministry.

This is not to say that widespread support for an organization like SAM was a foregone conclusion. Not all congregations within Lutherton are equal partners in community problem-solving, and they do not support every service endeavor that residents suggest. In this case, SAM was successful in part because it solved a problem that churches themselves faced—how to do "charity wisely," rather than hand out their benevolence funds in an ad hoc fashion.

But now that SAM is growing, it crystallizes years of private problem-solving efforts in Lutherton within one organization. Before SAM, Lutherton maintained a loose network of organizations that had the resources to provide social services as needs arose in the city. But with SAM, Lutherton now has a further institutionalized, centralized care network that operates outside of the city, county, and state governments.

Lutherton Residents' View: The Community as Problem-Solver

SAM's origin story illustrates the more general social process that helps sustain Lutherton's diagnostic frames: when a new social problem emerges, community leaders and residents fall back on private, collective resources to solve it; residents deem these efforts successful; and they diagnose similar problems as community challenges.

It was overwhelmingly evident in my conversations with Luthertonians that they feel their community is successful at meeting problems related to poverty. Patty, for example, is a teacher and union member who does not belong to a church but is worried about growing instability in her students' families due to the opioid crisis and housing precarity. When I ask her if she thinks the community is directing resources to resolve those problems, she responds: "You know, our community really does a good job at that [providing resources for people suffering from addiction or homelessness]" and then goes on to list four ways the "need is being met" by local churches and nonprofits. Many others I spoke to agreed with this idea: when Lutherton has a problem, local churches and nonprofits step up and resolve it.

These residents believe that church and nonprofit efforts are meeting local needs—even when they are not, by objective measures, resolving issues related to hunger, housing, or drugs. In part, this is because those efforts are so *visible*.

Eleven out of thirty residents I spoke to mentioned SAM's work with pride when I asked them if they knew of any challenges in the community. The fact that people tended to tell me about *solutions* when I asked about *challenges* underscores this visibility: residents often first learn about social problems from the people working to resolve them—friends from church or those volunteering with a local nonprofit. This creates a feeling that problems are being resolved. As such, residents' belief in the community's success persists despite Lutherton's ongoing challenge: as we saw in figure 6, Lutherton has not managed to resolve its many postindustrial social problems—nor has Motorville or Gravesend.

But to some extent, these objective realities are of secondary importance to residents' subjective interpretation of them. Residents' belief that their community's problem-solving is successful supports their local diagnostic frames, such that they categorize a whole range of problems as appropriate for private, collective response rather than public intervention. Mallory, for example, is a teacher and Republican who has lived in Lutherton County her entire life. When I ask her how she would go about addressing a new social problem in Lutherton, she explains:

> As far as like the housing issue, I think . . . that's something like churches do help with. And food. I mean, I think churches and those type of organizations, and other volunteer [groups] . . . I think they kind of rally together to address those type of issues of basic needs.

Mallory's thinking here is hypothetical—but she imagines the churches could take care of a future community challenge because she believes they have actually done so in the past. In this, Mallory echoes many other residents I met.

Even the opioid crisis, which is a particularly acute problem in Lutherton (per figure 6), does not destabilize residents' belief in the efficacy of local problem-solving. This is because, according to the residents I spoke to, addiction is an individual problem; as such, they don't blame the community's response for failing, as they don't think addiction is the community's responsibility in the first place.

This became clear in my second round of conversations with Lutherton residents, in March 2020. After hearing so many people express concern about the opioid crisis during summer and fall 2019, I started to ask about it more directly: had anything changed, was it still a concern for them, and were they aware of anything Lutherton was doing to address the crisis? When it came to that last question, few people I spoke to could pinpoint meaningful action. For example, when I ask Patrick—a non-churchgoing Democrat—if the opioid crisis is still a concern for him in March 2020, he tells me: "I haven't seen really any kind of major movement in that area. I know that there are a lot of groups still working on it, but there really hasn't been a lot of action taken. So, it is still a problem." Others offer similar responses.

Even so, hardly anyone I spoke to blames local government, the community, or its constituent organizations for this lack of action. Instead, they tend to recategorize the problem as an individual rather than collective one. Katherine, for example, recently participated in a NARCAN training that a local business owner and nurse have coordinated. She did so because her cousin died of an opioid overdose. As she explains, during those seminars the coordinators do advocate for people to go to rehab and "get help." But, she concludes: "Some people are ready and some people aren't." Note that Katherine's conclusion, while individualizing the crisis, is not an effort to distance herself from those struggling with addiction. In fact, given how much it has cost her family, she is full of compassion for anyone suffering in this way and, as described above, she volunteers with a church that provides meals to that community. In this respect, she is similar to many people I spoke with in Lutherton: while not necessarily blaming people struggling with addiction, whose names and faces they know, they tend to recategorize the problem as one not suitable for collective problem-solving at all. This recategorization helps explain why residents' belief in the efficacy of Lutherton's problem-solving persists, even when it objectively fails to solve problems.

While this is true on the whole, some residents—particularly on the left—did identify areas of failure in local problem-solving. Patrick, for example, is the Democrat we heard from above who has not seen much progress in resolving the opioid crisis. During the same conversation he also noted that the city needs more low-income housing to meet the needs of the local housing crisis. But even he has extensive knowledge of and praise for local churches and nonprofits: in the next breath he lists several organizations working to care for the hungry and unhoused, and then concludes: "So I feel like people wouldn't go hungry if they had a need in our community."

As such, we can see how the relationship between local organizational contexts and diagnostic frames is self-reinforcing: in Lutherton, when churches and nonprofits take visible action, residents deem their efforts as successful at meeting challenges related to poverty, such as hunger and homelessness—regardless of whether they are actually successful—and they continue to volunteer for and donate to those organizations. In doing so, they not only perpetuate their existing organizational context—as SAM's emergence shows—but also confirm their belief that problems related to poverty are community challenges rather than systemic or individual ones.

From Community Challenges to Anti-Statism in Lutherton

But perhaps most important for our understanding of Heartland politics, Lutherton residents draw on these local experiences when confronting national problems. For example, when I ask Mallory, the teacher quoted above, how she thinks society writ large can best take care of people's needs, she tells me: "I think the things we're doing now." She then goes on to again describe local churches and nonprofits and the work she sees them doing in Lutherton. In other words, local experiences serve as a reference point for political beliefs on both the local and national scale.[12]

As a result, when residents consider what role they want the government to play in their lives, they express a distaste for public intervention—particularly by the federal government—and a preference for churches and nonprofits to take over. Local government, as we will see, is often conflated with "not-government." And while residents do imagine a distinction between those who are "deserving" and "undeserving" of assistance, as we might expect in the national-institutional and racial context that defines U.S. welfare provision, they also distinguish further between the kinds of social problems that are suitable for private (local) and public (extra-local) intervention.[13] And it is this latter distinction that reveals the political importance of place.

Cal, for example, is a retired Republican who explains his own attachment to the Republican Party the first time we meet by saying:

> Republicans, I think, are more independent, and people doing things instead of government doing it. Individuals or local things. Food stamp programs and free lunches and all of that. You know, I don't think a government should be involved in any of that. In this country, I can't believe if you're able-bodied . . . that you can't make it if you're not worthless and lazy. But I also believe that in this country—and they don't do it as much as they, I understand, used to or what they should—is churches and social organizations and all should take care of that kind of thing rather than the government taking care of it. And they would do a much better job.

Cal's reasoning offers insight into how Luthertonians' local problem-solving experiences produce a particular kind of communitarian anti-statism. First, he articulates a language of deservingness, explaining that healthy people should be able to take care of themselves unless they are "worthless and lazy." This type of language is not uncommon among the people I met in Lutherton. Given the media's racialization of welfare recipients alongside Lutherton's own history with institutionalized racism, it's possible that Cal and other residents are thinking of Black Americans when they refer to "some people" as "worthless and lazy." But while concerns about undeserving people of color benefiting from federal welfare provision are important here, they do not fully explain Luthertonians' particular brand of anti-statism.

And that's because even when Cal recognizes a "genuine" need he prefers to meet that need through nongovernmental or local entities. More specifically, Cal notes that his preferred mechanism for providing social welfare is "individuals or local things" and "churches or social organizations." Like many people I met in Lutherton, he has a tendency to equate "local" with nongovernmental. As a result, these residents often had far less of an issue with their local or even state governments involving themselves in social problems than they did the federal government. And that's because, for people who live in Lutherton, hunger, homelessness, and other social problems are community challenges rather than individual or systemic ones. As such, they can and should be resolved locally and privately.

Moreover, the pervasiveness of the local, nongovernmental preference is so strongly linked to everyday experience living in a churchgoing community that it cuts across party lines to some extent, even in such a hyperpolarized era. Hugh, for example, is a lifelong Democrat from Lutherton who ardently believes in communities taking care of themselves. In other words, Lutherton's anti-statism is just that—Luthertonian.

This does not mean that everyone in Lutherton—or even everyone I met— thinks the same way. For example, there was more variation in the extent to which people applied local diagnostic frames to national politics: several people appreciated the community's ability to solve problems but did not evoke that line of reasoning when it came to the national welfare. And two leftists I spoke to preferred greater federal intervention for national problems. Place is thus not the sole reference point for how residents of Lutherton—or Motorville and Gravesend—make sense of social problems or derive political solutions; but in the case of Lutherton, it does create a tendency for residents to think of postindustrial social problems as community challenges rather than systemic ones.

Motorville: Local Opinion Leaders at the
Nexus of Organized Labor and Government

Motorville is a different story from Lutherton. As chapter 2 showed, it does not have nearly Lutherton's level of private and collective resources to address social problems. And although church leaders describe ongoing efforts to serve the community amid limited resources, I rarely heard about these from Motorville residents: they are less likely to be church members or know church members than are Luthertonians. Moreover, Motorville politicians rarely post on Facebook about community service activities, nor has the newspaper historically given them much front-page space.

And that's because Motorville's community leaders and information ecosystem are embedded in a different organizational context, where close ties between organized labor and local politicians encourage Motorvillians to conceptualize their problems as rooted in macroeconomic transformations that have disadvantaged their city. As such, residents understand other social problems as *symptoms* of their city's systemic decline, and they turn to the state government—and occasionally federal government—to help them combat these challenges. Although the outcome is different from what we saw in Lutherton, the process is similar: residents of each place learn to interpret postindustrial social problems through their experiences within stable organizational contexts. And just as this place-based process cultivates a particular kind of antistatism in Lutherton, it cultivates a particular kind of statism in Motorville.

We can observe this first at the level of local opinion leaders, who are themselves products of the local organizational context. During my first few weeks in Motorville I spent much of my time in the offices of elected officials and civic leaders, and I heard again and again that declines in domestic manufacturing are at the root of the community's challenges. As Elliot, who sits on the board of an economic development organization in Motorville, tells me: "We struggle in this area. We were built on manufacturing and transportation and that sort of started to shift and move away. We haven't fully recovered from that. We found some other ways to do it, but not fully." The way to recover is to bring "actually good jobs" back to the community, as a city councillor tells me.

Within this framework, Motorville's community leaders tend to understand their problems as rooted in a long-term drain of good jobs from the city. Challenges like the opioid epidemic are merely symptoms of these underlying systemic issues. Mayor Hayte, for example, explains the community's opioid crisis to me in the following way:

We get almost no assistance from the state of Wisconsin . . . some of the lowest Medicaid reimbursement rates in the country lead to a massive addiction crisis, one of the worst in the entire country. And our area with our much higher poverty rates is among the worst hit for addiction.

Mayor Hayte's comments echo a common refrain among Motorville's community leaders during the summer and fall of 2019: their lack of resources is compounding, as a dearth of good jobs leads to poverty, poverty increases the prevalence of addiction, the state does not help address the addiction crisis, and the community languishes further.

In other words, Motorville's community leaders understand that their city has been battered by a shifting political economy over the past several decades, a challenge to be addressed by rebuilding a foundation of good-quality jobs. This objective may seem somewhat unsurprising, but it stands out in contrast to Lutherton, where community leaders repeatedly affirm in the summer of 2019 that their biggest problem is too many jobs for their population, as we have already heard from the former mayor and DRG director. But even those whose job does not entail worrying about Lutherton's workforce echo these concerns. As Pastor Ron, who leads one of the largest congregations in Lutherton, explains:

And people who say that they can't find a job [in Lutherton] are just fooling themselves. They don't want a job, because there's plenty of jobs. We've got business owners in our congregation who are begging for workers and they have to increase their starting salaries just to compete with other businesses in town.

It's difficult to imagine a community leader in Motorville speaking about wage increases with the kind of concern that Pastor Ron invokes; in fact, the by-product that concerns him is the goal for Motorville's leaders. And in contrast to the unmitigated pleasure I heard from residents of Lutherton about their low unemployment rate, no one in Motorville characterized the economy as "booming," even as community leaders estimated that the city had three hundred unfilled positions when I began my fieldwork in summer 2019.

Moreover, many leaders I spoke with in Lutherton conceive of their local challenges—the housing and opioid crises in particular—as exactly the inverse of how Motorvillians view them: they are barriers to attracting and retaining employers, rather than symptoms of deeper social and economic issues. But this is not because residents of Lutherton don't recognize the human cost of addiction or homelessness; as we have seen, even those who have not been affected personally by these social problems are all too aware of the toll they are taking on their neighbors. And residents care deeply about this. But recall how Pam from the DRG thinks about the opioid crisis: it is both a challenge in its own right, one that is touching almost everyone in the community in one way or another, and a challenge for employers. Both can be true, and are true, for Lutherton's community leaders. But providing better jobs is not the solution for either.

The opioid crisis thus offers the clearest example of how a purely structural account, focused on the cities' divergent experiences of deindustrialization and different demographic composition today, fails to explain differences in the way that residents of Motorville and Lutherton interpret their cities' social problems: Lutherton is a city with abundant employment but stagnating incomes, persistent poverty, and an acute substance abuse problem (per figures 5 and 6), but its community leaders focus on bringing in more jobs rather than solving the public health crisis. And in Motorville, which has lower rates of drug overdose, higher real wage growth, and fewer employment opportunities than Lutherton, community leaders focus instead on the tragedy of the opioid crisis as a consequence of low-quality employment.[14]

This is because community leaders, who also serve as opinion leaders for other residents, are themselves products of the local organizational context—in two ways. First, even if Mayor Hayte wanted to solve Motorville's problems by supporting local nonprofits like Mayor Redner does in Lutherton, he would not be able to because he lacks the abundance of private human and financial capital that churches and nonprofits collect in Lutherton. There are simply different kinds of organizations involved in each city's problem-solving partnerships. But Mayor Hayte also wouldn't want to follow Mayor Redner's lead because he, like other community leaders in Motorville, believes that bringing good jobs back to the community *is* the best solution to the opioid epidemic. This is in part because of his current ties to organized labor but also because he grew up in Motorville and learned many of the same diagnostic frames that residents share today. Recall from chapter 2 how Mark, the former city councillor, caveated his obligation to local organized labor who helped elect him: "So I supported whatever they want—*not like blindly following them, but more, I agree with that*" (emphasis added).

Motorville Residents' View: Defining Postindustrial
Social Problems as Systemic

As ordinary Motorvillians make sense of their problems within this context, they tend to adopt community leaders' diagnostic frames, which define the city's challenges as systemic (i.e., beyond local control) and turn residents toward the government—particularly the state government—to solve their problems.

Brenda, for example, is in her mid-thirties and works three part-time jobs, most recently as a teacher's aide. In summer 2019, she describes feeling shocked by the amount of poverty and addiction she saw among children in the local public schools. As she explains her view of the situation, she echoes Mayor Hayte's comments: "So I am concerned because, again, if there is not a lot of good jobs and you are concerned about that, besides drinking, opioids are gonna be really cheap. . . . And so I can understand that, you know, these things just kind of keep this horrible cycle going." Later in the conversation, Brenda continues, also referring to the opioid epidemic: "And again, like what resources do we have, which isn't a lot, to deal with that?" Other Motorvillians agree with Brenda and their community leaders: Motorville is struggling under the weight of systemic challenges that can only be resolved through better jobs and more state resources.

As in Lutherton, this diagnostic frame is reproduced through both everyday experiences and specific instances of local problem-solving. For example, Motorville's community leaders routinely talk about their city's challenges as rooted in systemic economic decline, as we saw earlier, but they also prioritize this diagnostic frame when confronting challenges that pose trade-offs between good jobs and other outcomes that are consequential for the city. And in Motorville, where the economy is dependent on fossil fuels and Democratic residents are often hunters and fishers who love the environment, one such trade-off that emerges with some regularity is that between good jobs and the environment.

A vivid example of this kind of challenge took place just before my fieldwork began, when a train carrying crude oil through town derailed, caught fire, and exploded. Everyone has a story of where they were when it happened. Elaine saw the cloud mushrooming over the train while she was driving. Danny had to be evacuated but snuck back home in the middle of the night. The blast knocked Sybil's mother-in-law off her chair. Fear rippled through the city overnight until local authorities announced that the explosion had been contained and evacuees could return home.

In the wake of this incident, the railroad sought to rebuild. This was not uncontroversial, as it had likely harmed residents' health, polluted the air and soil, and, of course, put thousands of people's lives at risk. When the mayor in the neighboring city called for the rail line to permanently stop carrying crude oil and other hazardous chemicals through town, Motorville's Mayor Hayte—who ran for office with organized labor's support multiple times—stood in support of it. As he explained his decision to me in summer 2019: "No-brainer over here, everybody supports the railroad." Even in saying this, Mayor Hayte acknowledged some contradiction in his stance: personally, he considers himself a staunch environmentalist, but as Motorville's mayor, he also recognizes that he cannot pursue environmental goals at the cost of good-quality jobs for the city. And that's because, like other elected officials, Mayor Hayte understands that part of his raison d'être as mayor is to use local government to maintain and grow the city's good jobs.

Moreover, by rapidly coming down on this side of the issue, Mayor Hayte helped prevent other diagnostic frames—the railroad as an environmental or public health threat—from gaining ground. This is important because many Motorvillians I spoke to consider themselves environmentalists and there are several environmental activist groups in surrounding counties. And yet, members of these groups, whose advocacy I observed at a County Commission meeting when they spoke on behalf of other environmental issues, told me that they were not involved in any response to the explosion. Residents were thus presented with a clear diagnosis of the problem (a major employer was temporarily out of business) and the obvious solution (rebuilding). As a result, with the exception of three people (out of twenty), every resident I spoke to in Motorville wanted the railroad to rebuild because, as Spencer told me, "it's one of the biggest and *best-paying* players in town" (emphasis added). In Motorville, unlike in similar cities that are dependent on extractive industries, residents do not view jobs and the environment as a zero-sum game.[15] And by continuing to elect leaders with labor support, like Mayor Hayte, residents help perpetuate a "good jobs" frame for addressing emergent challenges.

But just as in Lutherton, Motorvillians' shared understanding of their social problems is reproduced not just in these rare incidents of collective problem-solving: it is also reaffirmed via the way residents interpret their own and others' experiences within the local economy during everyday social interactions, ultimately reproducing shared narratives about Motorville. While discussions in Lutherton are shaped by the church- and nonprofit-based social networks in which they are embedded, Motorvillians instead hear about their social problems from local opinion leaders like Mayor Hayte or from friends with ties to local unions. The result is that residents I met tended to describe

Motorville as underresourced, like Brenda, or "depressed," as Elaine said. Although Motorville is in fact not a depressed economy by standard measures of unemployment (below 4 percent in 2019), this objective fact has little bearing on how residents understand it.

Within this framework for understanding Motorville as a depressed place, residents regularly tell themselves that their own difficulties—and those of their friends, family, and neighbors—in finding good jobs are not their fault but the fault of the local economy. In other words, they refuse to individualize the problem. Renne, for example, is a county employee who watched many of her friends leave town even as she stayed after graduating from the local community college. When I ask her to describe Motorville's challenges, she reflects on her own experiences:

> Earlier when you asked why I had stayed [while others left], it was because—part of it was because I had found a good job. I feel very lucky to have the job that I have because I don't think a lot of people do. And I think there's a lot of people who struggle financially. So, you know, trying to get those nice jobs with good benefits is so important [for the community].

Like other Motorvillians, Renne explains that good jobs—those with benefits, wages that can support a family, and union protections—are hard to come by in Motorville. Renne is acutely aware of this because she lost her own union protections after Act 10. Even years later, as she tells me in summer 2019, that loss stings. But like other Motorvillians I met, she thinks about her own experiences not in the context of individual failing—or in her case success—but in the context of the broader challenges facing her community.

Motorvillians' desire to live in a city with good jobs may seem somewhat unsurprising. And yet, this is not how residents of Lutherton think about their local economy or how it fits into a broader system of social relations. Shannon and Ken, for example, are a couple who are self-employed and often piece together odd jobs that keep them working long hours. When I ask them about Lutherton's challenges, Ken tells me:

KEN: One of the things that's really good about Lutherton is they have a lot of employment here.
SHANNON: They do!
KEN: I've told her that I could go out every day of the week and get a different job every day of the week.
SHANNON: Mhhm. Factories.
KEN: We have plenty of economy and work.

Although Ken himself would prefer not to work at a factory because of how they treat their employees, he is one of the only people in Lutherton who mentions job quality to me at all. But even for Ken, Lutherton's economy is defined by the glut of jobs, not poor wages. As a result, Lutherton residents somewhat contradictorily see poverty, housing precarity, and addiction as features of their community even amid a booming economy. In Lutherton, these challenges are not interpreted as symptoms of systemic issues.

The State as Problem-Solver among Motorvillians

In contrast, many Motorvillians I met sounded a lot like Renne, offering similar stories about themselves and their friends. Through both their community leaders' repeated affirmation that Motorville's problems are rooted in systemic economic challenges and residents' own accounting to one another about their struggles to find good jobs, residents come to agree that a lack of good jobs is at the heart of the city's problems.

And to resolve these problems, Motorvillians argue that they need the state. In the case of local challenges like the opioid crisis, they typically mean the state of Wisconsin. Sybil, for example, is a lifelong Republican who, when faced with the deleterious consequences of the opioid epidemic in Motorville, argues: "We need more money from state governments for treatment." This is in fact the most common refrain I heard among Motorvillians regarding the opioid crisis: the state of Wisconsin needs to provide funds for in-patient treatment closer to home. In part, this is because they feel the state owes them. Much like Katherine Cramer (2016) identifies in her work, Motorvillians feel Wisconsin has long neglected communities outside of Madison and Milwaukee. They are "ignored statewide," as Isabelle says. But Motorville is also different from the places that Cramer studies: while they articulate a similar rural resentment, they do not turn against the state but toward it.

This is because, in a place where local challenges are understood as symptoms of systemic economic issues, residents believe they need help "from higher up," as Quinn tells me. And as we will see in greater detail in chapter 4, residents apply a similar diagnostic frame on a national scale: in a system of profound economic inequality, they and their community are among the disadvantaged, and the federal government should step in and level the playing field. Colton, for example, is an Independent in his early twenties who wrote-in Marco Rubio when he voted for president in 2016 and voted for a third party in 2020. In spring 2020 he's explaining to me why he *doesn't* like Bernie Sanders but ends up concluding he does favor a number of his policies, including

Medicare for All and raising taxes on billionaires: "I think the income inequality is pretty ridiculous. The top earners in our country are earning a lot of money, a lot of money, so much money, you don't even know what to do with it. So I think they definitely should be taxed more."

Contrast Colton's view to that of Cal, the Lutherton resident we met earlier. Even if both college-educated, White men were confronted with someone who had a "genuine" need for food, Colton might see this as the result of systemic economic inequality and evidence that the country needs better social programs, while Cal might view this as part of an occasional hiccup in an otherwise well-functioning system, which can be addressed by a local food bank. As chapter 4 shows, Colton's statism is further bolstered by Motorvillians' narrative of community identity, which tells them that they would likely benefit from state intervention to level the playing field.

We can further observe Motorvillians' turn toward the state, particularly relative to Lutherton, in the way some residents talk about private, collective problem-solving efforts in the city. Although it was rare for someone from Motorville to tell me that they would look to churches or nonprofits to resolve local problems, this did happen occasionally. And some people sounded like Luthertonians when they did so: two people, one who is actively involved in several civic organizations and the other who is a regular churchgoer, even expressed a belief that communities can and should take care of themselves. But other residents who were aware of nonprofit or church services in Motorville had ambivalent feelings about them. Jamie, for example, is one of a handful of people who is familiar with the local Catholic Aid Society's work to provide temporary shelter and assistance to people in need. But as she tells me when I ask her how our society can best take care of people's needs, that is not actually the way to address homelessness. Rather: "Well, if we had something preventative, I guess would be the best way to find a way to keep people from becoming homeless. If we have the social structures in place, that helps people to stop from becoming homeless or food insecure, why do we not have that?" Because Jamie, like many Motorvillians I spoke to, advocates for root-cause solutions, she sees other efforts in the city—even those led by an organization she trusts and admires like the Catholic Aid Society—as band-aids rather than solutions.

In sum, because many Motorvillians see their community's issues, and those of the country writ large, as the product of *systemic* challenges, they view the government as the only vehicle to rectify them—and on the local level they look to the state, while on the national scale they look to the federal government. Moreover, as the examples of Sybil and Colton indicate,

Motorvillians' willingness to call on both state and federal governments occasionally crosses party lines—although it does so to a lesser extent than Lutherton's anti-statism.

———

This chapter has shown how local organizational contexts help residents of Motorville and Lutherton cohere around place-based diagnostic frames, or ways of defining social problems and identifying political solutions. Within their organizational context, Motorvillians see their problems as systemic, rooted in long-term economic decline and a drain of good jobs from the community—a view that community leaders perpetuate in both their framing of social problems like the opioid epidemic and the way they address specific challenges like the railroad explosion. The result is that Motorvillians look to the state government to redress their local challenges—the "higher up" power in Quinn's language—and they look to the federal government to address similar challenges on a national scale.

In contrast, within Lutherton's organizational context, residents see social problems related to poverty as community challenges, which can and should be resolved through their local network of churches and nonprofits, perhaps with a little assistance from local government. Underlying residents' belief in the efficacy of community problem-solving are their experiences of highly visible nonprofit and church-based efforts to serve those in need. These visible actions are the flip side of what political scientists have referred to as the "submerged" and "delegated" welfare state: while middle-class families may not be able to see the myriad ways that the federal government supports them through tax credits and funding for nonprofits, those families do observe organizational activities within their communities.[16] It is thus both the *apparent* absence of the state and presence of local organizations that produces Luthertonians' particular anti-statism.

This argument implies that diagnostic frames are not determined purely by local structural conditions: Lutherton has more jobs of lower quality than Motorville, leading to greater challenges with hunger and overdose deaths. And yet, it is in Motorville that community leaders and residents focus on the need for "good jobs," while people in Lutherton focus on bringing even more jobs to town and "solving" the challenges that their churches are already working on—hunger and homelessness.

Nor can we reduce these diagnostic frames to direct political socialization within organizations. For example, residents of Lutherton tend to agree that their community can and should take care of their own, regardless of church membership or denominational affiliation: Patty, quoted above, articulated this belief repeatedly despite the fact that she does not attend church and belongs to a union. Individual organizational ties do matter, as we saw in the case of civically engaged residents in Motorville, but there is also strong evidence of city-level tendencies toward shared diagnostic frames. They even extend, to some degree, across partisan lines.

This means that local organizational contexts can shape political outcomes *far beyond their direct effects on members*. Moreover, my contention is that, to understand *how* local organizational contexts sustain diagnostic frames for organizational members and non-members alike, we have to consider not just quantitative indicators of organizational membership or revenue but also the different ways that organizations participate in community life and public problem-solving.[17] By expanding the analytic lens in this way, this chapter has shown how local organizations provide the context in which residents make sense of local challenges and how to resolve them—with or without government intervention.

This chapter thus departs from standard accounts of public opinion formation that emphasize the importance of national political party cues in guiding opinion. Although party cues are important, we have seen how routine dimensions of Americans' social context—in this case, local organizations—can *also* shape beliefs.[18] Following political scientists Michele Margolis and Michael Sances (2017), my argument is that the organization of social life often *precedes* politics, such that we can understand the emergence of "partisan" differences in political behavior in part through apolitical processes: Cal comes to sound like a communitarian Republican not because of some abstract ideological commitment but because his own life experiences, structured by Lutherton's organizational context, have taught him that this is how society should solve its problems.[19] As we will see in the next chapter, these experiences make Republican arguments about local control resonate with many Lutherton residents.

In short, residents' orientation toward state and federal governments develops partly within local organizational contexts that support different modes of problem-solving—turning Motorvillians toward the government and Luthertonians toward their community. But the very concept of "community" raises some questions. Whom do Lutherton residents imagine as part of their community? As political scientist Cara Wong points out, communities are often defined by members' subjective image of who does and does not belong. And when it comes to the social problems that residents of Motorville and

Lutherton are grappling with in this chapter, the central question becomes: "for whom am I willing to sacrifice and from whom should community benefits be withheld" (Wong 2010, 18)?

Chapter 4 takes up the answer to these questions. By describing the narratives of community identity that tell residents who they are as a community and where they fit into national party politics, we will see that the way residents of Motorville and Lutherton draw boundaries around community undergirds their ideas about problem-solving and, ultimately, reinforces their partisanship.[20]

4

From Place to Partisan Identity in Motorville and Lutherton

LUTHERTON USED TO BE a Democratic place, a fact that sweetens the Republican Party's victories every election cycle. Judge Meyer, an elected Republican in Lutherton County, explains her understanding of how this came about:

> I mean, traditionally, even probably as recently as twenty, thirty years ago, Lutherton County was a Democrat county. And it just swapped hard . . . I think it's because the Democratic Party has moved so far left. The Democrats here are what I refer to as old-style, labor-type Democrats. They were farmers and laborers that—you know, New Deal–type Democrats. And when [the] Democratic Party started moving into so many—what they would refer to as like far-left social issues—that's when I think they lost this county. I think the whole, you know, co-ed bathrooms in schools. People are just like, what? I mean, people are just really old-school midwestern [in Lutherton].

Later, she adds: "I think probably primarily what makes this community more conservative than a lot of other communities—both socially, fiscally, and religiously—is the tie to the church." Judge Meyer's summary proves insightful: Lutherton residents overwhelmingly agree that issues such as abortion and LGBTQ rights—what they consider moral issues—are fundamental to partisan divisions.

In contrast, many Motorvillians would disagree with Judge Meyer's characterization of the Democratic Party. When Motorvillians think about what is at stake when they cast a vote for one party or the other, they think about the divide between the "haves" and the "have-nots." Megan, who sits on a local industrial development board in Motorville, explains why she thinks Motorville is a Democratic town in this way:

All of my family was hardworking, hands-on industry, union family, right? So, I just grew up with—and I think a lot of—I can't say for sure for all families [in Motorville]—but I feel like there was this, what's going to be best for us, what's best for our community, and what's best for their families? . . . [Motorvillians] had a voice and I think because of those unions, too, of how to come together to have those conversations.

For Megan and other Motorvillians, the Democrats still feel like the "labor-type" party that Judge Meyer thinks of as a bygone institution. And even residents who are no longer blue-collar, union workers—Megan, for example, is college-educated and works in a white-collar job—often continue to identify themselves and their community with the working classes and organized labor.

———

Throughout this book, I have argued that structural and organizational dimensions of place produce two cultural frameworks that sustain partisan differences across Motorville, Lutherton, and Gravesend today. In chapter 3 we saw how organizational contexts produce one of these cultural frameworks: different place-based *diagnostic frames* turn Motorville residents toward the state to resolve their systemic economic challenges and Lutherton residents inward to resolve their community challenges. And now, in the differences between Judge Meyer and Megan, we can glimpse the second cultural framework: *narratives of community identity*. The two women understand partisan politics to be organized around different battle lines, and they locate themselves and their communities on different sides of those divides. The remainder of this chapter will show how these narratives of community identity help residents of each city locate themselves in the social and political world, ultimately sustaining their place-based partisanship.

As Judge Meyer's and Megan's comments indicate, the parties today represent a bundle of divergent issues. To an extent, the Republican Party is the party of Christian morality, business interests, White racial conservatism, and local rather than federal control, while the Democratic Party is the party of women's right to choose, the workers' side of the business-labor divide, racial equality, and federal intervention. These positions do not naturally go together: there is no reason why one party should stand for both organized labor and a woman's right to choose. But these diverse stances came to be bundled together over decades, as social groups mobilized politically and advocated for inclusion in party coalitions.[1]

Such macro-level party maneuvering vis-à-vis social groups indicates the range of possible interpretations that American voters might have when they think about what the political parties mean.[2] These interpretations are important because they shape the micro-level process of partisan identity formation: individuals form party attachments based on which party is home to their "kinds of people"—or others who share their social identity—rather than through a careful consideration of each party's policy programs.[3] For this process to occur, voters need "a particular kind of political knowledge about which groups affiliate with each party."[4] And according to scholars who argue that local and regional variation in the parties has waned in recent years, the question of which groups belong to which party should be easier and easier for Americans to answer, regardless of where they live.[5]

And yet, this is not true of Motorville and Lutherton, as Judge Meyer's and Megan's comments suggest. In many ways, the party evolutions generally thought of as historical processes appear here as contemporary differences in the parties' meanings across place.[6] As this chapter illustrates, this is because place leads residents to cohere around shared narratives of community identity, which tell them who they are as a community and which political party best represents their kind of people.

We can understand this process through two distinct phases: the construction of social identities and the way those identities are mapped onto the party system.[7] First, despite sharing similar social group memberships, residents of Motorville and Lutherton tell different stories about the kind of community they live in and who they are as people: residents of Lutherton understand their community as a German Lutheran town that takes care of itself, and Motorvillians understand theirs as a struggling working town that would benefit from state intervention. Second, within a two-party system where the parties represent multiple different groups, place helps residents figure out which party is most likely to represent them and their community, producing distinct, local interpretations of national party politics. This means that even if residents of Motorville and Lutherton were to share similar understandings of their social identities, they would disagree on which party best represents them. In Lutherton, people have learned through their churchgoing community that Republicans are the party of religion and local control in a political system divided by morality and the extent of federal government intervention. The Republicans are the party for them. And in Motorville, people have learned through experiences in their union town that Democrats are the party of the have-nots in a political system divided by economic inequality. Democrats are the party for them.

This is not simply an argument about Motorville containing more union members, who understand themselves and party politics in one way, and Lutherton containing more churchgoers, who think differently: if churches, and particularly White evangelical churches, have increasingly become sites of Republican partisan identity formation since the 1980s, and unions have long been sites of Democratic activism (although waning in recent years), then places with more churchgoers will have more Republicans and places with more unions will have more Democrats.[8] And the quantity of organizational ties does matter in both Motorville and Lutherton; but as we saw in the previous chapter, this is not just an argument about direct political socialization within organizations. Rather, local organizational contexts create shared cultural frameworks among residents, meaning that narratives of community identity extend far beyond individuals' direct organizational ties to churches and unions.

These narratives circulate through the same mechanisms we saw in chapter 3: residents' ideas about their community are reinforced through social interactions in which other residents describe themselves in certain ways—suggesting that this is a certain kind of place and, therefore, that they are certain kinds of people.[9] Amid a range of possible social identities for residents in Motorville and Lutherton, place helps make certain identities more salient than others. Amid a range of possible interpretations of party politics, place helps make certain interpretations more resonant than others.[10] In sum, place helps produce—and reproduce—residents' partisanship.

In a standard national survey or public opinion poll, the different ways that residents of Motorville and Lutherton think about themselves and the parties might appear as unexplained variation. It is only once we meet them where they live that we see how their interpretations are rooted in place.

Lutherton: The Republicans Are the Party for Us

The previous chapter documented how Lutherton's particular anti-statism emerges through their experiences of addressing postindustrial social problems within their community. These experiences also shape their community identity: they are a churchgoing town where, as Todd tells me, "we always take care of our own." This self-understanding is central to Lutherton's Republicanism, but it also suggests an important boundary between those whom they imagine are excluded versus included from the community's care.[11] And to residents of Lutherton, their community is defined along ethnoreligious lines: they think of themselves not just as a Christian community but as a German Lutheran community.

The Republican Party, home to White Christians and small communities who want to maintain local control without federal interference, is their home too.

A Community of German Lutherans
That Can Take Care of Ourselves

Recall how I spent my first afternoon in Lutherton: in the passenger seat of Wayne's pickup, getting a tour of the county in which German Lutheran churches were the highlight. As residents told me throughout my time there, Lutherton is a German Lutheran place. As we will see, ethnoreligious identity is central to how Luthertonians understand their community because churches are central to individuals' daily lives, to the community's way of solving social problems, and to how residents locate one another within a loosely agreed-upon social hierarchy.

Regardless of their denominational affiliation, the people I met in Lutherton often identified themselves as Christians without being asked, just as they identified their community as a Christian community without being asked. Harriett, for example, describes Lutherton through the lens of her experience growing up there: "We went to church probably three days a week, and like most families here in the community, their religion was very, very important to them." Harriett's description is common among other residents I spoke with in Lutherton: Christianity is not just a part of who individual residents are, it's a part of who the community is. This way of understanding themselves derives from residents' own practices and organizational affiliations but also their participation in a community that agrees on this defining feature. Individual and community identities reinforce one another.[12]

And at their maximum, the pervasive church ties in Lutherton lead to a kind of social pressure, such that church membership becomes a requirement for social citizenship. Oftentimes, the first question people ask newcomers to town is, "Which church do you go to?" During our conversations, many residents asked me a corollary version of this question, along the lines of "What's your religion?" with the assumption that religion is limited to Christianity. These questions remind residents in routine social interaction that they are Christians, reinforcing the salience of their Christian social identities.[13]

The importance of this assumed Christianity is most evident in the social pressure on those who buck the prevailing trend. Patrick, for example, is a non-churchgoer who "confessed" his status to me at the end of an interview, after I'd turned off the recorder. He only did so after asking me about my own politics. Finding out that I register as a Democrat, he breathed a sigh of relief, and then he spilled the details. When I first asked him if he attends a church in town, Patrick told me: "My wife goes to church, takes the boys there, [they] go as a family. I'm not practicing." At the time, I thought little of this response, only later realizing this was a carefully chosen phrase, as he explains:[14]

"When you asked me about where I go to church, I got a bit nervous," Patrick tells me. "Really?" I ask him. "Yeah," he says, "I think I might be a closet atheist." I laugh at the phrase, but he continues: "Honestly, it might be harder to be an atheist around here than to be gay!" He tells me that when he came back to town eight years ago, the first thing everyone asked him was where he was living; the second was where he was going to church. "For some people, the church question was the first question!" he adds. "And some people specifically asked if I was a Lutheran, because I went to a Lutheran church growing up and a Lutheran school until high school. I never wanted to lie," he explains, "so I always tried to avoid the question." He explains that citing his wife's church became a useful evasion tactic. "But," he concludes, "I really think there's a bit of a Lutheran mafia around here." He tells me the story of how two of his friends used to go to the biggest Lutheran church in town, and when they stopped going, the church announced it in their bulletin. They were small business owners and Patrick felt this was the church's way of telling people to stop shopping at their businesses.

Patrick's interpretation of this incident—that the church targeted former members—was salient enough that it shaped his future behavior—his interactions with me. And while Patrick was the only person who expressed this degree of social pressure surrounding church membership, he is also the only person I spoke with who grew up attending a large church *within* Lutherton and has since ceased practicing entirely. The other non-churchgoers I spoke to grew up elsewhere. Patrick's status thus raises questions among family, friends, and acquaintances, for whom church membership is a taken-for-granted part of their daily routines and social practices.

But Lutherton is not just a community that prizes Christianity and church membership: as Patrick's and Wayne's comments indicate, it's a Lutheran community—and, even more specifically, a German Lutheran community. And as with their understanding of the community as "faith-based," residents' recognition that this is a German Lutheran community is about more than just the number of people who attend Lutheran churches or who have German heritage, although adherents of the Lutheran Church-Missouri Synod (German Lutheran churches) do make up about one-third of all religious adherents in the county. But the ethnoreligious composition of the county is changing as largely Catholic immigrants from Mexico and Central America have joined Lutherton's ranks.[15]

And yet, amid these objective changes in demographic composition, the community's identity as a White, European place persists. In fact, residents reminded me again and again that Lutherton is a German Lutheran community, despite the fact that I never asked anyone about the city's denominational or ethnic makeup. For example, when I ask Larry what church he attends, before answering he recalls the exact number of Lutheran churches in the county— thirteen. There are also physical markers, in addition to church buildings themselves, that remind residents of their community's ethnoreligious identity: street signs and park names in German; large signs as you enter town from either direction proclaiming the names of the largest German Lutheran churches; and an annual festival celebrating the community's German heritage. And as Wayne did during our first drive through the county together, residents occasionally refer to these physical markers to explain what they mean when they describe Lutherton as a German Lutheran place. Through their efforts to explain to me—an outsider—who they are as a community, we can see how residents socialize newcomers into the fold: recall that it only took me a few hours to learn the salience of the community's ethnoreligious identity. As sociologist Japonica Brown-Saracino (2015) notes, this process of teaching newcomers about a place is essential to the stickiness of place character. The very people we might expect to disrupt old patterns (newcomers) become purveyors of those patterns (whether they like them or not) because they're the ones who are in the process of learning what their new community is all about.

Everyday social interactions further reinforce Lutherton's ethnoreligious identity when residents use church membership to locate each other within a local social hierarchy. Patrick is not the only person in Lutherton to describe something like a "Lutheran mafia" in town: several people explain that big Lutheran churches matter for social status. Fred, for example, is a member of the largest German Lutheran congregation in Lutherton. When I ask him where he and his wife attend, he cites their church's impressive membership numbers with pride. A few days later, I join him at a daily McDonald's breakfast composed of a handful of retired men. As they sit sipping coffees, Fred introduces us all, and then pauses to explain to me: "You know, all of us," he begins, gesturing toward himself and three others seated around a cluster of tables, "go to the same church. Immaculate. It's the biggest church in town. The current mayor goes to our church." As Fred points out each member, they smile and nod. A few months later when I return to have coffee with the group, another Immaculate churchgoer repeats a nearly identical routine.

The flip side of the McDonald's crowd's pride is the experience of social exclusion among those who do not share the prevailing ethnoreligious identity—people who are on the outside of the "Lutheran mafia," as Patrick and others described. There is racism and prejudice in all three cities, but in Lutherton this racism was institutionalized for much of its history, as we saw in chapter 1. James, an older Black man and one of the retired McDonald's attendees, recalls the segregated neighborhood he lived in growing up, the fact that he wasn't allowed to eat at a local diner, and his exclusion from the local Boys and Girls Club. While these experiences are seared into James's brain, they were news to the White members of the McDonald's club. Fred was shocked and horrified by James's account when he first heard it during one of these gatherings—despite the fact that they'd grown up going to school together. In some ways, this should not have surprised Fred, whose mother was of Italian heritage and who also described feeling that he was different when he moved to Lutherton at the age of five and found himself among so many Germans. And yet, America's system of racial oppression seemed far-off to Fred in the Lutherton he grew up in because it was 99.5 percent White at that time. Instead, he saw the community as one characterized by White ethnic and religious denominational divisions. And while some of those tensions have eased, their ongoing importance as community identifiers is revealed in both Lutherans' own feelings of social status and non-Lutherans' feelings of exclusion.

Even today, as residents grapple with a new color line amid the growing, largely Latinx, immigrant population, this ethnoreligious identity persists. In fact, the persistence of Lutherton's community identity may be one reason why the White residents I spoke to articulated almost no feelings of threat associated with a growing Latinx community in their city—despite the city's history of segregation and residents' present-day concerns about abstract threats from Muslims and "riots" in urban centers that emerged after George Floyd's murder. But most native-born residents I spoke to in Lutherton understood immigrants as the backbone of their local economy, did not support deportation, and even supported a path to citizenship for immigrants who had no criminal record but lacked documents.[16] All of this, even though they overwhelmingly supported Donald Trump as a presidential candidate.

In other words, racial politics in Lutherton is about more than just racism. Although there is plenty of evidence of racism at both the interactional and institutional levels, equally important is Luthertonians' ethnoreligious identity—a pride in who their community is.[17]

The Republicans Are the Party of Christianity, Local Control, and White People

As a result of the multifaceted role that Lutherton's churches play as community problem-solvers, social stratifiers, and, of course, religious edifiers, residents understand their community as a place where churchgoers—namely, White ethnic Christians—take care of themselves. Living in a community defined in this way informs how people understand what's at stake in national party politics: to them, partisan divisions center around race, Christian morality, and the appropriate role of the state, and Republicans are the party of White Christianity and local control. In other words, Republicans are the party for Lutherton.

This is not an argument about churchgoers voting for Republicans because they only care about abortion as an issue—although many churchgoers I spoke to do care deeply about this. Instead, what distinguishes Lutherton from Motorville and Gravesend is that, in Lutherton, residents tend to agree that Christianity is one of the centers of organized political conflict, and this understanding can cut across lines of partisanship, church membership, and formal political knowledge. In other words, it is place-based. Linda, for example, is a Republican who tends to stay away from politics and giggles with uncertainty when I ask her to describe the differences between the two political parties. Even so, she concludes that political divisions are rooted in biblical differences. As she describes the issues that most divide people:

> Again, I think it's those things that are like issues of faith. You know, like life issues, lifestyle choices, things that hundreds of years ago, when probably more of the nation was a Christian nation that people just took for granted. . . . And so I think going away from those biblical values is what's pulling people apart.

By "lifestyle choices," Linda later explains that she means sexual orientation. For many Lutherton residents I met, what they describe as "issues of faith" are the central fissures of American politics. And when it comes to putting formal labels on those divisions, residents further agree that the Republican Party represents the Christians—and, by extension, them.

And to a somewhat lesser extent, Lutherton voters also see Democrats as representing the opposite: un-Christian values. Amy, for example, identifies as a Republican but tends not to pay much attention to politics. She voted for Obama in 2008 and 2012 and Trump in 2016. When she describes what she sees as the major dividing lines in politics, she explains:

It's not really what's going on in our country with like our finances or with other countries. I think it's more, a lot of personal issues, like the "how I want to be perceived as a female or male or transgendered and other groups." . . . What people argue about in politics are like abortion and the gender things and more personal stuff instead of like what our country needs.

To her, the Democratic Party stands for those "groups." "It's like everybody's entitled. You know, and I don't feel like people are entitled to feel like you should just . . . like that's the way things are. Like hey, you're born a man, you're born a woman. That's what God . . . I feel like they try to take God out of our country."

Linda and Amy exemplify how place helps residents map their social identities onto party politics: the idea that party politics is organized around Christian values, with the Democrats on the side of trying to "take God out of our country," is *one possible interpretation* that Americans might have, given the amalgamation of social groups and issue positions that each party represents. Just as structural factors impose constraints on the diagnostic frames residents develop to understand their problems, political party maneuvering further constrains residents' understanding of what the parties mean and which social groups they represent.[18] As such, Linda and Amy's particular interpretation of party politics would be available to anyone who consumes right-leaning news sources routinely (although in this case, neither consumes much news because they don't have cable and don't read newspapers). In other words, place does not create party meanings—parties themselves do that.[19] But place helps ensure that certain interpretations of those meanings resonate with residents. This is true even if—as in Amy's concerns about taking God out of the country—those interpretations are not actually central to a party's platform.

Perhaps the strongest evidence of how place promotes specific interpretations of politics is a pattern of local counterpolitics in Lutherton: a handful of Democrats and Independents who reject the Republican Party precisely because of its "co-optation" of Christianity. Kyle, for example, grew up in Lutherton and has just finished his first year of college when we meet for the first time. Although politics is not a core concern of his, he has picked up several observations from his hometown. Republicans, he tells me, "stand for religion." This is the reason, he explains, that Lutherton is so Republican—it is a very Christian community. This single connection shapes a lot of Kyle's politics: if he had a "magic wand" and could change one thing about the country it would be to "keep religion out of politics." Other Democrats I met in Lutherton similarly describe how their voting behavior is more about disassociating themselves from a Republican Party that has co-opted Christianity than embracing the Democratic Party. In other words, Democrats in Lutherton are not drawn to their party for the same reasons as are Democrats in Motorville, as we will see: in Lutherton, religion is a core piece of party identification for both Democrats and Republicans. It is a feature of Lutherton politics rather than a feature of individuals' politics.

We can see why, for Lutherton residents who feel they are part of a Christian community, the Republican Party feels like the party for them. But they are not just Christians: they are German Lutherans. And in Lutherton, party politics does not just express moral divisions in society, it also expresses an essential racial division: between White people, whose home is in the Republican Party, and people of color, whose home is in the Democratic Party. This understanding, however, is not specific to Lutherton. In fact, residents of Motorville, Lutherton, and Gravesend—both Democrats and Republicans—routinely describe the parties in this way. Republicans, for example, occasionally argue that Democrats "use" people of color for their votes or lament Obama's presidency because he stoked "racism" against Whites, while Democrats refer to Trump's racism as representative of the Republican Party and describe the GOP as the party of racial oppression. The fact that this interpretation is shared across city and party lines suggests the overwhelming importance of racial divisions to American political divisions, perhaps even more so in the wake of Barack Obama's historic presidency.[20] But what this means for the particular case of Lutherton residents is that, while there is no political party that represents German Lutherans specifically, there is a party that clearly represents White Christians: the Republican Party.[21]

And if this were not sufficient reason for residents of Lutherton to find a natural home there, they have one more. Many residents also view Republicans as the party to represent places like theirs, communities that wish to take care of themselves without interference from the federal government. As we heard from Cal in chapter 3, this is exactly why he identifies as a Republican. And for many people I spoke to in Lutherton, the understanding that Republicans are the party of local control coincides with their view of Republicans as the party of Christian morality.

Katherine's description of the GOP exemplifies this combination. When I ask her what the Republican Party stands for in summer 2019, she tells me:

> They've always kind of believed, keep the government out of it as much as we can, that everything should be more or less on a local level. Let the states

or the local level take care of things and . . . let the federal government take care of things that nobody else can, like our national security. . . . And I think they believe in protecting the unborn. Definitely.

As Katherine's comments indicate, to many people in Lutherton, Republicans are the party that will defer control to the local level and follow "biblical principles," as another resident tells me. And for a White, Christian community that prefers to take care of itself, this is the party that best represents them.

Place-Based Mechanisms

For people like Linda and Amy, who both attend evangelical churches, it is easy to see how such an understanding would emerge despite their limited interest in politics. As one of their pastors told me, their church's approach to the Bible is "conservative," and while they don't routinely preach about politics they also don't shy away from political issues. But this is not just a story about organizations socializing their members into certain forms of politics. Other Lutherton residents who do not attend evangelical churches learn this tight link between Christianity and Republicanism in much the same way they learn about social problems and community identity: through social interaction with their neighbors and via local opinion leaders. Fred, for example, thinks of Republicans as "churchgoers." As he goes on to say: "Most of the people I know that are Republicans fall into that category." In a place like Lutherton, people like Fred only have to observe their neighbors to learn that churchgoing and Republicanism go hand in hand. For others like Jacob, who espouses Kyle's counterpolitics even more vociferously, local opinion leaders are more important. Jacob is enraged that Republicans have become the party of Christianity, and he is convinced of this fact because—as he returns to again and again in our conversations—local Republican politicians constantly campaign on their identities as "Christian conservatives."

The rare cases where individuals changed their party identification during the time I knew them illustrate these place-based mechanisms most clearly. In Lutherton, there were just two people whose party identification changed, and both were Democrats when I met them in 2019. Marie, for example, is a devoutly Christian resident of Lutherton who decided not to vote for Joe Biden in 2020 after a lifetime of Democratic partisanship and voting. As she told me repeatedly during our conversations, she is someone who tends to avoid talking about politics, and the differences between the two parties have long seemed somewhat "blurry" to her. But that was not always the case, as she told me in fall 2020: "When I was very young, I would have been listening to my dad more than anything." And according to him: "The Democrats were more for the little person. The Republicans were for the big corporations and the more wealthy people." But that was decades ago. Just a few months prior to this conversation, Marie had remarried and begun discussing politics with her husband after years of avoiding it. In place of the class divisions that had dominated party politics during her youth, her husband explained that moral divisions were now paramount: in particular, he told her that the Democrats are pro-choice and Republicans are pro-life. To Marie, who had always been concerned about the personal immorality of abortion, this became a troubling political problem for the first time. As she approached the 2020 election, she decided that she could not bring herself to vote for a pro-choice candidate again—a decision she now understood would take Democrats out of the equation. Although Marie still does not consider herself a Republican, and she refused to vote for Donald Trump, the suddenness of her disaffection from the Democrats is striking. And it happened because she started talking politics again after forty years, and the people who were surrounding her—other people who live in Lutherton—told her that politics was about Christian morality, not social class.

Motorville: The Democratic Party Is the Party for Us

In Lutherton, place helps organize residents' social and political identities, making it more likely that—within the constraints imposed by their social group membership and party politics—they understand themselves and their place in party politics through a certain framework. The same is true in Motorville, but here a different organizational and cultural setting produces a different narrative of community identity. As the last chapter revealed, the Motorvillians I spoke to agree that their community is struggling under the weight of systemic challenges that require better jobs and increased government intervention, at both the state and federal levels. And as this section will show, this diagnostic frame has become a fundamental part of how the community defines itself. For Motorvillians, the community's challenges are indicative of who they are: a community of have-nots. Like many other people and places, they are caught in a trap of systemic inequality that allows a few "haves" to horde most of the wealth while the "have-nots" like them struggle to keep up with the cost of living and pay for things like health care and housing. And the Democrats are the party that will wield the government—in this case, typically the federal government—to help them in that struggle.

From Systemic Problems to a Community of Have-Nots

Motorvillians' shared understanding that their community is among the "have-nots" is partly rooted in Motorville's proud legacy as a place that has fought against the "haves": Motorville was built on the back of organized labor, as Harry, the president of the MLC, described in chapter 2. Such a refrain was not atypical among the Motorvillians I spoke to—perhaps unsurprising given how local opinion leaders frame their city in this way. Echoing Harry, Isaac, a union member with the railroad, explains: "Motorville's always been a big union town." Even those who have never been in a union, like Carl, echo Isaac's assessment, explaining that Motorville is "a strong union area."

The pervasiveness of this community identity is rooted in unions' direct influence on their members and indirect influence on the rest of the city. For example, because Motorville has a relatively large quantity of union members, and because Motorville's unions have historically been politically engaged and active in community life, the *Motorville Tribune* has historically covered labor disputes, strikes, and labor-related decisions by the City Council with much greater frequency than either the *Lutherton Gazette* or *Gravesend Ledger*, as we saw in chapter 1. And just as local politicians in Lutherton post on Facebook about church and nonprofit service activities in town, Motorville's politicians post about labor issues—much more so than do politicians in either Lutherton or Gravesend (see figure A4). During election season in Motorville, yards are dotted with campaign signs that carry the endorsements of various labor unions.

Even Motorville's built environment reflects the image of a working town much more so than Gravesend's and Lutherton's. Regardless of the direction by which you arrive in Motorville, it is impossible not to be awed by the towering elevators that lift grain onto the Motorville River and the collection of ships huddled nearby to transport it. The railway that cuts through town regularly disrupts the rhythms of daily life—a reminder that it is one of the city's largest employers. In contrast, most of the manufacturing in Lutherton and Gravesend takes place in industrial parks containing long, flat, buildings that give away no sign of what goes on inside. While I had to go searching for the sites of the largest employers in Lutherton and Gravesend, I could see them the moment I arrived in Motorville. Just as churches and German park names do for residents in Lutherton, these physical landmarks routinely call to Motorvillians' minds that they are part of a blue-collar community.

As a result, beyond identifying Motorville as a union town, residents also describe it as a blue-collar town, defined by its hardworking residents. Luke, for example, is a lifelong resident who has recently moved to a neighboring city. He has never belonged to a union, but he offers this summary when I ask him to describe Motorville the first time we meet: "It's a good blue-collar town, you know, especially in comparison to Medford [the neighboring city] . . . we have factories, we have processing, you get all that. So if you think like almost the standard, like Midwest American town, it really does encompass a lot of Motorville." The other Motorvillians I spoke with overwhelmingly agree with Luke's definition. And when they describe Motorville, they similarly refer to the visible signs of the city's industrial and blue-collar employment or list the large union employers that remain.

Motorvillians thus share a pride in their blue-collar, union roots, but they also recognize that times have changed in ways that are not favorable to the local economy: as described in chapter 3, residents regularly recount the difficulty of finding good jobs with good benefits because, as folks like Tonja told me, the city's economy is "depressed" and "there's not a lot of opportunity." Each time residents interpret their own frustrating experiences of less-than-satisfactory employment within a broader narrative of national manufacturing decline and rising income inequality that have battered Motorville, they reaffirm the notion that Motorville is a disadvantaged place. This then further reinforces the framework within which they make sense of their own position in a broader system of social relations. Just as in Lutherton, individual- and community-level identities reinforce one another.

Christopher, a young professional, exemplifies this narrative practice. During our first conversation, he told me his view of the city's economy, weaving his story in as he went along:

> I mean, there's just the overlying theme that there's just a lot of people that live in Motorville and that have just been down and on the out for so long, that it's just rough. The general livelihood of a lot of the people that live here—not all, but a decent chunk—is just really not good, always has been.

Later, he continues, drawing on his own experience:

> I can tell you from trying to find a job in this market, in this area, it's really hard. It's very hard to find jobs. And anyone that will tell you, oh, it's super easy, no it is not. Because just due to the way this area is, your typical college level or non-educated level, entry jobs are usually getting filled by people that have much more experience.

Christopher describes his own challenges in finding a good job—at that time, he was doing a menial data-entry job that was both unfulfilling and offered low pay and expensive health insurance—as linked to a broader problem facing the city. Christopher's understanding of Motorville as a community of have-nots thus provides the context in which he understands himself as among the Americans who are struggling within the current economic system.

And much like in Lutherton, it is easy for newcomers to learn that this is the narrative through which Motorvillians understand their city. Recall how Elaine, a former bar-hopper who no longer drinks, introduced me to her hometown through the bar scene in chapter 1: in those few hours, I learned not only the various kinds of blue-collar employment and shiftwork that structured the rhythms of each bar but also the city's troubling underbelly of addiction that Elaine, like others, sees as a same symptom of the "depressed" economy. And what Motorvillians learn is that they are a community of have-nots, through no fault of their own.

Bringing the Government in to Level the Playing Field

And because Motorvillians understand themselves and their neighbors as among the have-nots, they also imagine themselves as beneficiaries of future government intervention to level the playing field. Moreover, as they shift the locus of their thinking away from local social problems to general concerns they have for themselves or the country, they tend to call on the federal rather than state government for assistance. Danielle, for example, is a county employee from Motorville who offers her take on the country's economic situation when we first meet in fall 2019. She is one of the two Motorvillians who think that the country could provide for its citizens' basic needs "if everybody in their community took care of each other." But when I ask her to think beyond the issue of basic needs and consider what she would change about the country if she had a "magic wand," she concludes:

> It's so divided between people that have money and people that don't have money. And then there's people like me who are in the middle where I'm making money, I'm middle class, if you will. But I cannot get any sort of benefit that the people that are making less money can. So I'm constantly struggling as well. I feel like everybody's struggling, except maybe the very, very top tier. And that is a huge issue in our country as well. Which kind of all of our issues come from that. We could have better health care, we could have better housing, we could have better rehabilitation, we could have better prison systems instead of there even being prisons. It all comes down to that, in my own opinion.

Danielle's comments are indicative of a widespread worldview among the Motorvillians I met. The country is profoundly unequal and "everybody's struggling"—even those in the "middle class" like Danielle, who, without a four-year degree, still has a good county job with benefits. Fixing that inequality would, as she explains, fix "all of our issues." Moreover, because Danielle—like Christopher—locates herself among the struggling, she believes she would benefit from that fix.

Although Danielle and Christopher are both Democrats or Democratic-leaning Independents, the tendency to apply a lens of systemic inequality to the country's challenges and to locate themselves among the "have-nots" occasionally cuts across party lines, as we saw with Colton and Sybil in chapter 3.

But for some Motorvillians I spoke to, this line of reasoning also implies a limit to their statism: the state is a vehicle to right systemic inequality, not for helping those who haven't helped themselves. Elaine exemplifies this stance. Throughout our conversations, she expressed concerns about people taking advantage of welfare; and during the pandemic she worried in particular that the extra $600 a week in unemployment benefits was too much. But in the same breath, she also advocated for more money going to the people who need it, a general increase in unemployment insurance (to at least 80 percent of wages), and a general increase in wages for Motorvillians: "It's ridiculous what they expect people to live on, and even like our cost of living is so high in Motorville and the wages are still very low. It's a very depressed economy I'd say." Elaine has some abstract suspicion that people may be taking advantage of welfare, but this operates alongside her lived experience, which is that people like her family, friends, and neighbors living in Motorville will always struggle to make ends meet in a "depressed economy."

Several Motorvillians I spoke to, like Elaine, hold both of these concerns in hand and are far less likely to support government intervention when they don't see those actions as righting a systemic wrong that would benefit the broad community of "struggling" Americans. In other words, Motorville residents are not some aberrant group of Americans who limitlessly call on the federal government: just as their lived experiences teach them they are a community of have-nots through no fault of their own, those experiences also teach them they are different from the people who are at fault for their own struggles. In a country whose welfare state racializes and demonizes welfare recipients, as we saw in chapter 3, it is somewhat unsurprising that people operating within those institutional arrangements would draw these kinds of boundaries.[22]

That said, this is not true of all Motorvillians—in particular, the younger residents I met tended to express a belief that government support is a *right* rather than an *earned benefit*. Much as we saw in Lutherton, there are several reasons why individuals differ, but there is still evidence of an important role for place: Motorvillians see themselves and their community as have-nots who would benefit from government intervention to level the playing field.

Democrats Are the Party of the Have-Nots

But Motorvillians' belief in government as a vehicle to resolve inequality—to their benefit—does not necessarily indicate Democratic partisanship. For that link to occur, they must further understand Democrats as the party more likely to wield the government to level the playing field. And this is, in fact, the case across all three cities. Residents of Motorville, Lutherton, and Gravesend tend to agree that the Democratic and Republican Parties are fundamentally divided on whether they prefer public or private solutions to social problems, and whether they will lean on the federal rather than local governments. As Carl, a retired teacher and Democrat from Motorville, tells me when I ask him about the biggest differences between the two parties:

> I think certainly with Obama and Clinton, you saw an effort to try to use the resources of government, sometimes the private sector as well, to try to help people try to make people's lives better. I think Republicans are largely interested in letting the private sector do that work. And I think that's the big difference.

Although not everyone I spoke to shares this understanding of the two parties, there were few differences across the three cities in its prevalence. Where Motorville does differ is that residents tend to see the Democrats as the party of big government *for the purpose of helping the disadvantaged in an unequal system*. The Democrats, in sum, are the party of the "have-nots," and the Republicans are the party of the "haves." As Kate, who is a former union member and a current Catholic, tells me: liberals are the ones who "want to even out the playing field" by providing good public education, infrastructure, and access to basic necessities like food. Because this kind of intervention is precisely what Motorvillians want, they see the Democrats as the party for them and their community.

Even when they were not discussing the role of government, Motorvillians regularly indicated that they view party politics as an expression of class differences—not religious ones, as we saw in Lutherton. This belief extends from the same place-based processes that we have seen throughout the book. In Motorville, one of these is the political nature of union membership. Motorville's union members tend to agree that Democrats protect workers. Isaac, a member of the railroad union, thinks of a Democratic voter as "someone that's hopefully more labor, kind of like a labor-orientated person, obviously." This, to Isaac, is obvious. More generally, he explains, the Democratic Party stands for the people "that maybe weren't born on third base." Moreover, many residents who no longer have direct ties to unions have parents, parents-in-law, or siblings who were part of unions and have instilled in them a belief that Democrats represent labor. Isabelle, for example, was only briefly part of a union when she worked as a retail clerk in high school; she is now in her seventies. But when I ask her if she knows which political party her parents preferred, she tells me: "Democrats. Oh, I can say that very quickly, very easily. My father would have never voted for anybody unless they were a Democrat. He was a union man, true and true. And the Democrats protect the unions, so . . ." This kind of long legacy of union politics—extending over time or across multiple family members—is not uncommon in Motorville, where unions have been prominent in the public sphere for over a century.

Isaac and Isabelle's politics imply a direct—or nearly direct—effect of political socialization from within an organization. But the political importance of place is not reducible to the quantity of organizational affiliations: unions' capacity to deliver voters to the Democratic Party has severely declined in the past few decades, and relative to those in Lutherton and Gravesend, Motorville union members are much more likely to share Isaac's worldview.[23] This is not true of everyone in Motorville—I spoke to two former union members who had negative experiences with their unions—but most people I met view unions as both a positive economic force and an effective political one. This belief persists because Motorville's unions are themselves shaped by place: as we have seen throughout part 2, the political nature of Motorvillian labor is not a contemporary accident but a legacy of historical decision making and movement building in the face of external threats.

But what truly distinguishes Motorville's politics from Lutherton's and Gravesend's is the fact that many residents, regardless of their own union ties, agree that Democrats represent the workers and Republicans represent businesses and the rich. This shared understanding emerges through the same processes that we observed in Lutherton. Many residents, like Fred in Lutherton, simply connect their observation of their neighbors to national politics, putting two-and-two together that if Motorville is both a union town and a

Democratic town, then there is a link between unions and the Democratic Party. Republicans, for example, bemoan the fact that the town has been "brain-washed" with "union values," as Bill tells me, while Democrats like Kate proudly state that Motorville is Democratic because it is "a town that respects unions."

The way community leaders framed Scott Walker's anti-union measures as a political attack on union members' economic well-being also cemented the union-Democratic connection among Motorvillians. Renne, whom we heard from in chapter 3, is a case in point. She grew up in a Republican household in Motorville and now works for the county. Prior to Act 10, she was a member of the local AFCSME. When I ask her what the Republican Party stands for, her experience with Scott Walker colors her response: "I grew up in a Republican home," she tells me. "I still hold onto some of those values. But like, through things like Act 10, some of my opinions have changed." Renne, who has always identified as a Republican, is now torn. Much like the case of Marie above, we can see how place exerts its own influence outside of direct parental socialization. Not everyone in Motorville is as fond of their union as Renne, but the widely publicized attacks by a Republican governor and legislature on the unions cemented for many Motorvillians the notion that Democrats are, as Isaac says, more "labor-orientated."

Beyond describing the specific ties between the Democratic Party and organized labor, Motorvillians broadly agree that Republicans represent the "haves" and Democrats the "have-nots." This came up again and again in conversations over the course of a year and a half of interviews. Tonja, for example, is a hesitant Democrat who does not watch the news and thinks of Motorville's economy as "depressed," as we heard earlier. When I ask her what the Democratic Party stands for, she responds:

> I guess more of what I would like, people helping people. Because from what I understand they're more supportive of like the human services. And some people say, "well we're giving them handouts." But it's just more about giving resources to those less fortunate because not everybody is born with the support structure and what they need to thrive.

She further explains that Republicans, in contrast, stand for the idea that "people with opportunities get more opportunities." Tonja is typical of other Motorvillians I spoke to: they believe "those less fortunate" are struggling in an unequal economic system and that they deserve political representation, which they can find within the Democratic Party. This belief is further supported by the fact that Tonja, much like Danielle, sees herself as more closely aligned with "those less fortunate" than with the "people with opportunities."

Motorvillians' idea that Democrats represent people disadvantaged in an unequal system—the "have-nots"—is not just limited to class; among many White Democrats I spoke to, it also extended to race, gender, and sexuality. As such, the relatively common idea that Republicans represent White people and Democrats represent people of color does not push these Motorvillians toward the Republican Party, as it does in Lutherton. Take, for example, how Isaac—the union member whom we heard from above—talks about this racial division as compatible with his general understanding that Democrats are the party of the have-nots. The first time we meet, in fall 2019, I ask him: "To you, what does the National Democratic Party stand for?" And he responds:

> ISAAC: It stands for inclusion. Everybody. Not the 1 percent, but every-body. Old people, students, elderly. White people, Black people, brown people. Everybody. Everybody come in, everybody has a chance. The system's not rigged. You know. And they stand for the middle class, for workers. And you know, everybody.
> ST: And what about the Republican Party?
> ISAAC: The opposite, I think. Old, rich, White people. And, you know. I mean, you look at the tax plan that came out in 2017. The nonpartisan Congressional Budget Office came out and said—83 percent of the benefits went to the richest 1 percent corporations.

Democrats, to Isaac, are inclusive of "everybody"—a broad category of people whom he imagines in opposition to "old, rich, White people" and the 1 percent. White people can fall on both sides of the partisan dividing line, depending on their wealth. This is not to say that there is no racism in Motorville, nor even that racism is less severe in Motorville than in Lutherton or Gravesend. In fact, Jonathan, a Native American man registered with a tribe in the area, grew up in Motorville and describes the city to me, simply, as: "blue collar and bigoted." In other words, this is not an argument about White Motorvillians' racism (or lack thereof) but about their *racial and political identities*.[24] And among the White Motorville Democrats I met, the idea that the Democratic Party represents people of color is consistent with the idea that Democrats represent people dealing with systemic disadvantages, including people like them. In other words, Motorvillians often think of the Democrats as repre-senting a cross-racial working-class coalition.

Perhaps the most striking part of this understanding is that it appears across people with widely different levels of political knowledge and trust in media, which can create barriers to political learning and engagement.[25] Quinn, for example, is someone who trusts very little information from the media. She's passionate about the environment and making sure everyone has their basic needs met—homelessness, for example, is a problem she thinks the American government should just take care of—but she's often not sure how to map these concerns onto the party system. This, in combination with her uncertainty about what the "truth" is after hearing conflicting accounts from media, can make it challenging for her to form a political opinion. But amid mounds of uncertainty about her political opinions, she tells me twice that she sees the Democrats as the party of the have-nots. For example, in March 2020, when I ask what she thinks is the biggest difference between the two parties, she says:

> I tend to lean more toward the Democrats just because—again, I don't know that much, but the Republicans to me are just, it seems, this is a stereotype, but the rich people. That's what it seems to me like usually the Democrats are the middle-class people who are trying to get fairness for everybody and then the Republicans seem like the opposite. But again, maybe I could be wrong.

Even here, Quinn caveats her statement twice, concluding "maybe I could be wrong." But she returns to this point a few months later when we speak just before the presidential election, telling me that the Democrats are "more for the people, for middle-class and lower."

These interpretations circulate widely, not just through union members and local politicians but through everyday social interactions that are ordered by the local organizational context. For example, in summer 2019, I joined the Motorville Democrats to watch the presidential primary debates in a local bar called Johnny-G's, when the owner approached us and offered up a kind of confession, saying: "Growing up, as a citizen, I was always a Democrat! And now, as a small business owner, I feel myself pulling toward the red. You know? And I hate it! I hate it!" His confession indicates how widely understood it is in Motorville that Republicans represent business interests, but it also shows how easy it is for residents to come to this shared political subjectivity through casual conversation—in the same way I learned about Motorville's "depressed" economy from Elaine.

In sum, Motorvillians—often across lines of political knowledge, union membership, and partisanship—see party politics as an organized battle to perpetuate or mitigate inequality, in which Democrats are fighting for the latter—often by calling on the state or supporting unions. And this solidifies place-based Democratic partisanship—Motorvillians understand themselves as a community of have-nots through no fault of their own and believe Democrats will advocate for state-led solutions that will help them.

A Counterfactual

But this interpretation of party politics is fragile: as four Democratic-leaning residents (out of seventeen Democrats I interviewed in Motorville) explained, they still think of Democrats as the party of the have-nots, but they also know several people in Motorville *who are have-nots but are not Democrats.* As Quinn went on to tell me during our final interview before the 2020 election, part of her uncertainty about the party meanings stems from the people she knows. When I ask her what she thinks the Democratic Party stands for, she explains: "I know Republican is more of the higher class, but it doesn't have to be. My grandma and my dad are Republican and they love Trump." This is perplexing to Quinn. Her dad has been laid off during Covid and is still searching for a new job because "in some places, it's hard to get a job," she says. She tells me this story to explain why she thinks the federal government should extend the extra \$600/week unemployment relief—to benefit her father and others like him. In other words, Quinn understands her dad as someone who would benefit from further state intervention; and yet Quinn's dad loves Donald Trump. This makes her question what and whom the Democrats represent. If more union workers, working-class folks, and have-nots in Motorville start voting Republican, and social interactions like the one I had in Johnny-G's become less common, Motorvillians' narratives of community identity will no longer be so taken for granted.

And without this shared understanding that Democrats represent struggling communities, Motorvillians might be more like Fred, from Lutherton, the retired Republican who introduced me to the McDonald's club. The first time I spoke to him and his wife, Janet, he told me he was concerned about growing economic inequality in the United States:

> You've got to look at income equality. We keep hearing that you have the haves and have-nots. And when I was in Cuba, I saw that the haves had it all and the others were struggling. So that gap between the haves and have-nots. You know, I always consider ourselves middle class. So I think that is shrinking.

Fred and Janet were able to build their middle-class lifestyle without college degrees, in part because of a housing market that was much less expensive relative to the cost of living, which Fred also recognizes—in fact, it's a challenge he worries about for his grandkids. But note his reference to Cuba. He traveled there on a mission trip a few years ago, and he still carries one important lesson with him: socialism takes away opportunity from people who want to better themselves and exacerbates inequality. So when I ask him what the Democratic Party stands for, he agrees that the Democrats want to provide more public goods to people, but he does not think these "freebies" will address income inequality: "I just really think that you can't bring people up from where they are to a better standard of living by just giving them things." Fred is the same person who wants his church to do more to help the needy in Lutherton, so he is not opposed to the notion of giving per se; instead, he's opposed to giving when it's done by the federal government which, as he tells me during the pandemic, "can screw up a glass of water." On the other hand, Republicans *do* want to help the poor, by cutting taxes to spur on growth. This rationale leads a handful of Lutherton residents to conclude that "the Republicans are for the working people," as Art tells me. Art himself is a business owner, but because he sees workers' and business's interests aligned in politics, this does not deter him from identifying as a Republican.

In sum, the idea that economic inequality is a problem for the country, while foundational to Motorvillians' Democratic partisanship, is insufficient to secure it; they must also see the Democrats as the party to rectify that inequality, to their benefit. And for many Lutherton residents, Fred included, place factors are unlikely to create such a tendency toward Democratic partisanship, for several reasons. Residents of Lutherton rarely imagine themselves or their community as the people implicated in a systemic economic crisis—recall how the low unemployment economy is such a source of pride. And even if they worry about economic inequality and how it will affect their family, they do not see the political sphere as the place to resolve that inequality. In a Christian community that takes care of themselves, politics is about upholding Christian morality and protecting local control—not shaping economic outcomes.

This is not to say that Motorvillians' interpretation of party politics is unavailable to residents of Lutherton. Consider, for example, this exchange I had with Linda—quoted above—and her husband, Peter, who sat next to us at her kitchen table during our first conversation, as their children ran in and out. I ask, "And so how do you describe the average Republican voter?" She replies:

LINDA: That is interesting. I would assume that they're White. I don't know why. And I would assume that they are older than they are

younger. I would assume that more younger voters are not
Republicans, but I'm just like making it up. I don't actually know.
I have like no basis for this.

PETER: I would agree.

ST: And the average Democratic voter?

PETER: The opposite.

LINDA: The opposite. Probably younger, probably wealthier. Like I feel
like Republicans generally are going to be more like, your blue
collar, like salt of the earth, you know, that kind of a thing. Whereas
Democrats, I would see more like white collar.

PETER: [*whispers*] It's actually opposite.

LINDA: It's my answer, I need to say what I think.

ST: I actually just want to know if she thinks—

LINDA: I'm just guessing. I don't know.

ST: I think your best guess [*pausing, laughing at Peter's gesturing*]. . . .
That's funny [*to his reaction*].

LINDA: I mean, that's mostly my experience, right? My experience is
mostly blue collar, White, middle class, you know, and most of the
people that I've known have be1234en Republicans.

Linda and Peter agree that Republicans tend to be White. But then Peter intervenes to tell Linda that Democrats are not the wealthier, white-collar folks
but rather the blue-collar workers. She stands firm, explaining: "that's mostly
my experience, right?" This was a not-infrequent line of reasoning among the
Lutherton residents I spoke to: many people were aware that others associate
Democrats with the have-nots and Republicans with the haves, but this association was counterintuitive to them. In their blue-collar community—or
similar blue-collar communities in which they grew up—everyone is Republican. Note also that Linda, like Quinn, keeps returning to phrases like "I'm
just guessing" and "I have no basis for this." But she does have a basis—her
experience growing up in a city she describes as much like Lutherton, then
spending the last ten years in Lutherton with her family.

Similarly, Motorvillians are not unaware of the Lutherton belief that party
politics is about Christianity, nor is Motorville a place where issues like abortion are irrelevant to residents' politics. Several residents in Motorville mentioned
abortion or Christianity as central to contemporary political divisions. In fact,
each time I arrived in town over the course of two years, I was greeted by a
large billboard portraying an image of a fetus at various stages of gestation,

designed to discourage abortion. But Motorville lacks the local processes that reinforce these associations for residents in Lutherton: churchgoing does not go hand in hand with Republicanism in a place where, for example, two Catholic Democrats I interviewed consider themselves pro-life *personally* but pro-choice *politically*, and two Republicans who were raised Christian but do not currently attend church consider themselves pro-choice. And where social interaction in Motorville reaffirms that politics expresses a class divide, it helps submerge the idea that politics expresses a religious divide. For example, Motorville has a crisis pregnancy center where volunteers work to persuade women against having an abortion, and they entered a float in the town's Fourth of July parade in 2019. As the float passed by me, a young Asian American man to my right commented on the irony of their float preceding the Democrats'. When the older White woman seated next to him did not react, he scoffed: "because the Democrats are for abortion." Rather than rise to the comment, she merely retorted: "So? So am I." The conversation ended there.

———

Chapters 3 and 4 have described how residents' understandings of what their problems are, who they are as a community, and which political party best represents them are supported within their distinct cities, which we saw emerge in chapters 1 and 2. I have also suggested that we can think about this process as a set of self-reinforcing relationships among the three dimensions of place (see figure 1): the structural and organizational dimensions of a place support its cultural dimensions—diagnostic frames and narratives of community identity—which over time take on a life of their own and help sustain both local organizations and partisan ties. It is clear, from examples like Fred, Art, and Linda, that each of these place factors can help make residents into partisans; but it is also clear that place is not the only (or even the most important) explanation for partisan identity. As we saw with Kyle in Lutherton, individuals have various reasons to identify with a different party from the one their friends, family, and neighbors prefer.

In sum, the comparison between Motorville and Lutherton shows how the meaning of an individual's social and political identities is co-produced by local and national factors: within the constraints of individuals' social group membership and national parties' maneuvering, place makes it more likely that residents will adopt certain social identities and interpretations of party politics. Motorville thus produces a working-class, Democratic community out of much the same demographic material that Lutherton creates a Christian, Republican one. Moreover, the place-based tendency toward Democratic partisanship in Motorville is so strong that it persists even amid many countervailing forces pulling residents in the opposite direction.

But what does this tell us about partisanship more broadly? Scholars have offered increasingly detailed accounts of the macro- and micro-level processes that lead certain kinds of people to identify with one party or the other. Motorville and Lutherton show us how place intervenes in this process, helping each resident understand who they are and which party best represents "people like me."[26] This means that place may have particularly important consequences among individuals whose political loyalties are contested by both parties. In such cases, there will always be multiple pathways for how those individuals situate themselves within party politics. Place makes it more likely that people will follow a particular path.

In developing this account of the factors that explain place-based partisanship, I've set aside what partisanship itself explains. This may seem like a glaring omission, as partisanship has become "one of the most important explanatory variables" in American political behavior research (Huddy, Mason, and Aarøe 2015, 1), a fact that poses challenges for researchers trying to understand what explains partisanship.[27] This means that partisanship itself might explain why Motorville and Lutherton residents have different beliefs about the appropriate role of the federal government in their lives—simply because people in Motorville tend to be Democrats and people in Lutherton tend to be Republicans. Nothing that I have argued in the previous chapters is an attempt to negate the idea that party attachments, once formed, create an important lens through which voters see the world. As such, in the feedback loop of structure, organization, and culture that sustains place-based partisanship, we can also add partisanship itself, which may reinforce certain political beliefs and even help sustain local organizational contexts.[28]

In short, I am not arguing that partisanship has no explanatory importance in these cities, but I am arguing that place *also* has an explanatory role in sustaining residents' political beliefs and partisan attachments and that it is particularly important for understanding political identity formation among cross-pressured groups. I have further shown *how* place accomplishes this, through local organizational contexts that support particular diagnostic frames and narratives of community identity. As the next chapter will show, it is when the relationship between these dimensions of place breaks down that place-based partisanship may shift.

5

Politics in a Dying Place

ORGANIZATIONAL INSTABILITY AND
POSTINDUSTRIAL POPULISM IN GRAVESEND

IN FEBRUARY 2020, I arrive at a community development meeting in Gravesend just as the head of the Economic Development Association, John, is fin-
ishing his presentation. The meeting is being held in a conference room at the
local country club, where eight large, round tables are full of residents watching intently as John clicks through his slides. As with most public events I've
been to in Gravesend, the majority of the crowd looks to be retirement age or
older. John is presenting the community's strategic economic plan, and when
I arrive he's focused on childcare, housing, and transportation as barriers to
maintaining and growing Gravesend's workforce.

But when John cedes the floor, the audience questions focus on more immediate ways to attract both people and jobs to Gravesend: bringing in new
retailers, drawing in higher-income people from nearby cities who could work
remotely from Gravesend, and developing tax incentives for real estate and
business development. As he deals with each question, John returns again
and again to the city's plans to compete with other similar places—through its
amenities, an attractive Main Street, high-speed internet connections, shovel-
ready land for development—to win both businesses and people. As he concludes in response to a question about crime: "We're doing all these different
things that make us a more viable place for people to live, essentially—live,
maybe not work."

But the crowd is not quite buying what John is selling. Several questioners
shake their heads as he speaks, others murmur disagreement under their
breaths, and occasionally John recognizes their discontentedness, noting that
"it's okay" to disagree with him. Even so, a woman at the table in front of me

seems to capture the audience's sentiment best when she says: "When I first came here and saw the empty buildings a few years ago and they said, 'oh, we have plans for that. We have plans for that. We have plans for that.' That was three years ago, I'd say. And *nothing is ever done*" (emphasis added).

––––––––

The Gravesend residents who attended the economic development meeting were angry not just because their city was facing an uphill battle for economic revitalization but because, as the woman seated in front of me noted, it seemed that no one was doing anything to prevent the city's demise. This was a common refrain I heard from Gravesend residents: where was their leadership? Even the solutions John offered had an air of incoherency to them, as though the city's economic development leaders were throwing everything at the wall to see what might stick. They even imagined, as John suggested, a jobless future—one in which Gravesend becomes a place that people "live, maybe not work." A city of retirees and remote workers. It is difficult to imagine that community leaders in Motorville, with their focus on good-quality jobs, or community leaders in Lutherton, with their focus on expanding the quantity of jobs, would articulate such a vision for their future.

But leaders in Motorville and Lutherton differ from those in Gravesend in two key ways. First, they are operating under different structural conditions, in that neither Motorville nor Lutherton is facing the level of economic and demographic threat that imperils Gravesend. Second, they are operating within different organizational contexts. The decline of the organizations that used to structure daily life in Gravesend—including Rivervalley, its unions, and local churches—means that Gravesend's leaders are *not* embedded within long-standing organizational contexts that provide them with shared diagnostic frames for addressing postindustrial social problems.

Although this poses challenges for Gravesend, it also means that this city is indicative of an important trend among postindustrial, Heartland cities. As chapter 2 described, the combination of Reagan-era restructuring of federal policy and deindustrialization meant a dual drain of both public and private resources from the Heartland at the end of the twentieth century. And in largely White places like Motorville, Lutherton, and Gravesend, people also stopped joining the many civic organizations whose federated structures had connected their members within and across cities.[1] Across the country, union membership and church attendance declined precipitously—though beginning at different points—between the postwar era and the end of the millennium.[2] This means that Motorville and Lutherton are, in many ways, anachronisms relative to other postindustrial, Heartland cities.

This narrative of decline—described as a trauma that "left behind" postindustrial and rural America—and Americans' interpretation of it has been recounted again and again in recent years.[3] Katherine Cramer (2016) has offered perhaps the best-known of these accounts: as she argues, rural resentment has fueled the rise of Republican Party support in Wisconsin because rural residents view the Democrats' government largesse as a means of propping up urban centers at the expense of outstate communities. Others, like Arlie Hochschild (2016), have argued that this kind of populist anti-statism is the result not of rural resentment but of racial resentment, as Whites in postindustrial places come to view the government as a vehicle for supporting racialized minorities at their expense. But both accounts agree that the decline of White, postindustrial cities has fomented anger at the government as part of the problem, not part of the solution.

And yet, as we have already seen, this explanation of contemporary Heartland politics does not fit either Motorville or Lutherton: Motorville residents tend to look toward the state to help them and their community, while in Lutherton, residents feel their economy is booming and churches are solving any problems that do emerge. But many residents in Gravesend *do* conform to prevailing accounts of White, postindustrial populism. Why is this the case? When we consider Gravesend in comparison with Motorville and Lutherton, it becomes clear that the city's emergent right-wing populism is not a *necessary* consequence of the city's population and economic decline or of White racial threat in an increasingly multiracial society.[4] Just as in Motorville and Lutherton, Gravesend's politics are the product of an interaction between local and national factors, as residents make sense of political and economic transformations from within their local context. And in Gravesend, residents lack the organizational stability that in Motorville and Lutherton provides a coherent diagnostic frame for understanding their social problems. As the community has suffered loss after loss, Gravesenders disagree about the best path forward, as we saw during the community development meeting.

But there is one thing that Gravesenders can agree on: the city's survival is under threat. Each time a new challenge appears and goes unresolved, they integrate it into their existing narrative of decline. As a result, emergent social problems are not just stand-alone issues but further evidence that Gravesend's survival is threatened and there is little anyone is doing about it. Gravesend residents thus represent the White Americans most susceptible to feeling threatened by racialized others: they are people who have observed objective declines in their community's material well-being over several decades; who subjectively feel their own social status and that of their community have declined; and who worry about falling to the very bottom rungs of the social hierarchy.[5] When politicians like Donald Trump embrace a populist rhetoric that implicates socialism and immigration as threats to the "great" (White) American way of life, that rhetoric appeals to Gravesenders. Gravesend is a *threatened community*, par excellence.

Changing this dynamic, finding ways to turn Gravesenders toward the state or toward multiracial working-class identification, is not simply a matter of injecting more organizations into the city—as we have seen in Lutherton, greater church embeddedness in civic life can turn residents inward, rather than outward.[6] In other words, Gravesend and cities like it are missing more than just social capital; they are missing an organizational context that provides them with a model for how to solve problems and whom to blame when those problems mount.

This chapter thus provides the final pieces of evidence for two of the book's three main arguments. First, that the historic and ongoing reddening of the American Heartland is rooted not just in national economic and political transformations but in how cities responded to them at different junctures, carving out distinctive place-based politics from within regional similarities. And second, that place is still shaping partisan attachments today, insulating people in both Motorville and Lutherton against populist resentments but fomenting them in Gravesend. To highlight this second argument, the chapter ends by returning to the exceptional case of Motorville—one case of just 4 percent of White, working-class, New Deal counties that have remained Democratic—to consider what changes might finally turn Motorvillians to the right.

Taken together, both arguments can help us understand Donald Trump's success in places like Gravesend, which had previously resisted the Republican Party's pull (per figure 3): it was the product of decades of decline in postindustrial cities that *both* chipped away at the local labor movement, an organizational link to the Democratic Party that helps promote cross-racial working-class politics, *and* left residents feeling threatened by other forces.[7] Although Donald Trump may not have been responsible for a sea change in the voting behavior of working- and middle-class Whites, his rhetoric did attract sufficient people living in threatened cities like Gravesend to win him the key Heartland states that paved his pathway to the White House in 2016.

The Demise of Gravesend

Almost everyone I spoke to in Gravesend locates the story of their terminal decline with Rivervalley. Although many point to the fire as the city's death knell, others look further back, to the 1979 bankruptcy declaration that lowered wages by more than 25 percent in one fell swoop. At the same time as wages were slashed in town, farms were struggling in the countryside. Scott, who lives in a small town on the outskirts of Gravesend City, describes how farm agglomeration has sucked the resources out of the rural communities and small towns that surround cities like Motorville, Lutherton, and Gravesend:

> There [were] so many farmers when I was a kid, there used to be three to four farmers in every section. You know what I mean, everybody had cows. . . . And the farming has gotten so big that there [are] no more farms. . . . And all these farmers went to Gravesend township to do business. Went to the creamery with their milk, went up to the elevator and bought feed, go to the shoe store. . . . And now there's no small farmers around anymore. There's probably . . . probably 90 percent less farmers now than there was when I was a kid.

Scott himself tried to sustain a small farm when he was younger but ultimately gave it up—it was not enough for him and his family to live on and yet too much work to maintain alongside his full-time job. Now he and his wife, Lisa, live in a house surrounded by corn and soybean fields, none of which they own. Most of the homes dotted throughout the countryside surrounding Gravesend are like Scott and Lisa's: "acreages" carved out from the harvestable land and sold as family homes while the fields around them were bundled into larger and larger farms.[8]

The result is that the generation that came of age with Scott—now in his sixties—and the one below him could no longer sustain themselves by farming, just as it became more and more difficult to find good-paying jobs in Gravesend. Ray's working years were splintered by these shifting dynamics. He grew up on a 160-acre farm outside Gravesend and hoped to have his own farm as an adult. Like Scott, he found small farming was not economically feasible by the time he was old enough to try it. Instead, he moved to town to work at Rivervalley, where he benefited from just a few years of the foundry workers' high wages before they were slashed in 1979.

Although the decline of Rivervalley and the demise of family farms were long, drawn-out processes, for most people I met it is the fire that marks

Gravesend's turn toward irrevocable decay. Most residents mention it the first time I meet them—it is a defining feature of the town, a piece of history that these Gravesenders view as essential learning for newcomers if they are to understand their community. Marge, the former United Way director, thinks of it as a community trauma that has still not healed.

As any number of residents would say, that's in part because the site where the plant once stood still sits vacant—a testament to Gravesend's struggles with revitalizing its economy. Michelle, for example, describes how her hometown has changed since she was "little":

> Well, our big companies closed. . . . There was a fire—you probably heard about that already—several years ago. And they just never reopened. . . . And I think that was a real blow to the community . . . you still drive through town and you see the big open space where that factory used to be, and the parking lots. . . . Nobody's doing anything with it. Yeah. So. It's sad to a lot of people who lived in Gravesend for a long time to see that big open space.

Note that Michelle assumes I've "already heard about" the Rivervalley fire: the loss is that central to understanding contemporary life in Gravesend.

Michelle also draws my attention to the "big open space" left in Rivervalley's wake, a concern raised by other Gravesenders, as we saw at the economic development meeting. Other residents recalled seeing workers walking up Oak Street with their lunch pails, headed toward the plant for their shifts. A row of small, square homes was built without garages near the plant, explicitly designed for employees who could make the short walk on foot. Like the empty lot where the plant once stood, the homes stand as a physical monument to both the city's past economic vitality and the fact that, as Michelle notes: "Nobody's doing anything with it." As residents tell me again and again, Gravesend has suffered not just from economic decline but from a lack of leadership: "the powers that be," according to Melissa, don't seem engaged in helping Gravesend survive, let alone thrive.

And while many organizations could provide that kind of stable leadership in Gravesend, several residents indicate that—much like Motorville and Lutherton today—it used to come from a combination of Rivervalley, unions, and churches. Kim, for example, is a retiree whose family has deep roots in Gravesend and the surrounding area. Below, she weaves in the story of church decline with the story of small-town decline:

> Well, of course, the demise of the small town. . . . Gravesend, it's a sad town. They lost the foundry. And the land Rivervalley sits on, they haven't done

a goddamn thing. . . . There's just no leadership. And that is very distressing
to all of us. . . . And the churches are just about empty.

Most people, like Kim, focus on Rivervalley as the symbol of Gravesend's decline because, as her comments indicate, the city lost more than jobs: it lost
good jobs over the years when "the union was busted and wages dropped," as
Derek explains; it lost sufficient population to sustain local churches, as Kim
tells me; and it lost the kind of leadership that could help residents make sense
of how to address their problems.

This outcome provides a useful counterfactual to Motorville and Lutherton: as we saw in chapter 1, several decades ago Gravesend shared many of the
structural, organizational, and cultural dimensions that today provide stability
and offer a layer of protection against postindustrial populism in Motorville
and Lutherton. But that is no longer the case.

In this context of great loss, and devoid of stable leadership, each time a business
closes or jobs leave town, Gravesenders incorporate these incidents into their
narrative of decline—it becomes yet another loss rather than an isolated oc-
currence. On my third visit to Gravesend I watched as residents invoked this
storytelling practice to talk about FreshFoods, one of the city's two supermarkets, which was closing for a few months in order to reopen in a smaller space.
Despite these plans, people feared it would not actually reopen. For weeks, residents told me their concerns about FreshFoods, even though I never brought it
up myself. During fellowship after Sunday services at a country church, congregants
worried about where they'd get their doughnuts and rolls once FreshFoods went
out of business. At a local coffee shop, a group of retired friends pondered its fate.
In interviews it was one of the only things people could think of as a "change"
since I was last in town. For example, when I asked Ken what had been going on
since I saw him last, he told me: "Oh, just more things closing. You know . . ."

But for Gravesend residents, the closure of a grocery story is not just a
single incident—it reminds them of all the loss they've experienced in the last
two decades, Rivervalley chief among them. Since that time, even much
smaller losses like this one bring people back to the fear that's been eating at
the edges of the city: that this place is dying. Even in casual encounters with
folks around town, people regularly told me that Gravesend is a dying place.
At the YMCA pool one morning, an older man asked what brought me to
Gravesend, and when I told him I was doing a research project on the city, he
responded: "Are you studying what it's like in a dying town?"

Gravesenders, in sum, are converging on a narrative of community identity
that describes their city as a place that is dying without any clear sense of how

to prevent this from happening. This narrative is rooted in real declines: not only did the Rivervalley fire destroy the city's largest employer, but the county-wide population fell by 16 percent between 1980 and 2019 and those who remained aged significantly—the portion of the population that was retirement age grew by almost seven percentage points. But because the narrative of Gravesend's death is so widespread, it also means that residents are more likely to latch onto incidents like the FreshFoods closure as confirmation of what they already know about their community; it is also easier for them to ignore the positives, like their relative immunity from the worst of the opioid epidemic (see figure 6). Just as in Motorville and Lutherton, the stories Gravesenders tell about their community are partly rooted in objective facts and partly rooted in their subjective interpretation of them.

Problem-Solving in a Dying Place

This is also true of how residents view their leadership: Gravesend does not *actually* lack leadership. In fact, their nonprofits and businesses have exceled at revitalizing the city's Main Street and developing local amenities, often by working in partnerships to win public grants. But every time they do so it is a novel configuration of organizations—rather than an institutionalized problem-solving arrangement that is highly visible to residents and conveys a shared vision for the city's future.

But in 2019, in the face of yet another loss, Gravesenders scored a meaningful victory that did begin to shift residents' thinking. Two years earlier, the town's primary care clinic—owned by a statewide group, MinnReg—announced that it would be consolidating its Gravesend-based health-care services with those of another clinic in a town thirty miles away. MinnReg explained that it was no longer financially feasible to keep the clinic open in a city as small as Gravesend. The clinic was home to primary care physicians and low-cost mental health treatment, and Gravesenders were overwhelmingly concerned about having to travel so far for essential services that have always existed within their city. As Jennifer, a young attorney who practices in town, explained her concerns: "I mean, if my child struggles with mental health at some point, I'm driving hours to find them help. Which is crazy to me."

The clinic's departure also hit a nerve because it was *yet another loss* for Gravesend, which some residents directly linked to the other factors that threaten Gravesend's survival. Mary, for example, sums up the city's challenges this way: "In the last five years, we've lost two of our major employers. The clinic and the foundry." Although she has inadvertently shortened the timeline between the two incidents, which were closer to twenty years apart, they are clearly linked for her. As most Gravesenders I spoke to would agree, the external resources that used to infuse city life with good jobs and necessary services have been slowly withdrawing for decades. Now any new loss feels like it carries the potential to pull the rug out from under the city.

It is thus unsurprising that the loss of the clinic triggered a groundswell of anger among residents. But it also triggered a groundswell of activism. As soon as the clinic consolidation was announced, a handful of people—business owners, school board members, and other concerned citizens—called a meeting in the high school cafeteria. The meeting gave rise to Protect Gravesend's Clinic (PGC), an informal organization built to fight the clinic's decision. The first time I drove into Gravesend I was immediately struck by the blue signs proclaiming PGC's logo, which were stuck into lawns and pressed against windows all throughout town.

In PGC's fight, ordinary Gravesend residents were a crucial resource. Every week for two years after the conglomerate's announcement, Natalie, the head of community engagement for PGC, led a group of five to ten residents in a Wednesday afternoon "turnout." Standing in a park on the edge of one of the busiest roads in town, they wave Protect Gravesend's Clinic signs above their heads. Natalie tells me they haven't missed a Wednesday in two years, even during the frigid Minnesota winter. On the sunny summer days when I joined the turnouts, the regulars included some people accustomed to activism—as Natalie says, this is "the least controversial" thing she does—and others for whom this is a first-time affair. Daniel, a retiree who uses a cane to support himself and prefers to bring his own homemade signs, had never participated in anything like this before. But, he explained, he relies on the low-cost preventive services that MinnReg used to provide to keep on top of his health. And as we stood waving at the passing traffic, it was clear how much support PGC had: almost every driver that passed honked or waved, and as Daniel said, for every thumbs down, there were a hundred signs of support.

Then, just as I was preparing to leave Gravesend in fall 2019, PGC announced their first victory: a new clinic, MedStar, was coming to town. PGC itself was buying an old retail building and renting it to MedStar—an assurance that Gravesend would never again lose their clinic as the building would be "community-owned," not owned by the city government or the clinic. By the time I returned a few months later, fundraising for the new building was well under way and residents had added green placards reading "I bought a square of the new PGC clinic!" to their windows alongside the older PGC signs. PGC also recruited local businesses, the Chamber of Commerce, and other well-known residents to their cause, hoping to ensure the new provider's success.

In this instance, the city was able to forestall further decline, and many residents rejoiced. Tina, for example, is a retired Gravesend resident who has lived in the county for her entire adult life. She could barely contain her enthusiasm when she reflected on PGC's accomplishments during a conversation in February 2020: "So I think Gravesend has already been setting [an example], you know, giving people hope and so on. But [if people in other cities want to accomplish something similar] they've got to have a community like Gravesend to do it. I think you've got the idea—I'm proud of my community, the people in it."

As Tina's comments indicate, PGC's success has shown Gravesenders that they are not just subject to the whims of global and national forces but that they can fight back. By scraping together the resources within their city they were able to claim a victory. But in contrast to Lutherton residents who have many experiences of local problem-solving within their nongovernmental network, this is a relatively new experience for Gravesenders. Even so, residents are beginning to draw lessons from this experience as to how they might resolve future challenges. For example, when I ask Melissa who she thinks could best help the community respond to a new challenge, she tells me: "I think the community themselves. I go back to PGC that, OK, we've got a problem here. We're losing our clinic. What do we need to do? So it was the community. It was this grassroots thing that came together and said, OK, what are we going to do?" As she explains, she gets annoyed when people inaccurately attribute PGC's success to the "city of Gravesend" when, in reality: "It didn't have anything to do with our governing people in Gravesend. PGC just came together and says we need to fix this. And that's been awesome." Melissa's assessment of what happened is correct: throughout the process, PGC sidelined local government. While partnerships flourished among civic leaders, political activists, and ordinary citizens who showed up each week to protest, local government involvement was limited.

Melissa's pride in the community's response is shared by several other Gravesend residents. These responses stand in contrast to how residents feel about the Rivervalley lot, which indexes only the city's lack of leadership. Although Gravesend's leaders have long been involved in creative problem-solving, these actions are not *visible* to residents—no one I spoke to, for example, had any sense of what John was doing as the new head of economic development. In contrast, almost everyone I spoke to was aware of PGC and proud of its success. We can imagine how further visible successes could, over time, lead residents to learn that the community can address its own challenges, ultimately moving them to embrace a kind of Lutherton-like antistatism. But for this to happen, PGC or other organizations must coalesce into a stable arrangement that routinely and visibly works toward resolving Gravesend's problems.

Republicans Are the Party of the Threatened

But this possible future cannot explain why, in Gravesend and cities like it, White voters have moved decisively toward the Republican Party, helping secure Donald Trump's victory in 2016. Ever since then, social scientists and pundits have been trying to figure out how Trump's candidacy swept these voters into the Republican column. The answers thus far have been twofold. First, as political scientists Nicholas Carnes and Noam Lupu (2021) argue, the fact that Trump won the majority of White, working-class voters is not indicative of his "unique" appeal relative to other Republican candidates. Rather, this constituency has been moving away from the Democratic Party for decades. Even so, we have to ask what brought them *into* the Republican coalition under Trump rather than out of politics entirely.[9] And here, the consensus seems to be that Trump was able to pull White, working- and middle-class voters to the right because of a discourse that valorized native-born Americans as hard workers who have been victimized by immigration and globalization.[10]

We can see why this discourse would be a powerful attraction to Gravesend residents, not only because of their race and class but because they live in a "dying" town without a stable organizational context. This creates, on the one hand, disagreement about how to solve the city's problems—as we saw at the development meeting—but it also produces a small but meaningful contingent of residents whose sense of threat becomes central to their politics. And as Republican Party elites during the Trump era have embraced a rhetoric of immigration and socialism as twin threats to White, Heartland cities, this rhetorical shift resonates with this group of Gravesenders—more so than in Motorville or Lutherton—because they live in a dying town.[11]

Moreover, a particular version of this Trumpian discourse is embraced by Gravesend's local politicians, who routinely emphasize a defense of the "small-town, American way of life" and appeal to anti-immigrant feelings among White, native-born residents. During the 2020 election, Democrats and Republicans representing Gravesend flooded Facebook with populist posts echoing these sentiments. Six of the top fifteen most popular topics among Gravesend's politicians were about urban versus rural divisions, gubernatorial overreach affecting rural communities, agriculture, "defending our values," or simply launching populist appeals framed as "us" versus the establishment of politicians in Washington, D.C.[12] A typical post embodying these concerns from the Republican candidate for the U.S. House of Representatives might read:

> If you're wondering why our opponent loves Pelosi and Kamala so much, I can spell it out for you: They support Medicare for All, including free healthcare for illegal aliens. They also support open borders. They support the Green New Deal, which includes a carbon tax that will destroy agriculture. And they support liberal judges who will fund late-term abortions and confiscate guns. And our opponent is a Democrat like them, who also supports making America into a socialist state. But here in Minnesota, we don't want America to be a socialist state. So vote for Republicans up and down the ballot if you want to protect our values and our way of life.

Although many of these inflammatory statements would only appeal to Republicans, one portion of the post would resonate with many Gravesenders I spoke to, regardless of their partisanship: the idea that "our way of life" is under threat. Democratic politicians also post regularly about how their opposition's policies will threaten small-town ways of life, suggesting that Gravesend's elected representatives from all parties recognize that this appeal will resonate with their voters. Much as in Cramer's (2016) study of Wisconsin, rural identity—and in this case, the specific identity of living in a dying place—plays a powerful role in shaping Gravesenders' politics, one that local politicians recognize and attempt to cultivate for their own electoral ends.

But as we have already seen in Motorville, such an identity does not necessarily indicate anti-statist populism or Republican partisanship; in fact, in Motorville, concerns about local decline turn residents toward the state and the Democratic Party. The Republican candidate's Facebook post points to what is different between the two cities: for some Gravesend residents, it seems that state expansion will likely help some racialized other, at their expense. So when Republican politicians link these otherwise unrelated issues—socialism and immigration—as dual threats, this makes a compelling case to certain Gravesenders.

Scott is emblematic of this. We've already heard from Scott: he is a lifelong Democrat who worries about the long-term decline of his community and now considers himself a Republican. Almost all of Scott's politics, both past and present, have emerged as the result of local conversation and experiences; he watches the news occasionally but does not have cable. Scott had a particularly formative political experience when he was young and belonged to a union, working for a boss who he felt mistreated him. That solidified for him that Democrats represented workers, and Republicans represented people like his former boss. But now, the more he talks to people in Gravesend—two particular friends, both Republicans—he is increasingly convinced that the Democrats and Republicans are no longer divided around class issues but around issues of immigration and socialism.

As we sit in his living room the first time we meet, Scott indulges in a lengthy reflection on his experiences growing up in Gravesend, what has changed for the worse in the country, and what he learned from his time in the union. In the midst of this, he tells me:

> I try to be a reasonable person. And I think a lot about this stuff. And like I said, I used to be a pretty strong Democrat. That's just 'cause my family always was. And now . . . and I'm getting older. I think we all get more conservative when we're older. But the Democratic Party has definitely changed. Used to be Democrat-Farmer-Labor. And, you know, the Republicans was more business. You know what I'm getting it. Just like me with my old boss. He was a strong Republican. And I was a Democrat. You know what I mean? And he didn't give a shit about his employees. You know, and that used to be, you know, labor and farmers and management, you know? And now it's gotten more where the Democratic Party has gotten for more of a giveaway thing. You know, by letting all these illegals in and all this kind of stuff. And I have got absolutely no problem with immigrants, people coming in. I have absolutely no problem whatsoever. But, all you got to do in my book is come in legally. Speak our language. Pay taxes like the rest of us do. Don't come in and think that you're gonna get a big handout. And that's what I think the Democratic Party is focused more toward. And that's why I think, I don't know which is left or right. But I think the Democratic Party is getting too far this way. And then I think the people, all of us in the middle are maybe gonna start voting back more conservative.

Later, the conversation turns to other topics, but Scott keeps bringing things back to this formative story. For example, when I ask him, "How would you describe the politics of the people who live around here?" he responds by saying:

> The Democratic Party has changed so much that I think Gravesend is lean-ing more to the conservative side. People in this area are not for—um, we want to help people. There's no doubt in my mind. But we can't expect everybody to flock in and not do nothing and not speak the language and pay their way. I mean, around here, I think, I know we would have, the area would have no problem with some immigrants, you know, these people from these other countries coming in. If they come in and spoke our lan-guage and wanted to work here and be part of the community. But when they come in and want us to change, they maybe should've stayed in their own country. . . . Don't expect all of us to change because you've got a dif-ferent religion. You can have your whatever religion you want, but don't go telling us in school we can't say the Pledge of Allegiance, or sing "Star-Spangled Banner," or you can't pray in school.

Trying to understand what he means when he uses the word "conservative," I ask: "And so when you say you feel people are pretty conservative around here—you talked about the issue of immigration maybe as part of that. Are there other things you think of when you say 'conservative'?" Scott again turns to a local example, of how "people don't want to pay any more taxes than they have to" but they want the city to maintain basic services. Conservatism for Scott is about not just small government but a government that is not frivo-lously throwing money around, especially not at immigrants.

For Scott, this understanding is new: he used to agree with Motorvillians that Democrats were the party of the have-nots. What has replaced this un-derstanding is one that resonates with him because of his specific fears about the future of his community: that Democrats are now the party of handouts, not just for anyone but for immigrants who threaten the American way of life, the way Scott and his community have been doing things "for generations." When Republicans, like Gravesend's congressional representative and Donald Trump, present their party as the party to protect small, White towns from these threats, that resonates with voters like Scott.

Scott's turn to the Republican Party is thus driven by two interrelated factors: a belief that immigration and socialism are an intertwined threat to his near-extinct community, which produces an anti-statism that is tinged with racialized fears; and an understanding that these issues—rather than social class—are now at the center of partisan conflict.

———

Immigration and socialism as twin threats. Lutherton's communitarian anti-statism provides a useful contrast to help us understand what is distinct about Scott's racialized anti-statism. For Lutherton residents, as we've seen, the federal government is not so much threatening as superfluous, because they are a community that takes care of itself. And in Lutherton, native-born Whites are hardly concerned about immigration as a threat to their way of life: economically, residents recognize that immigrants are essential to their success; and symbolically, they still feel they are living in a German Lutheran community. In fact, as noted in chapter 4, Lutherton residents I spoke to tended to converge on the idea that the best immigration policy would include both a border wall and a path to citizenship for undocumented immigrants who had not committed any crimes. We can see how this idea emerges from an amalgamation of two contradictory images that native-born Luthertonians hold about immigration as a political issue: the first, which comes from the media, of "illegal immigration" as a border problem to be resolved by building a wall that will keep future immigrants out; and the second, which comes from their lived experience of Mexican and Central American immigrants within Lutherton, which teaches native-born residents that immigrants are hard workers who should not be deported (and, further, that their deportation would destabilize Lutherton's economy). For example, in a conversation I had with Fred during the early days of the pandemic, I asked him how he felt about the growth of immigration in Lutherton in recent years, and his response toggled back and forth between these two images. He began by saying that "illegal" immigrants have a cultural problem of machismo that permits abuse against women. But then he reverted to thinking about Lutherton itself:

> The people that I know that are here, are family people and are continually sending money home . . . we [native-born Whites in Lutherton] don't have any real issues with 'em . . . they're good people. They're hard workers. They show up every day and I think are generally pretty well accepted here in the community. But illegal immigration is still an issue that conservative people here in Lutherton County are concerned with.

Trying to understand this conflation of Hispanic ethnicity and immigration status, I then asked: "Do you think the Hispanic population in Lutherton, do you think that they're all there legally?" He considered this and concluded that "a significant population of those individuals are not legal." He then went on to say that he gets annoyed by other White residents who think of Hispanic immigrants as criminals. As he said, "when I read the paper, I count the police activity. And you know what? There are more male Caucasians that are arrested for either domestic violence or being drunk than there are Hispanics." In other words, Hispanic immigrants in Lutherton are decidedly not criminals, not even the kinds of criminals that Fred has just said they were (domestic abusers). Finally, when I asked Fred what he thought should be done about immigration policy, he said: "I think we ought to give these people who are here an imminent path to citizenship or legal green cards or whatever it is . . . if you have been here, and you haven't been in trouble, you ought to have an opportunity, a path to citizenship."

Contrast this to Scott's view of immigrants as recipients of "giveaways" by the federal government—a view that Fred might not disagree with on one level but which in Lutherton is also counterbalanced by the lived experience that native-born, White residents have with immigrants in their city, which teaches them that immigrants are hardworking and family oriented. In Gravesend, where there is much less immigration, the image of immigrant-as-threat can go unchecked.

In sum, despite the fact that Republicans in Lutherton and Gravesend often watch the same news sources, it is easier for Republicans in Gravesend to conclude that the federal government is not just superfluous but threatening: their interventions not only fail to benefit Gravesenders in their many crises but also *appear* to support an immigrant community that is a symbolic threat to Gravesenders' way of life. The result is that several residents construe socialism and immigration as intertwined threats: that the federal government's reach is dangerous precisely because it will support immigrants rather than native-born Whites. Melissa, echoing some of Scott's concerns, tells me again and again that the Democrats "want to help everybody. And I says, there's gotta be a line. We can't help everybody." As she goes on to explain, she sees immigrants as a particular stress on the system:

> My sister works as a teacher [in a neighboring town]. . . . She's told me they have fifty-plus different languages in the school. . . . We can't take care of these people. And allowing children to become American citizens just because they were born in this country has got to stop. . . . We can't keep having people flooding our borders and, and it's not even taking away jobs. It's, you're overloading our system, our school system, our health-care system, our welfare system, everything. It's just, you're overloading.

Gravesenders are not alone in seeing a link between state expansion and support for immigrants at their expense. As Jonathan Metzl (2018) has shown, Whites are often so concerned about this possibility that they are willing to vote against social policies like Medicare expansion, even when their own health is at stake. The idea that racial resentment drives Whites' anti-statism is, of course, not new, but the effectiveness of this specific association between immigration and socialism in places like Gravesend points to more recent developments: even in places without large immigrant populations, like Gravesend, the threat of a multiracial society posed by growing immigration is palpable.[13] We get a sense of that fear in Scott's comments: he mentions immigrants wanting to prevent people from praying in school, despite the fact that organized school prayer has been illegal.

What the Democrats "used to be." The second facet of Scott's turn toward the Republican Party—that "Democrats used to be for the worker"—is also indicative of broader trends in Gravesend. The historical processes that have led unions to recede from public life in Gravesend may play a role in this, as I heard this same refrain from two other former union members.[14] Keith, for example, is a retired union member and former Democrat who tells me: "When I was Democrat, the Democrat Party was for the workers. They're not anymore, you know, that's gone." When I ask Keith to explain how his view of the Democrats changed, he tells me it was right after he retired and expanded his worldview beyond the unionized plant where he'd spent his career.

Among the handful of people I spoke to who have switched party affiliations, this kind of "awakening" is a common experience. Recall Marie's story from chapter 4: for Marie, the awakening occurred because she entered politics for the first time since childhood—she is now retired—and she did so in a place where residents agree party conflict is centered around Christian morality. Keith, in contrast, exited a lifelong union affiliation, which threw him into a period of questioning that eventually resulted in strong Republican partisanship. But both processes are specific to the places where Marie and Keith live: if Marie had lived in Motorville or Gravesend, she may have remained a Democrat. And if Keith had lived in Lutherton, he would likely never have been a union member or a Democrat.

But among Gravesenders like Keith and Scott, leaving a union job leads to the realization that the "Democrats are no longer the party of the worker." These very revelations suggest that the decline of churches and unions in Gravesend may have created not just a lack of coherence about what the parties mean at the local level but also a kind of instability within people over time. I did in fact speak to many more party-switchers in Gravesend than any-where else (seven out of thirty-two interviewees). These residents explained that their own views were stable but their partisan identities had shifted as they understood the parties themselves to change—much as Keith describes.

Today, Gravesenders are observing new shifts in the parties' meaning. As they come to understand Republicans as the party of threatened places and Democrats as the party of socialism and immigration, it seems increasingly sensible that the Republican Party is the party for them. This is not an uncontested point of view, however. Unlike in Motorville, and especially in Lutherton, where residents typically agree about what's at stake in party politics, Graves-enders often articulate different points of view on this. Some continue to believe Democrats are the party for the worker or, more typically, that Democrats are the party of "rights" and equality broadly conceived—along lines of class, race, gender, and sexuality. Others believe Republicans are the party of Christian morality, individual liberties (usually gun rights), and small government. This kind of incoherence and contestation explains why Gravesend has been a swing city for so long; but it is the undercurrent of racialized populism that explains their current trend toward the Republican Party.

Where Is Motorville Going?

Although there is still relative incoherence among Gravesenders, we can see how areas of agreement are beginning to emerge, through processes similar to those we observed in Motorville and Lutherton: within the constraints implied by so-cial group membership and political party rhetoric (in this case, the Republicans' move to construe immigration and socialism as a threat), place makes certain interpretations of social identities and party politics more likely. In a dying place, Gravesenders move to protect their White racial identity against perceived threats and embrace the Republican Party as the political vehicle for accomplishing this. As we have seen, the Heartland has become overwhelmingly red because of *both* places that cultivated White, Christian identities, nudging residents into the Republican column after the Racial Realignment and the rise of the Religious Right—like Lutherton—*and* the places that have more recently turned Republican amid a tide of racialized populism—like Gravesend. Just 4 percent of the 467 White, working-class counties that made up the New Deal coalition remained Democratic despite these forces and still vote majority-Democratic today.

What does this mean for Motorville's future? Can a place like Motorville continue to keep its residents in the Democratic fold despite state-level attacks on unions and national forces that have created strong pulls to the right in other, similar places? We've seen how place prevents Motorville residents from embracing both versions of Republicanism represented by Lutherton and Gravesend: one grounded in ethnoreligious identification with a party that represents White Christians and one grounded in racialized populism that identifies with a party catering to White places under threat. Are either of these a possible pathway for Motorville to turn to the right?

Based on the evidence presented thus far, it is unlikely that Motorville will follow Lutherton's path. While several residents I spoke to in Motorville thought of Christians as more likely to be Republicans, or referred to Republicans as pro-life, this was not the through line that led them to identify with one party over another: I interviewed several people in Motorville for whom Christian identification or pro-life politics did not map neatly onto their partisan identities. As such, for Motorville to become like Lutherton, it would require *both* a decline in unions' political mobilization *and* a shift in residents' church participation that would lead to a consolidation of ethnoreligious identity. Although such a shift is not impossible, declining church membership in Motorville suggests that this is unlikely.

But while Motorville will probably not become Lutherton, it may become Gravesend. As we've seen, the local organization of union politics leads Motorvillians to understand themselves as among the have-nots who would benefit from Democrats bringing in the state to level the playing field. But such an outcome is tenuous, on both an organizational and cultural level. In fact, during my last trip to Motorville in summer 2021, I attended the MLC's monthly meeting to share my findings with them. At the time, they were distressed because one of the largest private sector unions in the city had left the MLC. The union didn't see the point of paying the dues to the MLC when they had their own, internal political apparatus. At the meeting, the representative from a local retail workers union expressed empathy with this stance—as she pointed out, her members made the least money of anyone's in the room (teachers, postal workers, and several building trades representatives were also present). She could barely justify the current dues her members paid, let alone a proposed increase that was on the table, if the organization did not do a better job of telling the rank and file what its purpose was. In other words, Motorville is not immune from the many forces that have troubled unions elsewhere, both internal and external to the labor movement.

But even if there were instability in Motorville's organizational context (i.e., a decline in labor's political engagement), we should expect that the cultural dimensions of place would persist for some time, as residents and community leaders continue to tell each other stories that locate their community within a narrative of systemic economic disadvantage and remind each other that they would benefit from government intervention. But these stories would not persist forever without the anchoring organizational context that supports them. And as we have seen, there are already signs that the cultural dimensions supporting place-based partisanship in Motorville are tenuous: Quinn, whom we heard from in chapter 4, is one of four Democrats I spoke to whose association of Democrats as the party of the have-nots is somewhat troubled by their interactions with workers and union members in Motorville who are not Democrats.

If more people have interactions like Quinn's, it could ultimately reshape place-based partisanship in Motorville: Motorville residents might understand themselves as disadvantaged but no longer link that identity to Democratic partisanship as the way to redress inequalities. If that happens, they will sound much more like Gravesenders. In fact, political scientists Paul Frymer and Jacob Grumbach (2021) have found precisely this relationship at the individual-organizational level: union membership decreases racial resentment among White workers. When unions disappear, for both White individuals and communities, there is less contextual material preventing the kind of racialized populism we heard from Scott.

––––––

Motorville has retained important place characteristics that have held residents back from past and present pulls toward the Republican Party, but they are rare for a reason: such characteristics are difficult to maintain under constant political and economic threats against unions and sustained efforts by the Republican Party to attract places like Motorville, Lutherton, and Gravesend and the kinds of people who live there. For these reasons, we can see why certain pathways are more likely for similar cities in the postindustrial Heartland. As unions, churches, and other resources recede, instability and loss are likely to characterize more residents' experiences of postindustrial decline.

My argument is that this shifting local organizational context is the key piece of the puzzle missing in existing accounts of postindustrial populism among White voters in the Heartland. Trump had somewhat more success with this constituency, relative to other Republican politicians, because his rhetoric of immigration and socialism as threats to hardworking, native-born

Whites resonated not just with people like Scott but *in places like Gravesend,* where local organizations no longer provide coherence to local civic life.

This also means that bringing Gravesend back into a working-class coalition with places like Motorville requires more than just a new campaign strategy by political elites. Pundits often blame the breakdown of working-class politics on the Democratic Party, arguing that they focus too much on "social issues" that appeal to liberal, college-educated voters rather than the bread-and-butter issues that motivate workers.[15] But if Americans overwhelmingly vote according to their partisanship, and if partisan ties are formed as voters figure out which party best represents their kind of people, then these fluctuations in issue salience will only ever move the needle at the margin. The real question is, what would make voters in places like Gravesend think of themselves as workers operating in an unequal system who would benefit from state intervention to level the playing field? And the answer, as evidence from Motorville and survey evidence from the United States and other countries suggest, is *not* the parties, it's the unions.[16] Another way to think about this is from a historical perspective: the connection between unions and the Democratic Party is what cemented the working-class politics of the New Deal era, and that connection persists in many forms today. But unions are no longer able to deliver voters the same way they once did, as membership has declined and the quality of unions' engagement in their members' lives has altered dramatically.[17] Consider for a moment what it was like to live in Gravesend in the mid-1930s, when the UGWA was advocating for a broad, working-class movement that brought workers together across factories, drew women out of their homes and into the movement, and told the community as a whole that it would benefit from a more just version of capitalism and a more involved state. Regardless of whether FDR tweaked his rhetoric in 1936, relative to 1932, the UGWA ensured that Gravesend residents knew which party would represent them and their community. Even though unions have persisted in Gravesend today, they no longer accomplish this same kind of city-level, working-class mobilization.

This discussion also points to a broader argument about how the relationship between place and politics might change: a destabilization of local organizational contexts that eventually changes narratives of community identity. Political party maneuvering also matters, but its effect on place-based partisanship will depend on whether party positioning resonates within local contexts. Republicans saw an opportunity to cultivate a new political subjectivity around the "left behind" White Americans in the postindustrial

Heartland, but that subjectivity took hold in Gravesend because the destabilization of local social organization had already left residents feeling they were part of a threatened community. In contrast, in Motorville and Lutherton, residents are less likely to interpret their social position in this way because they make sense of themselves and their social problems using different cultural frameworks.

Throughout parts 1 and 2, I have argued that place matters for understanding the historical and ongoing reddening of the Heartland because it provides the context in which voters make sense of postindustrial decline, partisan politics, and their place in it. We can see from Motorville, Lutherton, and Gravesend how place-based partisanship is constituted by both national party politicking and local processes of political sense-making. Part 3 will address the final question we began with: will local processes continue to matter despite growing trends toward the nationalization of politics? Through the case of the Covid-19 pandemic, chapters 6 and 7 explore how nationalizing forces— economic crisis and elite polarization, respectively—affect the local processes that produce and reproduce place-based partisanship. We will see how residents of Motorville and Lutherton deploy place-based diagnostic frameworks to think about how the federal government should intervene to take care of its citizens amid skyrocketing unemployment (chapter 6) and how they continue to fall back on narratives of community identity to make sense of who they are and which party best represents them (chapter 7).

PART III

The (Possible) Future of Place

6

Local Contexts amid National Crisis

ECONOMIC DOWNTURN IN MOTORVILLE, LUTHERTON, AND GRAVESEND

IN MARCH 2020, as Covid-19 raced through the United States, I called Hugh, a law enforcement officer in Lutherton. As we discussed the state and federal government responses to the pandemic, he repeated the exact story he'd told me eight months prior: "I mean, we have a tornado come through here, [the local people are] the ones that go out first thing. We're the ones that protect the people and lock it down." As Hugh concluded on both occasions, the federal government is just too big. When there's a problem, "the local people respond." This was the same thing he'd told me when we first met, in July 2019. As he explained at that time:

> And I think by giving stuff away, it's pushed people away from what our country was built on. Our country was built on small communities taking care of each other. And now everybody thinks the federal government's got to take care of it. And that's not the case.

Hugh, like Cal from chapter 3, prefers for communities to take care of themselves, as they do in Lutherton. And even as the pandemic caused an unprecedented spike in unemployment, this did not shift his thinking about the relationship between the federal government and its citizens.

In fact, seven months into the crisis, just before Hugh—a lifelong Democrat—cast his first ever vote for a Republican presidential candidate, he expressed the same belief about the appropriate division of responsibilities between local versus national and private versus public entities. And Hugh was not alone in this: throughout the months leading up to the November election, other residents in Lutherton echoed Hugh's sentiments, articulating similar beliefs about the limited role of the federal government in taking care of Americans, even during a time of economic crisis.

————

This is, in some ways, unsurprising—several people from Lutherton offered similar commentary in chapters 3 and 4. And yet, even as Hugh and his neighbors remained stalwart in their beliefs, social scientists and political observers were predicting the opposite response: that the economic crisis would cause a rupture in Americans' anti-statism, leading to a rare moment of national unity as people called on the federal government to intervene. As historian David Blight wrote in *The Atlantic* in March 2020: "it is in our most profound crises that we discover, against the suspicions and beliefs of millions, that government can be our friend, even our savior." And yet, this was far from the case in Lutherton. What can explain the durability of Lutherton's particular form of anti-statism?

The account that Blight and others offered makes sense given the national-institutional argument about how citizens orient themselves toward the state, which chapter 3 revisited: the public's ideas about what the government should do are shaped by what the government already does, creating a degree of stickiness in beliefs about both the state and state institutions.[1] For this reason, crises such as war and economic depression are thought to create opportunities for change in the public's demands on their government because they can break down old institutional arrangements.[2]

And during the early months of the Covid-19 pandemic, the federal government *did* embrace novel forms of intervention to keep Americans afloat financially, including direct payments in the form of stimulus checks and the expansion of unemployment insurance. Moreover, these took place under a *Republican* president. We might expect that this eased some of the partisan divisiveness about the appropriate size and scope of the federal government, at least with respect to these specific interventions and, perhaps, that it even brought Americans to call on their government in new ways.

But transformation is always a contingent outcome during crises; and in what follows, I argue that attentiveness to place allows us to better understand pockets of stability amid national rupture. As we will see, some portion of the stability within individual residents of Motorville, Lutherton, and Gravesend has to do with how their partisan identity guides their thinking about political issues.[3] But we will also see that, particularly in Motorville and Lutherton, residents continued to deploy local diagnostic frames to make sense of how the federal government should intervene—even during a time of acute crisis.[4] This is because, when employment fell away, federal government programs helped stabilize individuals' lives and the broader economy. As a result, local organizational contexts were not undermined and, in Lutherton, local service provision did not *visibly* fail. The federal government's contemporary hodgepodge of social relief—even if ungenerous in comparison with peer countries—is what differentiates the pandemic from David Blight's example of the Great Depression: local organizations were not alone in helping people stay afloat this time.[5] Instead, the direct influx of federal dollars to individuals, alongside the government's long-standing and less visible forms of support to middle-class families, helped sustain the local status quo.[6] As a result, the pandemic created an opportunity for residents of Motorville and Lutherton to apply existing diagnostic frames when thinking about how the federal government should intervene, thus reproducing rather than eroding their place-based (anti)-statism.

Beyond Motorville and Lutherton and the specific case of the Covid-19 pandemic, this suggests that any attempts to incorporate citizens into the U.S. polity through national welfare reform will come up against ingrained local modes of social service provision. But this is not impossible to overcome: with repeated evidence that familiar models are not able to solve new problems, or that other models work better, the public should change their beliefs. Up to that threshold, however, national ruptures may reaffirm local processes rather than disrupt them.

This chapter also begins to develop the final argument of the book: that place will likely continue to matter for American political outcomes because many factors we may expect to nationalize politics do not actually destabilize the diagnostic frames or narratives of community that sustain place-based partisanship. In this chapter, we will see how national disruption can reinforce diagnostic frames, and in the next chapter we will examine how narratives of community identity persist even as individuals polarize on novel issues related to the public health dimensions of the Covid-19 crisis.

Experiencing the Economic Crisis

In March 2020 the pandemic provoked a rapid spike in layoffs, furloughs, and cutbacks that transformed the local economies of Motorville, Lutherton, and Gravesend. During the earliest days of the crisis, just as schools and businesses were closing in late March, I spoke to residents of all three cities who almost uniformly expressed profound concerns about the economic crisis.[7] Kate, for example, is a Democrat from Motorville who works as a retail manager in a popular shop. When I asked her in mid-March how concerned she was about the pandemic, she, like many people, broke her worries into two buckets— health and economic. After explaining her precise level of concern about catching Covid-19 and how it might affect her and her husband, she continued:

> I'm extremely concerned about the economic impact it's going to take on the community because like for right now, [our] store is closed for browsers. . . . I am concerned, but it has more to do with the economic stuff because I work every day with a lot of people that if something happens and they can't collect unemployment, they'll be in really dire straits. And I'm very fortunate that the store is responding very well . . . but there's going to be some long, long reaching implications because they're saying that the economic impact of this could last into the fall.

Kate, like many people I spoke to who lost hours at work or watched others get furloughed, felt the crunch of the pandemic's economic costs immediately. There was little question that it was more than a public health crisis; it was also an economic crisis. And this was particularly true in Motorville and Lutherton, where the rise in unemployment between 2019 and 2020 was more than twice what it was in Gravesend.

But despite recognizing similar levels of need, residents described living in cities that responded differently to that need: Lutherton residents praised their community for taking care of itself; Motorvillians saw little evidence of a co-ordinated, local response (nor did they expect one); and Gravesenders continued to fall somewhere in between, some recognizing that churches and nonprofits were helping and others feeling—much as we saw in chapter 5— that local leadership was nonexistent.

Lutherton's persistent awareness of local efforts to help those in need stood out more than ever in this time of crisis, as people sat closed off from one another and their usual forms of volunteerism. The day before Governor Holcomb issued Indiana's first stay-at-home order on March 23, I asked Todd from Lutherton if he'd heard of any local people or groups "stepping up" to help out those affected by the early days of school and work closures. He replied quickly: "They've never stepped down. They've never changed anything. [Even as the need has grown] the organizations here in town are still doing exactly what they've always done. It's been business as usual. There's been hardly any hiccup."

Todd learned of several activities through his own church and his involvement with SAM. His assessment is consistent with organizational activity reported by other residents, volunteers, and local media. Across Lutherton, the networks of churches, ministries, and nonprofits extended the work they were already doing to meet the community's growing need. SAM went from serving 35–50 people each Wednesday night to over 100 people, according to one volunteer's estimate. The organization's leadership discussed leveraging this opportunity to deepen their ties with local churches, investing further in existing problem-solving strategies rather than searching for new ones.

Even beyond those directly connected to service groups like Todd, many residents I spoke to in Lutherton continued to express appreciation for and awareness of local churches and nonprofits serving the community during the pandemic. Often, they learned of these efforts via the same communication networks as they had previously: local news and social media. Even amid the many other sensational events of 2020, Lutherton's politicians continued to post on Facebook about churches and nonprofits helping their communities, and residents liked and commented on those posts. The *Lutherton Gazette* continued to cover these activities, and residents continued to attend church online.

The result was that residents still felt that Lutherton was taking care of itself. As Emma explained of her hometown in March 2020, it's different from a lot of other places in this way:

> Because, you know I think a lot of people would wait for FEMA or they'd wait even for the national governments to say, here's what we're giving everybody. Everybody was all about their thousand-dollar checks that have yet to hit the mailboxes. And so, I think a lot of people would wait for that.

Note how similar Emma's view of her community is to the one that Hugh expressed at the beginning of the chapter: in Lutherton, the local people do not wait for the federal government but instead take care of their community as they are accustomed to doing. Many others agreed with this assessment.

Luthertonians' narrative about what kind of community they are was thus *reinforced* during the crisis. Even as these residents recognized the dire economic fallout from the pandemic, they continued to feel that their network of nongovernmental social provision was successfully meeting community needs, thus removing things like food insecurity—and, to an extent, housing—from the list of social problems that require government intervention.

Did SAM or other local organizations actually stem the tide of need during the pandemic? It's difficult to answer this question. According to the

Point-in-Time (PIT) Count by the Department of Housing and Urban Development (HUD) of unhoused people, which is conducted each January in cooperation with local nonprofits, the size of Lutherton's unhoused population relative to the city as a whole was cut by nearly two-thirds between January 2020 and January 2021.[8] But SAM opened a housing shelter during this time and did not participate in the PIT count. As such, it's possible that several people were counted in 2020 because they were staying at a local nonprofit that did participate in the count and then were left out in 2021 because they were staying with SAM. Even so, as we saw in chapter 3, the question of whether or not these groups were actually successful is often secondary to their visibility; to Lutherton residents like Emma and Todd, they were doing excellent work.

Contrast this to Motorville, where residents—despite racking their brain—could not think of much that local groups were doing to meet the need in spring 2020. And they may have been correct: according to HUD's data, the number of unhoused people relative to the total population reached a five-year high in 2021. As Isabelle, who has lived in Motorville her whole life, explained: "I know there's people that have food insecurity and what have you. And I haven't heard of any food drives here at all. I haven't heard of anything." Although Isabelle is referring to food drives here, which are ostensibly run by nonprofit organizations, she concludes her statement by noting, as she had several times in our past conversations, that Motorville is often "forgotten about" by the rest of the state—a reference to public resources. As Isabelle's response indicates, when Motorvillians think about their lack of resources—even when considering a lack of nonprofit resources—they often locate the problem as a public one.

Although a handful of residents with direct ties to local organizations were more aware of their activities, most Motorvillians I spoke to echoed Isabelle's sentiment. Even Kate, a member of a local Catholic Church, had little knowledge of her congregation's efforts to provide for the community. As she told me: "I feel like kind of the culture of Minnesota and Wisconsin is kind of helping people out on more of a smaller scale. . . . I think there's a lot of smaller, you know, helping out kind of things that doesn't necessarily get reported or shared."

This does, in fact, seem to be what happened in Motorville—or at least what was most visible to residents. Many people I spoke to pointed to two Facebook groups that emerged shortly after the stay-at-home orders, one dedicated to supporting local businesses and the other that filled with posts of residents' needs and others' offers of assistance. Danielle recalls seeing people post offers for car repair, childcare, and so on and concludes: "I know a lot of the community itself is opening their doors to fellow community members."

But while many Motorvillians lauded these groups, both had tapered off by the fall of 2020 as residents tired of the many calls for help.

Gravesend was much the same. Several residents, primarily churchgoers, noted in spring 2020 that churches and the Salvation Army were continuing their usual work of providing food and toiletries to needy families. But for the large majority of people I spoke with, nonprofits and churches were not a visible presence—even among churchgoers. Ben, echoing many Motorvillians, explained: "I think churches are still trying to go out to the community and kind of minister to the community. Although not being super connected with the workings of the churches anymore, it's harder to see what's been going on." Ben used to be a much more active participant in two local evangelical churches, but during spring 2020 he was working three part-time jobs amid the pandemic and was less attuned to their activities. Even so, much like Luthertonians, Ben takes for granted that churches *should be* stepping in to help their neighbors during an economic downturn.

But it was only in Lutherton that the ongoing *visibility* of local efforts created a shared sense among residents that the community was taking effective action to meet the crisis. Even more so than in Motorville, many Gravesend residents I spoke to felt a lack of local leadership from both the private and public sectors—much as they had prior to the crisis. Zack summarized this view in April: "in terms of actual leadership [locally], in terms of addressing the health concerns and the economic fallout and the well-being of the community. No."

As we have seen again and again, Zack's comments do not mean that Gravesend's leaders are *actually* "worse" than those in Motorville or Lutherton; rather, it indicates that residents are less aware of their actions and that this lack of awareness leaves them feeling rudderless. In sum, while residents of Motorville, Lutherton, and Gravesend faced the same national crisis, they experienced it from within different places—where residents learned different lessons about how well the community was meeting the growing need and what additional assistance they might need from the federal government.

A Moment of Agreement

This became clear during my third and fourth conversations with residents in April/May and September/October 2020, when I began trying to disentangle their views on the complex and federated government response to the pandemic. I asked about what residents thought could be done locally to address the crisis; what they though their states could do; and what they thought the federal government could do. I also asked them to evaluate what the state and federal governments had already done. And despite the ongoing differences in how residents of each city viewed *local* responses in the early weeks of the pandemic, I heard some degree of agreement across all three cities in spring 2020 about how the *federal government* should respond: that it needed to intervene to address the mounting economic crisis. As Lutherton residents described it in March and April, there was a growing group of people who probably needed more than what the community itself could provide. Veronica, a Republican from Lutherton, felt that the federal government's stimulus was necessary: "You know, I think it's a good thing, especially for those individuals that aren't able to continue working. And it should hopefully help them." Most Motorvillians I spoke to at this time agreed, often advocating for federal relief before the CARES Act was passed.

Veronica's comments also pick up on the near-universal claim circulating at this time that there was a clear division between the people who "needed" federal relief and the people who did not. For example, Paul, a Republican from Gravesend, was livid about the stimulus package when we spoke in early April. As he told me:

PAUL: This is supposed to be stimulating stuff. Why in the world does the Kennedy Center get it? Oh, isn't Pelosi's daughter on the board of trustees or something? . . . I didn't read a lot about it. I'm like, oh my gosh. This stimulus should be stimulating the people. Why are these museums and stuff getting all this money? Why'd Amtrak get a billion dollars? Why? Well, because they have special interests in it.

ST: So in terms of the checks, the thousand-dollar checks to the regular people, that to you seems . . . good, or . . . ?

PAUL: Better than nothing! We didn't have that in the past. So, I mean, it helps. There's a lot of people, you know, single moms who . . . are trying to make it, now they're staying home. Now they don't have money coming in.

ST: So you feel like the part that's going to the people is good.

PAUL: Yes.

ST: But the part that's going to the museums is bad. What about the businesses, like the airlines and things like that?

PAUL: Ridiculous. Absolutely ridiculous. They don't need the stimulation.

ST: So you would just say give all the money to the people?

PAUL: Yes.

ST: OK. And do you feel like it should be more than a thousand dollars?

PAUL: I don't know. If we didn't give away, what, 2.3 trillion dollars? It probably could have been.

Paul's comments summarize the concerns of many people I spoke to whose immediate reaction to the CARES Act was that big corporations should, under no circumstances, receive assistance from the federal government. As Paul explains, there are trade-offs between supporting "the people" and supporting corporations, and the federal government should prioritize those who "need the stimulation."

It was rare, in those early days of the shutdowns, that I heard from anyone who did not share this view. Although people drew different boundaries between who was and was not truly "needy"—between rich and poor; the working and unemployed; and families and single people—almost everyone I spoke to agreed that there were people who "needed" federal relief and people who did not. As a result of these needs-based distinctions, many people—like Mallory, a teacher from Lutherton who was still fully employed, as was her husband—grouped themselves in the category of those who did not "need" the funds and felt uncomfortable receiving them. As she explained of her feelings about the stimulus check she received: "I mean, we were not affected financially at this point. So it made me feel a little bit guilty that we were even getting anything." Mallory's guilt over receiving the stimulus payments was overwhelmingly common among those who remained employed full-time during the early months of the pandemic.

But even among those who were unemployed, several people expressed qualms about making more money staying at home than they did working. In late May I spoke to Scott and Lisa, who live outside Gravesend; we heard from Scott in chapter 5. In spring 2020 Lisa's receptionist job had temporarily disappeared; later, the loss would become permanent. Lisa, like Scott, was a lifelong Democrat until 2016, when both voted for Trump. She joined our conversation over the phone in May, and as we were concluding, I asked them both, "Is there anything else that you would want to see the federal government doing right now that they are not doing?"

SCOTT: I don't think so. The only thing I wondered about is they've got that $600 thing in for everybody on unemployment. People are making more money when they're home than when they're working, and that's not right.

LISA: Yes. We do kind of wonder how that got passed.

SCOTT: It would be the liberals who did that, got it in somehow or another.

LISA: Yes.

SCOTT: It was something that got slipped through that there weren't a lot of thoughts on how it works. I don't know.

LISA: The nurses and doctors, they should be getting hazard pay as well.

SCOTT: Right, instead of the people getting paid $600 extra a week sitting at home.

LISA: Yes, a week? I mean, I couldn't even see it if it was a month, but it's every week.

ST: [*referring to a comment she'd made earlier*] So you're making more money now than if you were at work?

LISA: Yes. [*laughter*] Yes, I am.

SCOTT: Absolutely, way more.

Scott and Lisa, along with several others who lost their jobs, felt they did not need the extra money; in fact, like Mallory, they felt guilty.

But this guilt was not just due to needs-based concerns: as Scott and Lisa's comments indicate, it was also about residents' feeling that the benefits were *unearned*. Scott and Lisa wonder: why spend resources on the people "sitting at home"—even if that's them in this case—instead of the frontline workers? In contrast to other universal social programs, like Social Security, which were designed on a contributory basis precisely so that recipients would feel it was an earned benefit upon retirement, the stimulus checks that flowed nearly universally to Americans in spring 2020 felt unearned to many people I spoke to—in other words, they felt they did not deserve them.[9] As we will see, and perhaps somewhat unsurprisingly, this point of view was least common among Motorvillians who occasionally embraced a more universalist logic of welfare provision. But for the most part, my interlocutors reacted to these new forms of government intervention with similar caution and confusion, regardless of where they lived: as the government provided funds to those who did not "need" them, and even to people who had not earned them, their typical categories for making sense of state support no longer applied. The result during the early weeks of the pandemic was a minimum degree of cautious support for federal intervention across all three cities, at least for those in need.

The Limits of Crisis as Transformational Opportunity

But these similarities proved to be short-lived. As the economy began to recover, residents of both Gravesend and Lutherton wondered if the unemployed were needy or simply lazy—taking advantage of free-flowing government money.

And Lutherton residents further made a specific, place-based claim: there are people who are needy and people who are not needy; but there are also types of need that are suitable for government intervention and types of need that are not. Most importantly, those needs that can be addressed within the community, should be. The result was that, by fall 2020, many people I spoke to in Lutherton felt there was no further need for public assistance, except in the case of small businesses: small business loans were not something the community could take care of itself. Thus, even as both Lutherton and Gravesend residents became increasingly focused on articulating deservingness rather than needs-based criteria for public assistance, it was only in Lutherton that this local anti-statism continued to shape residents' claims on the federal government.

Meanwhile, many Motorvillians (particularly Democrats) wanted the federal government to provide a second stimulus bill that included all elements of the first and more. In fact, as they experienced the government making an unprecedented foray into Americans' livelihoods, some residents saw this as evidence that they were right all along—*the government could always have been helping the working and middle classes more than it had been.* The result was that, particularly between Motorville and Lutherton, participants' views of the state's responsibility for its citizens diverged further than ever.

From Need to Deservingness:
Lutherton and Gravesend

By the fall of 2020, residents across Motorville, Lutherton, and Gravesend were returning to work as the shutdowns eased. While this was true everywhere—only two of my interlocutors suffered permanent job loss by the time of the election—it was only in Lutherton that residents had come to view the local economy as entirely recovered. In contrast, Motorvillians offered up a lengthy list of people they knew personally who were still suffering and Gravesenders continued to think of their economy as in a state of permanent depression. As a result, Lutherton residents—and, to an extent, Gravesend residents—became increasingly wary that the people claiming a need were really lazy or unmotivated to return to work. In other words, they were undeserving.

Consider, for example, how Ashley, a Democratic-leaning Independent from Gravesend, responded in October when I asked if she would like to see the extra unemployment relief extended: "Yes. If they are unemployed because of Covid, yes. If they're unemployed because they're lazy, then no." And as she contemplated continuing the extra $600 a week, she added:

> It's kind of tricky for me. I had a coworker who chose to take a leave of absence—not a leave of absence. She chose to be laid off or whatever, furloughed for it just because she didn't want to work but she wanted to make that extra money. I mean, as long as they're not making more than they normally would at work, I'd be definitely okay with that, but there's people who are just lazy and want the money.

By fall 2020, many people agreed with Ashley that government relief should be limited to those who were unemployed directly because of Covid-19. This was distinct from the most common needs-based claims evoked by participants in the spring, which focused primarily on income and wealth as a dividing line between the needy and the not needy. This is because concerns about deservingness had crept into their thinking. As Ashley said: "there's people who are just lazy and want the money." As we saw in Scott and Lisa's comments above, these kinds of concerns didn't disappear during the early days of the crisis, but they were submerged because residents suspected that "real" economic need was pervasive.

Note also that Ashley, much like other people who shared her concerns, refers to her own experiences when she thinks of a person who is undeserving of government assistance. Similarly, the very notion that "need" had declined tended to come from residents' observations in their own cities. For this reason, concerns like Ashley's were even more prevalent in Lutherton because residents overwhelmingly concluded that their economy had returned to its pre-Covid robustness by fall 2020—a view that crossed party lines. For example, Kevin, a Democrat who runs an assembly line in Lutherton, told me in October, "I really feel like anyone who wants a job around here can get one." As a result, he did not support another relief bill, explaining that he knew it would go to people choosing not to work. Lutherton residents tended to repeat this idea despite the fact that annualized unemployment in the county rose about 4.5 percentage points between 2019 and 2020; this amounted to a 180 percent increase in the unemployment rate, compared to a 119 percent increase nationally, a 130 percent increase in Motorville, and just a 63 percent increase in Gravesend. But as with Ashley, who observed a coworker choose not to work because of the generosity of unemployment, the myriad "Help Wanted" signs around Lutherton told residents that there must be "people who are just lazy" and therefore do not deserve more government relief. As I've discussed throughout part 2, social scientists have long argued that such notions of deservingness are foundational to U.S. welfare provision and are particularly salient for White Americans with concerns about racialized others receiving undue benefits with their tax dollars. But here, as in previous chapters, we can also see how local contexts also matter. And as a result of both factors, many of my interlocutors across Lutherton and Gravesend agreed: as the economy recovered in summer and fall 2020, the truly needy—and the truly deserving—were a dwindling bunch.

But for many Lutherton residents, that circle of people "truly in need" of government assistance was even narrower: it included *only those directly impacted by the pandemic who were not being served by the community.* If, as many residents told me, the local economy had rebounded, the usual patterns of local provision should suffice to meet any "normal" levels of need. This line of reasoning helped residents parse out where and how they wanted the federal government to continue intervening. For example, when I asked Harriett, perhaps the most active and staunch Republican within my sample, about further federal stimulus in October, she was adamant that it should not happen because of the local economic recovery. I pressed her further: but what about those who "really do need help"? She replied: "I just think that communities take care of one another. We've got a shelter. We've got food pantries . . . if they're really in need, we help. I just don't think another stimulus check or anything from the government is necessary." Harriett's response perfectly encapsulates the narrowing window for federal intervention for many Lutherton residents I spoke to at this time: it lies between what the market (through jobs) and the community (through nonprofits) can provide.

By November 2020, this logic led many people I spoke to in Lutherton to agree on two things: that the federal government should prioritize those in need; and that those in need were small business owners. Marie, the Democratic-defector we heard from in chapter 4, who pays little attention to politics, exemplifies this stance. When I asked her in fall 2020 if she would like to see another round of relief passed in Congress, she considered it and then replied: "I'm not sure if that's a good idea because what's happened is this caused people not to go back to work because they're enjoying payments. Around here, almost every business you pass is hiring. They can't get people to work." I then turned to the specific elements of a possible bill and asked about more loans for small businesses. This time her response was different: "I think I would. A lot of small businesses just didn't make it because people can't go there."

In sum, because Lutherton residents tended to define "need" so narrowly—as those directly affected by Covid who could not receive help within their community—they increasingly saw little role for government provision. Employment had picked up, local organizations continued to provide food, and only small businesses still needed help. This perspective was almost entirely limited to Lutherton. Only one person from Gravesend expressed a similar notion in September when I asked if the government should pass another round of stimulus checks—but she was one of the most civically engaged people I met in Gravesend.

From Need to Universalism: Motorville

But there was an even greater contrast between Lutherton and Motorville, where even residents who were aware of nongovernmental service efforts saw these as evidence of public failure—just as they had done before the pandemic. Christopher, for example, was one of a handful of people who knew of a Catholic charity providing financial and food assistance in Motorville. But after he told me about this in September, he continued: "It's still not as much as we need. I've known two different people now who because of this have not been able to get their jobs back and have been evicted from their homes." He went on to describe a cascade of issues he saw tumbling from the lack of help for people like his friends, and I finally asked, "So, what would you like to see done?" He replied: "Realistically, more stimulus money going out to people, the unemployment benefits brought back. People need financial assistance right now from the government, and that's not been happening."

During the pandemic, Motorvillians like Christopher did not categorize private assistance in the same way as Lutherton folks did—as an example of communities taking care of themselves—because this is not how they had categorized such actions in the past. Instead, Motorvillians turned toward the federal government. And even as most people I spoke to continued to articulate a preference for needs-based public relief, some were also beginning to make appeals for further state intervention on the basis of universalist principles. Isabelle, for example, is a Democrat who argued in September that everyone needed another round of stimulus checks. As we discussed what she would like the government to include in a second relief bill, I asked: "Okay, and in that bill, would you like to see another round of those $1,200 stimulus checks go out to everyone?"

ISABELLE: Absolutely. Prices are so ridiculous in the grocery store. I've never spent so much money on services and on food than I have these last several months.

ST: Oh, interesting. So, you feel like that money could help people make up the difference?

ISABELLE: Oh, yes. I'm getting a regular source of income, I'm getting my retirement income in, but it's not covering anywhere near what it did because hamburger has doubled in price now. Everything has gone up.

Isabelle's claims for a universalistic approach are couched in needs-based language: she believes everyone has at least some increased financial cost from the pandemic. But later, when we talked about the idea that unemployment benefits might deter people from working, she first expressed concern and then concluded that some people, like her sister-in-law who was deeply afraid during her shifts at Wal-Mart, might be uncomfortable going into work because of the virus. As she did so, she shifted into an even more universalistic logic: "Until this gets straightened out, I think the government's going to have to foot the bill." In an instance of national crisis, the federal government simply has to take care of all its citizens.

But others in Motorville—particularly younger residents—took this even further, drawing lessons from this experience about how the state should relate to its citizens in general. As Quinn told me in September, she supported another round of stimulus checks and greater resources for a whole host of people in need: "Because I feel like we all pay the government our whole life so I think they should give us a break right now and give us some stimulus checks, and obviously what they can. Because I just think that the ones that really need it the most, it would help a lot." Quinn, like others, recognizes that there are some who "need it the most" and others who don't; however, she also argues that if people pay into the system they have a right to government relief.

Motorvillians who shared this orientation also saw the stimulus as evidence that the government could always have been doing more for people, if only politicians had chosen to do so. Jamie, who continued to work during the crisis but feared for her coworkers at a local brewery who were furloughed, explained in May:

This pandemic is really exposing how many of our institutions are just . . . it's all bullsh*t. There have been states where they just passed laws saying guess what? You can't evict somebody for being late on your rent this month because of the pandemic. . . . The federal government could easily, say, look, nobody is going to work, but you're going to pay. And that's just the way it is.

For Jamie and several other young Motorvillians, the crisis revealed a lie that they had long suspected: that the government was *unable* to provide more for the people. As Danielle wondered aloud while we discussed the stimulus in spring 2020: "If America could have done this to begin with, why weren't they doing it all along?" Like Jamie said, "it's all bullsh*t." By the fall, this group of Motorvillians were focused on the possibility of not just widespread, but universalist, interventions.

But these were not entirely new beliefs for this group of Motorville residents. Note, for example, a comment from Danny, who felt the stimulus checks supported his preexisting belief in a universal basic income: "it opened my eyes to confirm what I already had somewhat of a belief in." Danny already believed the public sphere should be expanded significantly. For folks like him, the notion that the "government can be a force for good," as Carl put it to me, was commonsense long before Covid-19. The pandemic proved their point rather than taught them this lesson.

But importantly, their willingness to call on the state to provide for the things they already wanted—particularly universal health care, universal basic income, and student debt relief—evolved as the federal government actually took up similar policies. Free school lunch for everyone and universal basic income suddenly seemed politically and pragmatically feasibly. As Luke explained in May: "I'm a big fan of the idea of a universal basic income. So that was the first moderate steps to implementing that. So it was nice to see that it could actually work and have a plausible effect."

Outside of Motorville, I rarely heard similar claims. Only a handful of Gravesenders called for universalistic policies, and when they did so it was usually on terms that focused on the federal government's responsibility in times of crisis rather than on claims of citizenship or fairness. And as we saw above, many residents of Lutherton and Gravesend increasingly embraced deservingness as a boundary line for government provision. In fact, by fall of 2020, Todd—an erstwhile progressive Independent—was the only Lutherton resident I knew who firmly supported another round of stimulus checks.

———

The economic crisis wrought by Covid-19 reproduced differences in beliefs about the role of the federal government across each city—differences that had previously been particularly stark between residents of Motorville and Lutherton because of their stable organizational contexts that sustained distinct, place-based diagnostic frames. During the pandemic Motorvillians learned that the government could take care of a whole range of social problems that had long plagued the country, exposing the lie—or the "bullsh*t"—of the system, in Jamie's words. Meanwhile, Lutherton residents learned that the status quo worked: a combination of local, private solutions and a national spigot that could be turned on in times of crisis.

In other words, residents' experience of the national economic crisis from within their local contexts shaped how they interpreted the federal government's interventions and ultimately proved their previous beliefs right. When Covid-19 brought the economy to a standstill, certain organizations in Lutherton, like SAM, continued to visibly deploy existing strategies for taking care of the needy and, according to residents' view of the situation, were able to meet the rising local need. If the government had not stepped in with the CARES Act, those local systems may have been overwhelmed as they had been in earlier eras of economic downturn, like the Great Depression. But in this instance, the balance of public and private provision sustained Lutherton's community problem-solving enough so that residents were not forced to question its validity.

In many ways, this arrangement was not that different from what always supported Luthertonians' experience of social provision: a balance of invisible, public support for the middle class by the federal government and visible, private support for the needy within their community.[10] Although public support became more visible than ever during the pandemic, this did not change the way Lutherton or Gravesend residents thought about the federal government. This is because, unlike in Motorville where residents always felt the federal government owed them a debt for redressing systemic inequalities, many Lutherton and Gravesend residents felt these new benefits were *unearned*.

As we've seen throughout the book, place was not the only factor that shaped residents' reaction to federal pandemic relief: age proved an important dividing line in Motorville, for example, where the younger residents I spoke to were consistently the most pro-government intervention of anyone during the eighteen months of my study. We can also see how partisanship and ideology are, unsurprisingly, key: Todd, a progressive Independent from Lutherton, was the most pro-relief person I spoke to in that city (but note that he is not a Democrat—in fact, he voted for a third-party presidential candidate in 2020).

Even so, we've also seen evidence of how place-based diagnostic frames can occasionally extend across party lines. Consider, for example, what it sounded like to be a Democrat in Motorville versus Lutherton in fall 2020: Hugh, Marie, and Kevin are lifelong Democrats from Lutherton (although Hugh and Marie were leaning toward defection by fall 2020) who wanted less federal relief because they felt "anyone who wants a job around here can get one" (Kevin) and "our country was built on small communities taking care of each other" (Hugh). And then there's Isabelle—not one of the younger progressive Democrats in Motorville; instead, a retiree—who said: "Until this gets straightened out, I think the government's going to have to foot the bill."

In sum, the national economic crisis of the Covid-19 pandemic did not produce convergence, in part because of entrenched lines of partisan division but also because it did not undermine local organizational contexts. As such, residents continued to deploy local diagnostic frames that told them what role the government should play in responding to the crisis, and those frames continued to "work"—in other words, there were no visible failures. But the pandemic also brought up a host of new issues, on which political elites polarized rapidly. Such polarization presents another potential threat to place-based partisanship, which the next chapter examines in detail.

7

The End of Place?

HOW THE NATIONALIZATION OF POLITICS SHAPES PLACE-BASED PARTISANSHIP

IN MID-SEPTEMBER 2020, the United States was facing the beginning of its third—and at that point deadliest—wave of Covid-19, which did not ease up until vaccines became widely available in spring 2021. At the same time, the country was hurtling toward the 2020 presidential election. And after several months of focusing on racial inequality after George Floyd's murder, the media's attention had turned back to the pandemic's progress. Then, on October 2, the politics of Covid-19 took another dramatic turn: President Trump and First Lady Melania Trump tested positive for the virus.

On that day I had a midafternoon phone call with Mary, a Democrat from Gravesend. We discussed how Covid was affecting life in Gravesend and how she felt Governor Walz had handled things in Minnesota, and finally I asked about President Trump, a topic I knew was a sore spot for her:

ST: How are you feeling these days about how the Trump administration has handled Covid?
MARY: I don't think the Trump administration has handled Covid. I think he has pushed it off. He admitted on tape [to Bob Woodward] that he was lying to the public. He knew how serious it was and he chose not to tell people how serious it was because he didn't want to cause a panic. I'm sorry [*she pauses, frustrated*]. I'm not using the language that is going through my head right now.
ST: You feel like the Trump administration really hasn't done much of anything?

MARY: Well, I don't think they have done enough and I don't think they have done the right things. I think he has politicized this. He helps the governors in favorable states politically to him and criticizes the governors in the states that are led by Democrats and the cities where the mayors are Democratic. He's done nothing but criticize the way they've handled things. He pits the governors against each other to get personal protective equipment. They were in bidding wars with providers because he set it up that way. He said, "Go get it yourself."

Mary's response is overwhelmingly typical of what I heard from other Democrats at that time, regardless of where they lived—in their view, the Trump administration had abdicated responsibility for taking care of the country. Many, like Mary, expressed concerns about Trump's delayed response to the pandemic, which he famously discussed on tape with journalist Bob Woodward, who then published his comments just a few days before I spoke to Mary. Others were similarly angry because Trump appeared to politicize the response, failed to listen to experts, or, as Mary tells me, pushed responsibility onto the states. Among the Democrats I spoke to on the eve of the 2020 election, President Trump's handling of the pandemic was a complete and utter failure. Even as many were also angered or saddened by his response to George Floyd's murder, it was in these remarks about the pandemic that their sense of abandonment came through more clearly than at any other time during the previous eighteen months.

About a week and a half later, I talked to Veronica, a Republican from Lutherton. I asked her the same question I'd posed to Mary, and she responded:

Again, it's similar . . . with the governor. It's very difficult, I think, trying to strike that balance of protecting us as individuals but not totally destroying our economy because in essence, our economy is part of taking care of us too with our livelihood. Overall, I think he did the best he could—as anybody could have done. I don't know that anyone else would've done anything better or different. . . . I think he tried to lean on the medical professionals to help guide him through that. Even some of them, I know there's a lot of controversy on who's the most, I guess, knowledgeable on what we should be doing. I think it changes every day because they're learning more about it. I think they did the best they could, honestly. If a Democrat would've been in there, I would've not been one to be overly critical because I just don't know how a president can really control the virus.

Veronica's response, like Mary's, is typical of what I heard from her co-partisans at the time: the pandemic was a challenging situation that any leader would have struggled to address, given trade-offs between public health and economic health; Trump "tried to lean on the medical professionals" and listen to the experts, but there was disagreement over who the true experts were; and in the end, it was hard to judge him critically because "I just don't know how a president can really control the virus." In other words, the president did not abdicate responsibility—stopping a virus wasn't his responsibility to begin with.

———

In the preceding chapter we saw how national economic crisis did not destabilize local organizational contexts, enabling residents to continue answering questions about the scope of federal intervention by drawing on preexisting diagnostic frames about how to solve social problems. But other threats to place-based partisanship loom on the horizon. Mary's and Veronica's comments indicate one: that individual partisans will be drawn out of their cities' organizationally embedded communication networks and into a national media environment that focuses their attention on issues such as those publicized by Bob Woodward.

This kind of process was a threat to place-based partisanship long before the pandemic—not just because local associations have been in decline for several decades but because social media and other forms of digital communication appear to be erasing the distinctiveness of the local, weaving an invisible web of transnational connections that blurs the boundaries of physical geography.[1] As local media outlets disappear or cut their budgets and Americans get more news online, the public has less knowledge about local politics and tends to fall back on partisanship to guide them in state and local voting decisions.[2] Moreover, these processes are accelerating: in 2018, for the first time, social media outpaced print media as a primary news source for Americans. And in 2020, with the Covid-19 pandemic racing through the country, political campaigns shied away from in-person canvassing operations, relying increasingly on digital strategies to get out the vote.[3]

Such changes seem to leave little role for local experiences in shaping Americans' political identities or behavior. According to political scientist Daniel Hopkins (2018), the result is indeed an increasing nationalization of American politics, in which the two political parties have "national brands" that mean the same thing to people regardless of where they live or the level of government at which they are seeking office. Taking this argument to the extreme, it means that a Democrat would never vote for a Republican, and vice versa, even for dog catcher.[4]

But as Motorville, Lutherton, and Gravesend have already shown, this nationalization argument only captures part of the story. Residents' votes are indeed tied closely to their partisanship, a relationship that largely holds at the local level. This was clear when I canvassed in Lutherton for the Democratic mayoral candidate in 2019 and found that Republicans were just as likely to say something along the lines of "Democrats are baby-killers" when I told them about the candidate as they were to recall her well-known family name and view her as distinct from the national Democratic Party. And yet, as preceding chapters have also shown, residents of Motorville, Lutherton, and Gravesend tend to disagree about what it means to be a Democrat or Republican.

In other words, while residents of these cities are subject to the same nationalizing impulses as are other Americans, there is reason to doubt that these changes will completely erase the role of place in shaping their politics. But thus far, we have only encountered residents in "settled times," as in part 2, or when they confront issues to which they can apply existing diagnostic frames, as in chapter 6.[5] This chapter thus takes up perhaps the most pressing threat to the future of place-based partisanship: how individuals form opinions on *novel* national issues. Why might this be a threat? If residents self-select into a national media environment that confirms their partisan biases, then routinely form partisan opinions on new issues, this may lead all co-partisans to care about the same issues and view the parties in the same way.[6] Democrats in Motorville and Lutherton would no longer sound as different as they did in chapters 3, 4, and 6.

In what follows, I examine the extent to which this occurs in Motorville, Lutherton, and Gravesend using the case of novel public health issues raised during the Covid-19 pandemic. I show that, while strong partisans did polarize *temporarily* on issues related to Covid-19 containment strategies—typically by following national news outlets—these new opinions emerged alongside, rather than in place of, the narratives of community identity that they use to situate themselves within national party politics. And as the national media moved on to other concerns, residents moved on as well.

What does this mean for place-based partisanship? Because the media does not undermine the place-processes that sustain local cultural frameworks, it does not undermine place-based partisanship: by the eve of the 2020 election, Motorville residents were still workers who wanted the Democratic Party to level the playing field; Lutherton residents were still Christians in a community that takes care of itself and favors the Republican Party; and Gravesenders were still threatened by immigration and socialism, tending toward a Republican Party that seemed to echo that sentiment.

Emplacing the Public Health Crisis

I began many of my conversations in spring 2020 by asking residents how their communities were handling the Covid-19 pandemic, and many people weren't sure—they'd been holed up inside for days or weeks, trying to protect themselves and their families. But others offered detailed responses. Just as they always had, residents of all three places continued to learn about their cities through local news, social media, and—even during the pandemic—in-person observations.

In those early days of fear and uncertainty in March and April 2020, many people I spoke to explained that they used the time gained from forgone work commutes or shortened work hours to stay up to date on the virus's spread within their states and counties. They tuned into local news outlets that reported case counts, hospitalizations, and deaths. Lutherton residents, for example, proudly reported that they had yet to have a death by late April; in Gravesend, residents noted that the quick jump from zero to thirty cases in early to mid-April had been largely confined to a residential treatment facility; and in Motorville, people assured me that their first few cases had all been out in the county, carried in by people traveling from out of state. Amanda, for example, is a Democrat from Gravesend who could cite chapter and verse the state of the virus in Minnesota when we spoke in late April:

> Minnesota has seen an increase, although I don't think today was a new high. The past two days were new highs, though I don't think with a new high in deaths, which is good. That's a good thing. But the two previous days, I think we had beaten the record beforehand for a number of deaths in a day.

Like Amanda, many people learned about the virus's progress through their cities and states via their governors' daily press conferences. But as was the case prior to the pandemic, they also learned about local developments from social media, particularly Facebook. Lutherton's mayor even began posting daily Covid case counts on his official Facebook page.

Nearly universally, interviewees described dedicating more time than usual to consuming news, particularly state and local news, so that they could collect accurate information about the pandemic's course. This tapered off after a few months: by the fall, few people were following the pandemic's progress as closely as they had been in the spring, nor were they as attuned to local case counts. But for a brief period of physical isolation, state and local news became a much more regular feature of many people's lives than it ever had been.

In some ways, residents of Motorville, Lutherton, and Gravesend were more emplaced than ever. Many residents also described being hypervigilant about their neighbors' reactions to the pandemic. Early on, people described the frenzied dash for toilet paper and other basics that emptied shelves in supermarkets across the country. Kevin, for example, is the assembly line supervisor from Lutherton whom we heard from in chapter 6, describing the local economy as recovered. But on March 20, as he sat in his car parked outside the Home Depot, he was not so assured. As he described the crowded parking lot and his recent challenges finding flour and ground beef, I could almost hear him shaking his head. He went on:

> There's a guy that works for me and he was like, "Hey, I need a vacation day tomorrow." And I always like to ask 'em what they're doing. I was like, "So, what are you gonna do man? Anything fun?" He's like, "No, I want to get"—he has five kids. He's like, "I want to get to Wal-Mart early and make sure I get what I need." And I thought, oh my God, you have to take a vacation day to go to Wal-Mart now. And he sent me a picture. I'll send it to you later. But it's Wal-Mart at 7 o'clock in the morning and there's like forty people in line. It's like Black Friday. But they're trying to buy like milk and eggs and shit. Like you can't find eggs.

At that point, Kevin's company had yet to shut down their operations, and his voice was dripping in anxiety over the entire situation: that people had to ask for days off to get eggs; that he had to field questions about public health issues from his workers that he could not possibly answer; that he had to have his temperature scanned on the way into the facility each morning; that he had to go into work at all when the other plants in town had closed. His response was not uncommon at the time across all three cities: a mix of anxiety and fear, focused on the most visible sign of the pandemic's reach into the city—a long line at the Wal-Mart.

Within a few weeks, the focus of that anxiety had shifted from bare shelves to neighbors' mask-wearing, but the principle remained the same: through some combination of in-person observations during limited trips to the supermarket, extra attentiveness to local news, and scans of neighbors' posts on Facebook, residents of all three cities got a sense of how their neighbors were responding to the pandemic. For example, when I ask Rose how she thinks Motorville is doing in May 2020, just after Governor Evers's stay-at-home order in Wisconsin was overturned by the state Supreme Court, she offers a response that exemplifies how these overlapping communication flows kept residents tied into their cities amid the pandemic. As she tells me:

ROSE: The governor's stay-at-home order was overturned by the Wisconsin Supreme Court. And I realize, if you have been unemployed for the last, whatever, six weeks, two months, it has taken a financial toll on you. But I think because people are in such dire circumstances, they feel, we've got to restart the economy right now. But it was ironic because on the local newspaper, front-page picture was a bar in Motorville already last night that had patrons in it.

ST: Oh, wow.

ROSE: If you go on Facebook and—you know, I'm not reading all of it 'cause I don't want to waste time. It's just depressing. I mean, everyone, of course, is adding their two cents. And regardless of what side of the fence they're on, they're very passionate in how they feel. And no matter what one would say to the other, I think one's feelings are so ingrained, no way would they change their mind.

ST: Right. Right. So you're seeing people on Facebook fighting over whether or not people should be going to the bars right now?

ROSE: Right. And let's just say it's maybe fifty-fifty. People are saying, you're endangering the health of others. No way would I go out. Other people are saying, it's about time. It's long overdue. Our freedoms have been stripped. You're hearing both sides.

In this conversation, Rose explains how she saw an image in a local newspaper that she then read about on Facebook. We also saw this in chapter 6, as many people I spoke to described learning about local service provision through Facebook. In other words, even as Covid-19 altered so many rhythms of daily life that had connected residents in these places, they continued to hear about their cities through many of the same mechanisms as they had previously.

Individual Partisan Polarization

It was during this period of heightened local focus in the earliest days of the pandemic that a moment of consensus about public health policies emerged, much like the consensus on federal fiscal policy that we saw in chapter 6. It wasn't just that residents of all three cities agreed—sometimes reluctantly—to adjust their own behaviors for the sake of public health or that they approved of the stimulus but also that they were worried about both public and economic health in the same breath. In fact, it was overwhelmingly common that when I asked people how concerned they were about the pandemic in March and early April, they would—without prompting—run through a list of their concerns for public health, personal health, the economy in the abstract, and their own personal finances.

Rose offers an example of this. She is the Democrat from Motorville whom we just heard describe her reaction to the lifting of Wisconsin's stay-at-home orders in May 2020. Two months prior to that conversation, in mid-March, we spoke on the phone as Governor Evers contemplated imposing those stay-at-home orders, and businesses in the city were already closing their doors. As she said: "Our life will be changed for a long time, especially up here where a lot of the jobs are paycheck to paycheck. There are so many people now without jobs and it's only going to get worse." This was not an indication of her lack of support for containment measures. As she went on to say, she and her husband were being particularly cautious because they lived with her elderly mother. "The last thing I want to do is expose my mother to anything," she explained. As Rose's example indicates, residents during these early days understood the pandemic as a dual challenge: to both the economy, including their personal finances, and public health, including their own. And this was true regardless of where they lived or what party they preferred.

In other words, public health and economic prosperity were not understood to be in opposition to one another. But already by my conversations in late April and May, this consensus had shifted. A sizable contingent of people I spoke with—those who were most politically sophisticated and regularly tuned into national news—had begun thinking along partisan lines: consistent with survey evidence, Republicans in my sample favored reopening sooner to protect the economy and Democrats favored extending stay-at-home orders to protect public health.[7] In sum, they had polarized rapidly. And they did so by many of the same pathways that lead to greater nationalization in American politics: self-selecting into a news environment that confirmed their partisan biases.

Many Republicans I spoke to in April and May expressed their readiness for reopening by explaining: "we can't stay locked down forever." In late April, for example, Fred described how he wanted Governor Holcomb of Indiana to approach the issue of reopening the economy:

Well, I think the governor has to talk to his experts and see what is going on in the state. And I think what he's gonna do is do a partial opening of the state. And I don't think that's too soon. I think, the longer we wait, the more damage is gonna be done. You can only run so far on the gas tank when the needle's on empty. And I think that's where we're runnin' right now, as far as the economy is concerned.

Fred is not opposed to the governor listening to "his experts"; in fact, he told me the month before that he wanted officials to follow the "scientific approach" in addressing the pandemic. But after a month of stay-at-home orders, he had begun to feel that scientific expertise had to be balanced with economic considerations.

Jeff, a Republican farmer from Gravesend, took this sentiment even further. As he told me during our conversation in late April: "I'm not concerned about the virus at all. Maybe 5, 10 percent of my thought is questioning how dangerous it is. You know, I know it's pretty contagious, but there's lots of things I figure are contagious. I'm more concerned about collapsing the economy and destroying a whole way of life here." Facing financial devastation as a result of the collapsing grain market, Jeff could only focus on the economic costs of the pandemic.

On the flip side, many Democrats like Isabelle from Motorville hoped that the government's response would prioritize public health. For her and others, the trade-offs from opening the economy could not be balanced by any economic gain. As she told me in mid-May after the state was summarily reopened by the Supreme Court:

> I'm just anxious for the election to happen . . . I thought we were gonna have some messed-up policies we were gonna have to fix—the environment's pretty much on the edge and if we had another four years, it might be too late for the environment. But I thought we could still. . . . We could still fix it. You can't fix dead people. And that's what's happened now.

Thus, despite the novelty and complexity of the issue, partisans like Jeff and Isabelle came to opposing views on what was at stake as the government responded to the pandemic. For Isabelle, the issue was not just health but keeping people alive—"You can't fix dead people"—she tells me; while for Jeff, it was not just the economy but small-town ways of life—"I'm more concerned about collapsing the economy and destroying a whole way of life here," he says.

To reach these opposing conclusions, partisans like Isabelle and Jeff quickly perceived and accepted the terms of the debate over pandemic policies (as a trade-off between health and the economy); simultaneously deduced which party supported each side by watching partisan news (MSNBC for Isabelle and Fox News for Jeff); and followed their party's position in forming opinions.[8] The result by the time of the November 2020 presidential election was that partisans, regardless of place, had reached starkly different conclusions about President Trump's handling of the pandemic, as we saw with Mary and Veronica at the beginning of the chapter.

This outcome suggests a possible pathway to the slow erosion of place-based partisanship: if residents are turning toward national, partisan-leaning media as their primary form of political information gathering and then developing opinions in line with the national parties, the place-based variation within partisans that we saw in parts 1 and 2 will eventually disappear. Democrats in Motorville would, eventually, be no different from Democrats in Lutherton.

Nationalization or the Same-Old Place-Based Politics?

But this was not what I observed over the course of four interviews, a pandemic, mass mobilizations for racial justice, and a contentious presidential election. Instead, elite-led issue polarization created individual-level variation (people who consumed partisan news tended to polarize, while others did not) as well as temporal variation (at various points in time, partisan residents of each city might disagree about any number of issues, based on what was in the news). But what stayed the same were the place-based cultural frameworks that told residents what kind of community they are, what their problems are, and where they fit into party politics.

We can observe this temporal variation by looking at how residents responded to questions about the top two or three issues they cared most about—which I asked in three interviews between June 2019 and November 2020. During my first interviews, immigration was a concern for people regardless of where they lived or how they voted: 50 percent of Democrats and 42 percent of Republicans mentioned it as a top issue for them. By fall 2020, the corresponding figures were 6 percent for Democrats and 17 percent for Republicans. Even Covid followed a similar trajectory—spiking as a public health concern for Republicans in spring 2020, then disappearing almost entirely and reemerging as a question of the country's economic well-being by the fall.

This also means that, each time I spoke to them, Republicans and Democrats—regardless of place, to an extent—often appeared sharply divided on issues they had not mentioned just a few months prior. For example, on the eve of the 2020 election, Democrats were overwhelmingly worried about five buckets of issues: protecting or improving government programs, including maintaining Social Security and expanding affordable health care (89 percent); mitigating class inequalities through living wage laws and redistributive programs (56 percent); mitigating racial inequalities, often through police reform (47 percent); climate change (39 percent); and the Covid-19 pandemic (39 percent). Republicans, in contrast, showed some degree of consensus (> 30 percent) in their concern about three buckets of issues: religious/moral issues, including abortion and electing conservative justices to the Supreme Court (43 percent); economic recovery, including "getting people back to work" and not imperiling the economy by a return to strict pandemic containment measures (43 percent); and reforming social programs and limiting the tax burden on the middle class (39 percent). These differences summarize the changes I observed quite well: after about seven months of the pandemic and a summer of mass political mobilization against racial inequality, Democrats—regardless of place—were living in a world where the country faced a dire public health crisis and a simmering racial reckoning, while Republicans were living in a world where the biggest threat to the country was anything that might destabilize economic recovery.

But these concerns about racial inequality and Covid-19 issues had displaced earlier worries about immigration and health care, as we saw above. Moreover, just a year later in summer 2021, both the pandemic and the Black Lives Matter protests had also receded from residents' list of concerns. In other words, this kind of issue polarization was temporary—even if new national issues evoked intense responses from participants during one interview, they were likely to have forgotten about it by the next.

But perhaps most important, beneath these shifts in issue concerns, the narratives of community identity that sustain partisanship in Motorville and Lutherton remained: Democrats from Motorville were worried about expanding government programs for the purpose of leveling the playing field, and Republicans from Lutherton were worried about reforming government programs and protecting the unborn. In sum, residents were overwhelmingly consistent in how they understood the political parties and which one best represented a community like theirs.

To illustrate this, consider how Jamie from Motorville thinks about what the two political parties represent. Jamie is the young woman we heard from in chapter 6, describing her concerns for her coworkers who were furloughed because of Covid. She considers herself to be a progressive Democrat and is an ardent supporter of Elizabeth Warren. The first time we met in late

June 2019, sitting in a coffee shop on Motorville's Main Street, I asked her: "So to you, what does the national Democratic Party stand for?" Jamie replies:

> Well, I think they stand for, I don't want to say like the little guy, because it's not necessarily the case, but they stand for the people, I guess they stand for—They're working toward making it so everybody can go toward that, you know, the American dream or whatever. Where, you know, it feels a lot like Republicans are like, "I can go toward the American dream," whereas *Democrats are everybody* . . . they want everybody to be able to—to enjoy the wealth of life, as it were [emphasis added].

In this example, Jamie articulates the common belief among Motorvillians I met that Democrats are the party to fight for the workers, the disadvantaged, "the little man." Republicans are just for themselves—"I can go toward the American dream," she imagines them saying. And in contrast, Democrats are "for the people."

About eight months later, in March 2020, Jamie and I are on the phone and I pose a slightly different question: "So what do you think is the biggest difference between the two political parties?" She responds similarly:

> JAMIE: I think it seems like a lot of the Republican motivations are very internally motivated, whereas the Democratic motivations are more generally all-people-motivated . . . not necessarily Republicans who are running for office or in office or anything like that, but like the ones that I talked to just generally in life: "How is this going to affect me personally?" Versus: "how is this going to affect the community as a whole?" I get a lot of guys [where I work] who complain about their personal paying out in taxes. And it's like, well, yeah, but, you know you pay for schools right now. Right? That's a thing that you are doing. So it's sort of almost like a cognitive dissonance between like, if it doesn't directly impact them, then they can't see what the use is.
>
> ST: And whereas you feel like Democrats . . . ?
>
> JAMIE: The Democrats are more like—don't get me wrong, I am fully aware that Democrats, politicians are going to be politicians no matter what side they're on. But it's sort of, you may or may not be able to think of some of the way that it affects you personally, but that doesn't mean that it's something that you shouldn't be doing.

In this instance, Jamie again articulates the notion that Republicans are selfish, focused on taxes as something being taken from them, while Democrats are more focused on "the community as a whole," and part of that entails thinking about how their taxes are a part of their duty as citizens—as she says, helping pay for schools.

And finally, in October 2020, I ask the same question I asked more than fifteen months prior—"What do you think the Democrats stand for?"—to which Jamie responds:

> JAMIE: I think that what they want to project that what they're about is for the people. It's a little bit vague, but like they're about helping everybody and not just the wealthy, the White, that kind of thing. I think that's what they're trying to project—now whether or not I agree with them, [if] they actually match their words . . .
>
> ST: Got you. So, then the Republicans, what do they stand for?
>
> JAMIE: [*laughter*] At this point, they stand for clinging to their desperate dying power to do what they want. Again, they put forth that we're here to protect the hardworking Americans who earn their money, it's like, "Do you though?" Because I think at this point, it's very clear that they are ruled by the almighty dollar.

In similar terms to those she uses throughout our conversations—in response to both these questions and others about political divisiveness, the biggest challenges to the country, and her concerns about the pandemic—Jamie again articulates the notion that Republicans "are ruled by the almighty dollar" while Democrats are "about helping everybody and not just the wealthy, the White . . ."

Even as Jamie's understanding of the parties extends to more explicitly incorporate her renewed concerns about racial inequality in the wake of Black Lives Matter protests after George Floyd's murder, it doesn't destabilize her core beliefs about what's at stake in national party politics. This was true of almost every Democratic Motorvillian I spoke to in fall 2020: because they understand Democrats as the party that should fight for "the little guy" on multiple axes—race, class, gender, and sexuality—race and class were not at odds as the organizing principles of their politics. As such, they tended to incorporate race more explicitly into their understanding of partisan divisions after the Black Lives Matter protests (although some did this before, as we saw from Isaac in chapter 4).

In other words, Jamie's understanding of partisan divisions is overwhelmingly stable—even if it's "a little bit vague," as she says in our last conversation, and even as she questions Democratic politicians' commitment to the cause. As is typical of Motorvillians I spoke to, Jamie does not see the process of paying taxes to expand government intervention as solely an unjust benefit for others but as a universal duty and benefit.

And although I focus at length on Jamie here, I do so because the stability she evinces was the norm among participants in Motorville and Lutherton, where local organizational contexts are stable. There were a handful of cases in which residents' understanding of the parties shifted during the course of our conversations—in Marie's particularly rare case, described in chapter 4, this resulted in a shift in partisan identity. But her shift was in the direction of conforming with place-based cultural frameworks. As such, the evidence suggests that residents' consumption of partisan media does not destabilize the organizational and cultural factors that create distinct place-based partisan ties in Motorville and Lutherton: how residents see themselves and their communities fitting into the political system.

———

In an era of increasingly nationalized political parties and media coverage, we may think it's time to do away with the old adage "all politics is local" and replace it with a new one: "all politics is partisan." But as we have seen from Motorville and Lutherton, place-based partisanship is relatively durable—it can survive even national crises, partisan media, and polarization on controversial national issues. When we look across each of the chapters that examined possibilities for change in place-based partisanship (chapters 1, 5, 6, and 7) it becomes clear that nationalizing forces are *most threatening* when they undermine the local organizational context, ultimately shifting local cultural frameworks. This process of local-national interaction—rather than partisan media—is what has produced a growing trend toward Republicanism in Gravesend, as we saw in chapter 5.

This is not to say that national media have no effect on local politics: as we have seen residents' concerns about new issues spiked with national media attention. But this did not displace their place-based partisanship: their narratives of community identity persisted over the course of eighteen months of fieldwork, four interviews, a life-altering pandemic, months of mobilization against racial violence by police, and a historically contentious presidential campaign. This suggests that elite-led issue polarization—although consequential for other political outcomes—is somewhat epiphenomenal to place-based partisanship. While Lutherton residents (particularly Republicans) may have forcefully disagreed with Motorvillians (particularly Democrats) about Covid containment strategies during summer and fall 2020, those issues eventually faded from their list of concerns. Already, when I returned to Motorville, Lutherton, and Gravesend to check in with several residents in summer 2021, the conversation had shifted to new topics.

In fact, while residents might be polarized on any number of issues at any given moment, focusing on this kind of issue polarization distracts from the social processes that sustain their orientation toward politics. For social scientists and political observers who are concerned about the consequences of mass polarization for a well-functioning democracy, this suggests that we need to shift the object of analysis away from documenting the ever-growing quantity of issues on which Americans may be polarized and refocus our attention on the forces that provide order to Americans' social lives, reinforcing the ways they make sense of party politics and their place in it.

Conclusion

THE FUTURE OF HEARTLAND POLITICS

IN AUGUST 2021, the 2020 presidential election was in the rearview mirror, Joe Biden was installed in the White House, and the Covid-19 pandemic had briefly receded from center stage amid the widespread availability of vaccines. That month, I spoke to Isaac from Motorville. Isaac is a Democrat who, during every single conversation we had from October 2019 through the November 2020 presidential election, was preoccupied with protecting the working and middle classes. Even more specifically, he was preoccupied with the Trump administration's 2017 tax cuts, which symbolized to him everything that was wrong with American politics: the legislation wielded government power to exacerbate economic inequality rather than mitigate it. So it was somewhat unsurprising when, in summer 2022, he returned again to the 2017 tax cuts in response to a question about the infrastructure bill that was, at that time, up for debate in Congress. At first, he explained his support, saying: "I wish it was bigger, but I mean, I hope they can pass something. I, you know, it'll be good for American workers, and obviously it'll be good for people that are invested in the stock market. It'll be good for the economy and for the stock market, I think in general. So yeah, I wish it was bigger." But then he went on to describe his frustration with those who oppose the bill and other social spending measures that had been floated by the Biden administration. As he said:

> Well I mean, people talk like we can't afford that. And I'm not saying that
> we can, but in 2017. . . . You know, they call those middle-class tax cuts. I
> mean, those weren't middle-class tax cuts. The corporate tax rate got
> dropped from 35 percent to 21 percent and the top tax bracket got dropped
> from . . . I want to say, 39 percent to 37.5 percent. . . . And the nonpartisan

Congressional Budget Office said that that's gonna add 1.7 trillion dollars to the national debt. Somehow, we could afford that and you know, 83 percent of that, or 84, 85 percent, they said, is gonna go to the richest 1 percent of the country. We can afford that, but we can't afford an infrastructure bill. . . . You know, it was the largest upward transfer of wealth. I mean, we can afford that, but we can't afford infrastructure.

Over the course of the two years during which we spoke on five separate occasions, Isaac's politics were unperturbed—despite the pandemic and a change in presidential administration. Not only did the broad brushstrokes of Motorville's working-class politics remain intact, but the specific experiences from which Isaac drew political meaning were the same. He learned a lesson from the 2017 tax cuts, one that resonated with his worldview so much that he returns to it again and again as a central political touchstone. The same was true of so many people I met in Motorville and Lutherton, and to a lesser extent in Gravesend.

But some things had changed by summer 2022. Just before I spoke to Isaac, I returned to Lutherton. Although it would be impossible to know the city had just survived an ongoing global catastrophe, some things had changed: a new café had opened up at the end of Main Street, and a handful of other businesses had shuttered. But the biggest difference was in what was top-of-mind for certain residents: critical race theory (CRT). Larry was among these residents. He is a retired educator and Republican. When I asked him if he had any new concerns about the community since we'd last spoken, he at first answered no, but then replied:

> Two of our school board members are members of our church. We have a country church. Lutherton is a pretty good-size school system. And I just made a comment to both of them that I would. . . . Hopefully they are aware of CRT . . . I simply say that, as I see it, from what I hear, I would not prefer that any of our students—I was a teacher for forty years. That was not my job [preaching politics]. Nobody knew—I did mock elections and everything all those years. No one knew my party right. Because I think it's important. I resent professors, teachers who are out there to do that [preach politics]. . . . That's [the job of] parents in their home.

Later in the conversation, when I asked if there was anything else we hadn't discussed yet that was concerning him, Larry again returned to the issue of critical race theory and his concerns about forcing this kind of education on members of the military and on public schoolchildren. From there, he continued, linking concerns about CRT to his other worries about race, education, and socialism in America:

> Another philosophy I have, is that six hundred thousand people died in the Civil War, and let's just say it's half-and-half, three hundred and three hundred. There were three hundred [thousand] White Northern people fighting to free the slaves, and they want to turn that history around as if. . . . That 1619 project, whatever it is, of changing the whole philosophy of the Civil War. And let me keep going. I'm on it now. And it's the fact that all this stuff, taking down statues and all that. There's a socialistic background in that. That's happened in all the nations that [socialism] ever happened. What you do, you tear down the history of the past. So there isn't that. And then you develop your own, which is your way. And then you go after the nuclear family and you go after the kids and their education system. And here we go. We're on a fast track to places I don't want to go.

Although questions of socialism, education, and the nuclear family were not new to my conversations with Larry, critical race theory certainly was. But as these examples indicate, it was a clear preoccupation for him in July 2022: he mentioned it in response to two extremely open-ended questions about his community and his current concerns about the world. He also articulated fairly well-developed opinions on the subject and linked it back to many of his preexisting political beliefs about American families and the appropriate scope of the state. Those beliefs did not change, but they expanded to incorporate this new set of concerns, much like what we saw with people's beliefs about Covid-19 mitigation measures in chapter 7.

A Theory of Place-Based Partisanship

These conversations with Larry and Isaac evoke exactly the pattern of continuity and change that characterizes the present dynamics of place-based partisanship in Motorville and Lutherton, which are summarized in figures 1b and 1c: the structural and organizational dimensions of place lead residents to cohere around shared cultural frameworks, including diagnostic frames for solving social problems and narratives of community identity that tell them what kind of community they are and which party best represents them; these place-based frameworks produce and reproduce residents' partisan attachments and political beliefs over time, as we can see in Isaac's case here; and even as residents take up the party line on new issues, as Larry does with critical race theory, these concerns do not displace the cultural frameworks that reaffirm place-based partisanship. This is not to say that these new opinions aren't important to residents—as Larry's comments suggest, they may feel extremely pressing, even urgent or all-consuming, when they emerge; and they may also be consequential for political outcomes. But the key is that they do not undermine the local organizational contexts or cultural frameworks that sustain residents' place-based partisanship: Larry's new focus on CRT did not displace his thinking about what kind of community Lutherton is or how they solve problems; rather, it displaced his more recent concerns about Covid containment policies.

This account of how place helps sustain partisan attachments—even in an era of increasing national and global integration, partisan division, and media fragmentation—answers two of the central puzzles I set out to address at the beginning of this book: the present operation of place in American politics and its likely future. Place matters for White, working- and middle-class Americans because they are cross-pressured: their racial and class identities each point them in different partisan directions as both the Democratic and Republican Parties court their loyalties. In this situation, place raises the salience of certain social identities over others and helps residents figure out how to map those identities onto party politics. As we have seen throughout the book, this does not mean that social group memberships and national party politics don't matter for Americans' partisanship; rather, I have argued that place helps cross-pressured voters navigate within these constraints, guiding them toward one partisan affiliation over the other.

This argument implies that place should *also* be relevant for political identity formation among other cross-pressured social groups whose votes are sought by both parties, like Latinx voters. For example, there are important regional differences in Latinx political behavior, suggesting that place itself might explain why certain individuals are less likely to identify with Latinx as a singular social and political group and more likely to identify as Republicans.[1] In fact, García Bedolla (2005) shows that local ethnic cohesion does shape Latinx residents' political participation and identity.

But this argument does *not* imply that every place with the same organizational context will lead its residents toward the same party—the constraints imposed by social structural divisions and national party politics still matter here. For example, we should not expect that Black Americans living in a churchgoing community would join the Republican Party because they may—as do many of my interlocutors—understand the Republican Party as the party of White people. But even social group memberships, which I've described as "objective," are themselves politically constructed: racial and ethnic categories are not transhistorical but shaped through the interaction of state policy, party tactics, and social movement mobilization.[2] As such, it is possible that over time the parties may work to create new social cleavages that support their electoral strategies, and the relationship between place, social groups, and partisan attachments may shift.

But perhaps the best argument for why place still matters is that it can provide a vital source of informal political knowledge for people who otherwise struggle to get a grasp on the slippery truths of contemporary partisan politics.[3] Remember what we heard from voters like Quinn, Linda, and Marie—people who repeatedly told me that they didn't know much about politics, didn't watch the news, and didn't know which news sources they could trust. As I later learned, this widespread distrust in media made it difficult for them to form opinions during the Covid-19 pandemic. This uncertainty resulted in some people, like Ben from Gravesend, concluding: "I feel like I'm unable to comment on the coronavirus hardly." Ben made this comment in May 2020—at the height of a global crisis that was receiving nonstop media attention. But his distrust of media made him wary of how to interpret the conflicting accounts he found in the media, landing him in a place of non-opinion. And yet, none of the residents I spoke to, regardless of their distrust in media, lacked all information about the political world: for example, Quinn, Linda, Marie, and Ben all learned from experience or conversation about which party represented which groups of people, even if they were uncertain about it. And as we saw in Linda's case in chapter 4, some of that uncertainty was actually a kind of false modesty: when her husband, Peter, told her she was wrong, she doubled down, insisting that what she told me was right because it reflected her own experience. And if figuring out which party represents which social group is how many Americans form their partisan attachments, then the fact that place can help them learn this means that it has a vital role to play in contemporary political outcomes.[4]

My theory of place-based partisanship suggests that place matters most among social groups that are cross-pressured, and among individuals who are uncertain about which party represents their group, but what does it tell us about the *kinds of places* that matter more or less for their residents' politics? A key piece of my argument about how place sustains partisan attachments is via residents' routine observations of problem-solving and social interaction within their cities. This means that place should also matter for residents' politics in suburbs or neighborhoods of cities with long-term residents, where many people buy homes, settle down for decades to raise children, participate in their schools, make friends at soccer games, and bake cookies for the church bake sale. But it may have less of an influence on residents' politics in places with exceptionally high levels of in- and out-migration. Although in-migration can actually bolster place character, extreme levels of transience may undermine it: in-migrants who do not engage at all with their new homes are unlikely to feel the effects of place, and if a community ultimately becomes full of transients, the distinctiveness of the place may deteriorate altogether. That said, these questions are still ripe for future research. For example, scholars might consider the kinds of places that we might expect to have the least effect on their residents' politics—perhaps city centers where young professionals move for short periods of time after college. Similarly, as rapidly growing suburbs and cities in the Southeast and Southwest become the new political battlegrounds, scholars should carefully consider the extent to which place is *acting on* the political behavior of new arrivals.

But the most ambitious lesson we can draw from Motorville, Lutherton, and Gravesend takes us even beyond the question of how place-based partisanship persists and toward the question of how social contexts sustain Americans' partisan attachments. This is of central importance to American political and social life, given that partisan attachments—once made—shape not only political decision making but romantic and economic behavior as well.[5] And while this book is a study of how place shapes the way people make sense of their social position and map that position onto the party system, my broader argument is that other forms of durable social organization are likely to play a similar role. Although we have plenty of evidence about how social contexts shape intergroup animosity, political participation, and even public opinion, rarely do these accounts extend to partisanship. This suggests that future research should examine the extent to which other elements of social context shape partisan attachments; for example, do social networks shape partisan ties, do partisan ties shape social networks, or both?

For now, what Motorville, Lutherton, and Gravesend have shown us is that for any of these factors to shape the formation of partisan identity, they must create durable social contexts that structure people's experiences in a way that helps them make sense of who they are, what their problems are, and how to resolve them through party politics.

From Motorville, Lutherton, and Gravesend to Heartland Politics

In sum, the many parallels across Motorville, Lutherton, and Gravesend, and among the people who live there, have provided a unique opportunity to understand how similar people can become different political subjects—not just through party elites' maneuvering or mass communication but through the social organization of their everyday lives. And for residents of Motorville, Lutherton, and Gravesend, a meaningful portion of that social organization is emplaced: their routines of work, leisure, social interaction, and associational life—even their social networks and engagement online—occur within a specific geographic area that is imbued with meaning for the people who live there. While an outsider might drive through each of these cities and write them off as just another small city in the American Heartland—with many of the same physical characteristics like struggling Main Streets, extensive corn fields, myriad churches, dilapidated housing, and sprawling industrial parks—residents take different lessons about who they are from living in each place.

This takes us back to the very first puzzle that this book has sought to resolve: how has the reddening of the American Heartland, as past and present process, been shaped by the interaction of local and extra-local forces? I arrived at Motorville, Lutherton, and Gravesend by searching for all the counties in the United States that had once been part of the White, working-class coalition that carried FDR to the White House four times and that remain overwhelmingly White and blue-collar. In effect, these cities are indicative of the kinds of places that were once at the heart of both U.S. manufacturing power and working-class politics. But among those New Deal counties, I found very few that still vote majority-Democratic. As that political coalition has broken down since the 1960s, Lutherton and Gravesend have followed two different but relatively common pathways toward the Republican Party. Motorville, in contrast, is a rare case where local processes have kept a White, postindustrial city in the Democratic Party.

As I have argued throughout this book, we can only make sense of the puzzle posed by Motorville, Gravesend, and Lutherton—and of the Heartland's reddening more generally—if we stop asking whether race, class, or religion is most important in shaping White voters' political behavior and start asking *in what contexts* are these voters more likely to understand social and political divisions as organized around race, class, or religion?

As we have seen in Motorville, place-based processes can be so powerful that they still hold White, working- and middle-class voters in a Democratic coalition that other members of their social group have been fleeing for decades, in search of the party that represents their racial or religious identities rather than their class-based ones. But in a social context like Motorville's, where unions are politically mobilized and active community leaders, class remains a salient organizing principle both socially and politically—one that is not in conflict with race. For people like Jamie in chapter 7, the Democrats are supposed to represent *all people* disadvantaged by systemic inequalities. In contrast, in a context like Gravesend, where local organizational breakdown has residents feeling there is no viable solution nor any local leadership trying to find one, residents feel their city's survival is under threat. The Republican Party's growing rhetoric around immigration and socialism as further threats to places like Gravesend resonates, pulling residents to the right on a tide of racialized populist resentment. Race also shapes Lutherton residents' Republicanism, but here it is less about racial resentment than ethnoreligious identity, as we saw in chapter 4.

In sum, to understand how national party politics reverberates down to individual voters, drawing them into working-class coalitions, ethnoreligious politics, or populist resentment, we have to understand how party maneuvering interacts with local ways of meaning-making.

But what can this local, contextual argument tell us about the prospects of reviving a national political coalition organized around class, like the one that existed (to some degree) during the New Deal? First, these cities indicate that the political mobilization of organized labor helps raise the salience of class identities and minimize feelings of racial threat among White voters. As we saw in Motorville, race and class are not at odds in residents' interpretation of party politics.

Second, this answer points us away from other mechanisms by which we might expect to cultivate class voting among White Americans. It suggests that social policy is probably not part of the equation. This is not to dissuade politicians from fighting for legislation that will improve the lives of America's working poor. But it is to say that this is probably not what will marshal people from Gravesend, and those like them, into a coalition with Motorvillians, advocating for government spending to benefit a cross-racial, working-class coalition. That's because Americans typically vote in line with their political party, and as we've seen throughout this book, they join a party based on their interpretation of their social group membership and the political content of that membership.[6] What social programs can do is increase voter turnout among their beneficiaries by increasing their resources, but this does not mean that those folks will go to the polls on behalf of the party that provided the benefit.[7] In fact, in other research projects, I've found that FDR's expansion of Old-Age Assistance programs during the New Deal cost him votes in elderly counties that had previously leaned Republican—in other words, he turned out the opposition.[8] If even a social program rolled out during the era of Democratic consolidation under the auspices of a pro-worker, pro–welfare state agenda did not mobilize welfare beneficiaries to their cause, it is unlikely that future social programs will have this effect.

These findings also suggest that political party maneuvering can only go so far in transforming White, working-class politics: since at least the 1960s, both parties have been vying for this voting bloc, leaving individuals to figure out which party best represents them and their kind of people. But Motorville, Lutherton, and Gravesend indicate that not all of these individuals— and not all White, postindustrial cities—will be susceptible to the same kind of political mobilization. In fact, the very notion of reviving a Motorville-style working-class politics may be inapplicable in places like Lutherton, where unions have taken a backseat in political life since the 1970s—recall that unions in Lutherton have been disengaged from local politics since that time, and they have also been disconnected from the regional and national umbrella organizations like the AFL-CIO that create a sense of labor movement identity among their members and involve them in both an economic and political project. In other words, as unions in Motorville discuss revitalization in the wake of the Scott Walker administration, they can only do so in reference to the historical legacy of labor organizing in the city; in a place like Lutherton, there is simply no corollary set of institutions or understandings to revive.

But in places like Gravesend—former union towns with some residents who are still part of unions, others who remember and have passed down the stories of unions' glory days, and a pool of potential leaders who believe in the power of unions as a mobilizing force for economic equality—such a revival is possible. One of the challenges, of course, will be how to build support for unions within the workplace. As Amazon's efforts to frighten and demobilize their workforce in Bessemer, Alabama, made clear in 2021, this is no small feat.[9] But part of my argument is that *community-wide* support for good jobs, good wages, and a better standard of living can actually be a source of support for unions within the workplace. This suggests that cities whose leadership engages with the politics of good jobs, the way Motorville's community leaders do, can create both a working-class politics that is not undermined by racial threat, as we saw in Motorville, and the social bases of support for unions that will further sustain this kind of politics in the future.

————

Motorville, Lutherton, and Gravesend are, in some ways, just three small cities. But my hope in writing this book is that they teach us lessons about American politics—both how we have gotten to this point in the ever-reddening American Heartland and where we might go from here. There is also a more subtle political message that I hope this text will convey: despite the fear, hatred, and resentment that motivate the most vitriolic scenes of American politics, like the January 6, 2021, insurrection at the Capitol, many of Americans' political differences are of a much more ordinary variety. They come from individuals' routine life experiences and the stories people tell themselves to make sense of those experiences. This fact should be front of mind when we speak across lines of political division—not because it makes people more persuadable; in fact, it may make them less so, because their beliefs are often deeply rooted in the way they experience their social and political worlds. Instead, the political differences among such similar people as those who live in Motorville, Lutherton, and Gravesend remind us that other people come to their political beliefs not for the purposes of disagreement or contention but because those beliefs make sense to them. They are the product of an often-invisible web of social organization, social structure, and party politics that weave all Americans into the polity.

Additional Figures Referred to in the Main Text

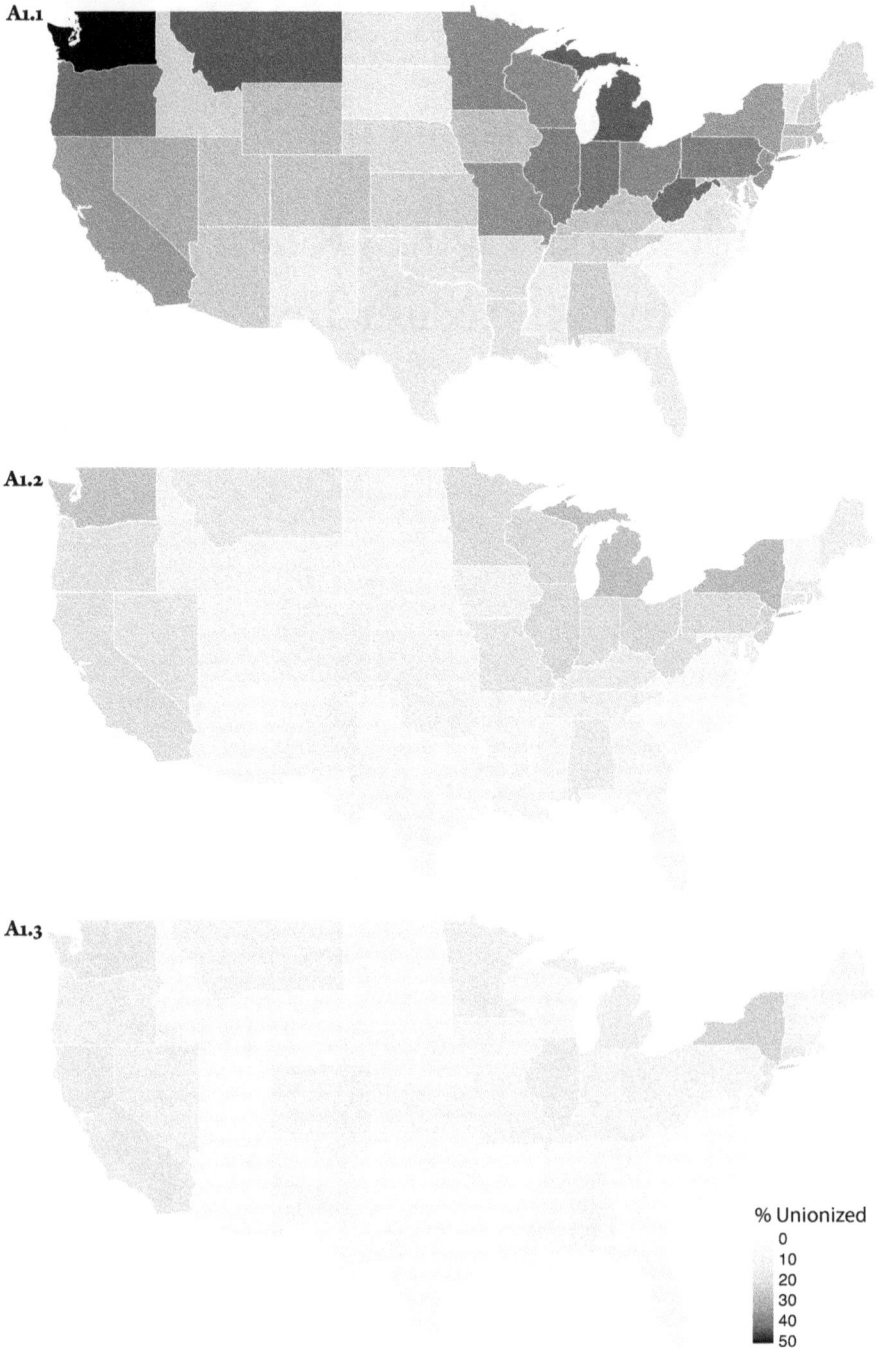

FIGURE A1 (*continued on next page*). Unionization by state in 1956, 1986, and 2016. Figure A1.1: 1956. Figure A1.2: 1986. Figure A1.3: 2016. *Note:* Union density data from 1965 to 2019 are from Hirsch, Macpherson, and Vroman's "Union Density Estimates by State, 1964–201" at unionstats.com. For information as to

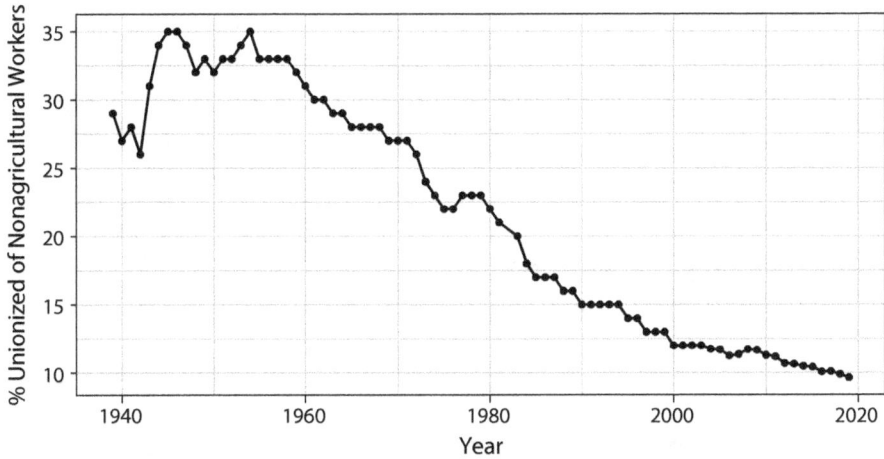

FIGURE A2. National trends in unionization, 1939–2019. *Note:* Union membership data from 2004 to 2019 are from Hirsch and Macpherson 2019. For information as to how they compiled the data, please see Barry T. Hirsch and David A. Macpherson, "Union Membership and Coverage Database from the Current Population Survey: Note," *Industrial and Labor Relations Review* 56, no. 2 (January 2003): 349–54 (updated annually at unionstats.com). Nonagricultural employed workers data from 2004 to 2019 are from the Bureau of Labor Statistics' Current Employment Statistics (CES) survey (https://www.bls.gov /ces/data/). Union density data from 1939 to 2003 are from Mayer 2004. Mayer also draws on Hirsch and Macpherson's data.

how they compiled the data, please see Barry T. Hirsch, David A. Macpherson, and Rob G. Vroman, "Estimates of Union Density by State," *Monthly Labor Review* 124, no. 7 (July 2001) (updated annually at unionstats.com). Union density data from prior to 1964 come from Leo Troy, "Extent of Union Organization, by State and Region, 1939 and 1953," in *Distribution of Union Membership among the States, 1939 and 1953* (Cambridge, MA: National Bureau of Economic Research, 1957), 17–27.

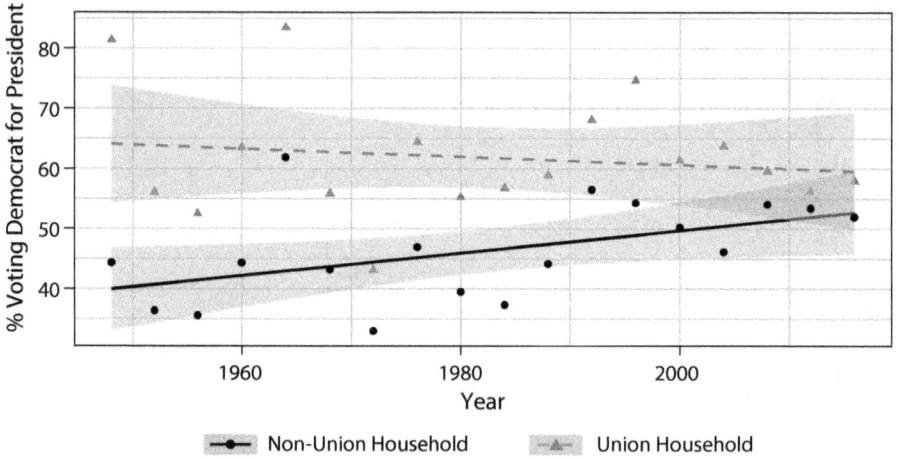

FIGURE A3. Democratic Party voting in union and non-union households, 1948–2016. *Note:* Data come from the American National Election Studies (ANES) Cumulative Timeseries file. In calculating percentages for each year, I have applied the appropriate weights.

Methodological Appendix

INTERVIEW AND ETHNOGRAPHIC
DATA COLLECTION AND ANALYSIS

I CHOSE MOTORVILLE, LUTHERTON, AND GRAVESEND because I wanted to study the contemporary ramifications of historical realignments that broke apart the White, working-class New Deal coalition. After I had identified the three clusters described in the introduction, I began by choosing Motorville from within the counties in the Democratic cluster, as there were far fewer Democratic counties than either swing or Republican counties. That helped winnow my options for choosing cases within the Republican and Lean Dem clusters, as I sought places that even more closely mirrored Motorville's size, density, and demographic composition.

Next, I presented a map of potential field sites to a working group of my colleagues in political science, asking if there were any theoretical reasons to prefer one county within the "Turned Republican" and "Lean Dem" clusters over another, when they were all so similar. One of the other graduate students excitedly pointed out that he had worked with the chair of the Republican Party in one of the counties. He offered to connect us, and then she offered to host me during my fieldwork. A similar happy coincidence led me to Gravesend. I had a list of several swing counties from which I could choose, and I sent out emails and Facebook messages to the Democratic and Republican Party chairs from the first county on the list. Soon after, I received an overwhelmingly enthusiastic phone call from the former chair of the Republican Party, who invited me to the picnic I described in the introduction—and who eventually invited me several times to stay on his farm during my fieldwork—and I decided to go there.

I did not design the study to examine place as an object of analysis; rather, I wanted to speak to White, working- and middle-class voters with different partisan attachments who may (under different historical conditions) have had the same partisan attachments, and I used aggregate voting statistics to locate them. When I began fieldwork and realized that place was a key piece of the reason for the individual-level variation I was interested in, I searched for work on the social and political meaning of place to help make sense of my findings. With key examples of this genre in hand—namely Molotch, Freudenburg, and Paulsen 2002 and Japonica Brown-Saracino's recent work (2015, 2018)—I realized that my study design in many ways mirrored theirs: comparing "like" places with different outcomes to identify the emergent properties of place that shape residents' social identities. Thus, while I did not intend for my study to imitate theirs, it's now clear that these kinds of Millsian paired comparisons are particularly fruitful for understanding how place operates in contemporary social and political life (per Paulsen 2004).

After identifying the three field sites, I made my initial connections in each place by emailing and Facebook messaging community leaders whose contact information was publicly available, as I describe in the introduction. I also asked residents to post on local Facebook community groups for me. I often met people just by spending time in public spaces: I never quite looked like I fit in in the city clothes I wore, as Elaine once told me, so I often received confused looks and, from some of the bolder residents, questions about who I was and what brought me to town. This rendered a handful of interviewees and some interesting ethnographic experiences. I particularly stood out during my morning swims at the YMCAs in Motorville and Gravesend, where I was usually the only person present below the age of sixty-five. Each time I made a connection with a resident or community leader, I asked to be introduced to friends, family, or acquaintances who would speak to me and who fulfilled certain characteristics I needed to balance out my samples. In particular, it helped me reach residents who don't watch the news and don't care much about politics (see Ternullo 2022b). It was also essential for my analyses that I spoke to both Democrats and Republicans (and both union members and churchgoers) in each field site. Although it did not prove difficult to recruit people in both organizations (for example, I met churchgoers in Motorville by chance, and union members in Lutherton by chance), it was difficult to meet Democrats in Lutherton. I found two through snowball sampling when I began asking people to introduce me to any Democrats they knew—one from the Republican Party chair who recalled a particularly obstinate Democratic constituent, and another through a candidate for City Council in 2019 who was a Republican but knew a coworker who was a Democrat. Table A1

TABLE A1. Sample Political and Demographic Characteristics

Political Characteristics (%)	Lutherton	Motorville	Gravesend
Democrat	20	54	44
Republican	63	13	31
Independent	17	25	25
If I/DK, % leans Republican	7	8	9
If I/DK, % leans Democrat	10	21	16
Don't know	0	8	0
Avg. political engagement[1]	2.6	2.5	2.9
Demographic Characteristics (%)			
Female	47	63	41
College graduate	53	50	53
Church member	87	25	75
Retired	23	21	41

[1]Respondents were ranked on a scale from 1–4, where: 1 = little sense of what differentiates the major parties, does not watch the news, may or may not vote; 2 = some sense of what differentiates the major parties, may watch the news, votes with regularity; 3 = knowledgeable about partisan differences, watches the news regularly; 4 = avidly attuned to politics.

describes the political and demographic characteristics of the samples in each field site.

Snowball sampling was essential to achieving a mix of political and demographic characteristics in each field site, but of course, it has its downsides. First, my sample is not representative of each city as a whole, nor is this the goal of qualitative sampling (Small 2009). Instead, as described above, I purposefully constructed a sample with sufficient variation across several theoretically important dimensions (partisanship, organizational affiliation, knowledge, and whether people lived, worked, attended school, or participated in organizations within the main city bounds or in the smaller outlying towns) such that I could see where place-based patterns did or did not extend to unexpected kinds of people. This also means that some of my interviewees knew each other; but as I snowballed from many different sources as well as recruited randomly and from flyers and Facebook posts, this was a small portion of my data.

After my initial interviews, I sent handwritten thank-you cards to all participants in the hopes that this would encourage them to participate in future interviews. Table A2 summarizes the interview timeline. I originally chose to

TABLE A2. Interview Timeline

Round 1 (June–October 2019)	78
Round 2 (February–April 2020)	71
Gravesend Covid 3b (April 2020)	4
Round 3 (April–June 2020)	66
Round 4 (September–November 2020)	66
Post-election undecideds (November–December 2020)	8
Summer 2021 follow-up (July–September 2021)	19
Total	312

include longitudinal interviews as part of the research design so that I could assess how residents responded to new issues that emerged during the 2020 presidential campaign. Although they did serve this purpose (see chapters 6 and 7), I also found that they were essential for theory building (Hoang 2018; Timmermans and Tavory 2012). This is because I was able transcribe and code all interviews between the first and second rounds, and then again between the third and fourth rounds. After taking a very inductive approach in the first round, I developed new questions to probe emergent patterns in the second round. At the same time, I introduced new questions about Covid-19 in the second and third rounds, which raised entirely new patterns about information gathering and processing during the Covid-19 pandemic (see Ternullo 2022b). I was similarly able to probe those more deductively in the fourth round. I also collected and coded local politicians' Facebook posts between the third and fourth rounds (see table A4 and figure A4) and used those to develop questions for the fourth-round interviews.

In addition to the semi-structured, longitudinal interviews that form the core of the data for this book, I learned a great deal about local life through more informal and ethnographic means. For example, it was during casual conversation among friends that I finally understood how devastating the loss of the supermarket was in Gravesend. I only participated in that conversation because I happened into a favorite coffee shop on my first morning back in town after several months away and was welcomed into the group I'd met a few months prior.

Although these unexpected moments often helped bring clarity to a puzzle I'd been grappling with, most of my argument stems from more direct efforts at triangulation. As I've noted throughout the book, a core analytic challenge for me was understanding how place was leading to these clear spots of coherence among the residents I interviewed. To figure this out, I often toggled back and forth between interviews with community leaders, objective data on social problems (per figures 5 and 6) and local organizations (from the Urban Institute or the Census of Local and State Governments), and what I found from my analysis of local newspapers and Facebook posts. For example, almost from the first moment I arrived in Lutherton, community leaders began telling me that churches were very important for local politics. Based on their own campaign experiences, churches were important because they provided large social networks that were crucial resources in elections. But this did not fit with what I heard from residents or observed during fieldwork. Only two people, among dozens of doors I knocked during canvassing in Lutherton's mayoral election, said they would vote for the Democratic candidate, Sondra, because they went to the same church as her husband. But even here, the role of church ties is ambiguous, because Sondra's husband attends the same church as the Republican candidate. In sum, the ways that leaders thought churches mattered didn't seem right in local elections, let alone national ones. But through my interviews I found that churches do matter for how Lutherton residents engage in national politics because they help shape the way residents understand their community, its problems, and which party will best represent them. I was able to arrive at this conclusion after hearing so much coherence from residents and community leaders that churches are important, ruling out the theories that community leaders themselves offered about why that is the case and then taking seriously the areas of agreement among residents about how they define their city.

But it was often in the more informal ethnographic settings—social gatherings rather than organizational meetings—that I caught glimpses into how different elements of my identity were interpreted and reinterpreted by residents and community leaders in each place. During one McDonald's kaffeeklatsch in Lutherton, I was asking the retired men clustered around the sticky plastic tables to tell me what they were most worried about for the country. It was summer 2019, and their answers were the same as everyone else's: health care and immigration. We'd thoroughly discussed the health-care issue, and were ready to take up immigration, when the oldest and most revered member of the group stopped everyone. "Where is your last name from?" he asked me. "I just want to make sure before we go on and insult her people." He said it as something of a joke, something of a warning to the other group members. I explained that my name is of Italian—not Spanish—origin, and the group carried on. In other words, I assuaged their concerns and assured them that I was in the category of "White, non-Hispanic"; but if I hadn't, I'm not sure how the conversation would have gone differently. This point of clarification was one of several that marked different ways in which I was both insider and outsider in these field sites. For example, Elaine noted that it was not only my clothes but my dark hair and tan skin tone that made me stand out in Motorville. But in a conversation with Rob, from Lutherton, my ethnoracial identity afforded me clear insider status: we were also talking about immigration, and he immediately launched into an invective against Muslims, explaining that the Quran exhorted them to kill people "like us"—as he went on to clarify—White, English speakers.

Such experiences helped shed light on the feelings of outsider-ness expressed by White residents of Lutherton who were not German Lutherans and also underlined the importance of that in-group identity in Lutherton. And, while community ethnoracial identity was not nearly as salient or consensual in Motorville and Gravesend as it was in Lutherton, my interaction with Elaine was a reminder that not just Whiteness but a particular kind of Whiteness was often the shared expectation during social interactions across all three places.

Interpretations of my religious and class identities offered similar lessons. In Lutherton, and occasionally in Gravesend, residents were relieved to learn that I attended a Catholic high school—even for non-Catholics, this fact gave them a point of reference for how to locate me within a Christian world. In Motorville, in contrast, my student status often became the focal point of my identity, which residents used to understand me: both young people with mounds of student debt and older residents worried about young people's student debt expressed concern that I was still in school in my late twenties. This, despite the fact that I grew up in an upper-middle-class household and had attended several "elite" educational institutions. These markers were not only not as salient to my interviewees (i.e., it would be difficult to know about my parents' occupation and income unless someone were to ask me directly) but, importantly, they were less legible. The distinction between the University of Chicago and other private institutions, for example, was less meaningful than the distinction between expensive private schools and less-expensive public schools.

In sum, the way my positionality shaped my data collection was not only multivocal (shaped by the intersection of my racial, religious, and class identities) but also situated (Reyes 2020)—it shifted both across the three field sites and in different social contexts within each community.

This raises one last point, about my ethical commitments during fieldwork. First, I chose to anonymize my field sites. This is a methodological decision that has several drawbacks, including that it requires the reader to trust that I have revealed the most relevant information about my field sites (Jerolmack and Murphy 2019). But I did so because I worried that making the names public would have posed challenges to recruitment for elected officials and political activists who may one day seek higher office. I am now in the process of conducting fieldwork for a new book, in which I have chosen to identify the field sites and provide anonymity for these kinds of community leaders only if they ask me to do so. Data collection is ongoing, but several have asked for anonymity so far. In sum, anonymizing the field sites probably granted me greater access but also poses challenges of trust for the reader. Rather than simply ask for this trust, I have attempted to earn it by sharing as much data as possible about each city and using national averages to preserve their anonymity.

To further protect my participants' anonymity, I also attempted to contact all residents and seek approval for the quotes I planned to use before publishing them. Although I have lost contact with several people (those who dropped off between first- and fourth-round interviews), this means that I was able to explicitly discuss with most participants whether they had concerns over anonymity after they saw the way I was using our conversations as data.

Data Collection and Coding of Local Newspaper Archives

I began collecting archival data in spring 2022, after I had already developed the presentist argument of the book—about the place-based processes that are still keeping Motorville in the Democratic fold. But what had happened between 1964 and 2016 that set the three cities and these other New Deal places on different trajectories? To answer this question, I took a more deductive approach in collecting data from the local newspaper archives.

My research assistant, two volunteer county archivists, and I collected the front and editorial pages from all three local newspapers during the days surrounding national events from 1932 to 2016 that are typically understood as part of the story of political realignment. Table A3 summarizes the dates of data collection for these events. We also conducted keyword searches for "Roe v. Wade," "strikes," and the names of the local labor councils in each city. These were particularly helpful for producing counts of strikes by year. Taken together, these searches rendered hundreds of pages of archival material, which I analyzed deductively to probe the findings from my interviews and fieldwork: first, I counted how often the local newspapers mentioned these major national events; second, I analyzed the content and political stance of

TABLE A3. Archival Data Collection

Event/Election	Date Range for Data Collection
National Events Central to Realignment	
AFL-CIO merger	12/1/1955–12/6/1955
Montgomery Bus Boycott	12/5/1955–12/20/1955
Birmingham Campaign (start through MLK's arrest)	4/3/1963–4/12/1963
Birmingham Campaign (children's demonstrations through truce)	5/2/1964–5/11/1964
Birmingham Campaign (KKK attack through MLK's eulogy)	9/15/1963–9/19/1963
March on Washington	9/28/1963–9/30/1963
Civil Rights Act passes Senate	6/19/1964–6/22/1964
Civil Rights Act signed into law	7/2/1964–7/6/1964
Bloody Sunday	3/7/1965–3/9/1965
MLK assassination	4/4/1968–4/6/1968
1968 Democratic National Convention	8/22/1968–8/29/1968
Roe v. Wade	1/22/1973–1/24/1973
Air traffic controllers	8/3/1981–8/7/1981
Presidential Elections Central to Realignment	
FDR 1932	11/7/1932–11/9/1932
FDR 1936	11/2/1936–11/4/1936
FDR 1940	11/4/1940–11/6/1940
LBJ 1964	11/2/1964–11/4/1964
Nixon 1968	11/4/1968–11/6/1968
Reagan 1980	11/3/1980–11/5/1980
Reagan 1984	11/5/1984–11/7/1984
Bush 2000	11/6/2000–11/8/2000
Obama 2008	11/3/2008–11/5/2008
Obama 2012	11/5/2012–11/7/2012
Trump 2016	11/7/2016–11/9/2016

editorials, letters to the editor, and local stories (as opposed to those written by the Associated Press and run in the local paper, for example) pertaining to those national events; and third, I counted front-page references to churches, service-oriented nonprofits, and unions during these dates. This last analysis allowed me to assess how frequently these organizations and their activities were

TABLE A4. Geography of Issue Content

Motorville		Lutherton		Gravesend	
Local-State-National	0.9	Local-State	0.9	Local-State-National	1.3
Local-State	3.5	State-National	1.4	Local-State	1.6
State-National	5.6	Local-National	3.0	State-National	2.6
Local-National	7.2	State	14.4	State	14.1
National	21.3	Local-State-National	15.8	Local-National	20.8
State	24.5	National	19.9	National	29.4
Local	37.0	Local	44.5	Local	30.2

part of local media portrayals without biasing the selection process, as the dates were determined by national rather than local events.

Data Collection and Coding of Politicians' Facebook Posts

Between the third- and fourth-round interviews, during summer 2020, with the help of three research assistants from the University of Chicago, I collected all publicly available Facebook posts from "local" politicians in each field site that were posted between March 1 and August 31, 2020. I used these data to develop questions for interviewees in the fall, and then I later extended the data to include all posts from January 1 to November 3 (the day of the U.S. presidential election). This included all candidates and incumbents from city and county offices, up to the community's U.S. House of Representatives seat. I focused on Facebook posts as interviewees had overwhelmingly indicated in previous interviews that this was their preferred social media platform.

I collected three pieces of information from each post: the text, the number of likes, and the number of comments. I then qualitatively coded each post for its geographic scope (table A4). For example, a post about Main Street development was coded as "local"; a post about a governor's stay-at-home order during Covid-19 was coded as "state"; and a post about President Trump or the impeachment as "national."

I also coded each post for issue content. The coding process was inductive, and many posts received multiple codes. "Covid containment" posts included any that advocated for social distancing, mask-wearing, or a test-and-trace strategy. Posts were coded as "populism" when were framed in an us versus

(a)

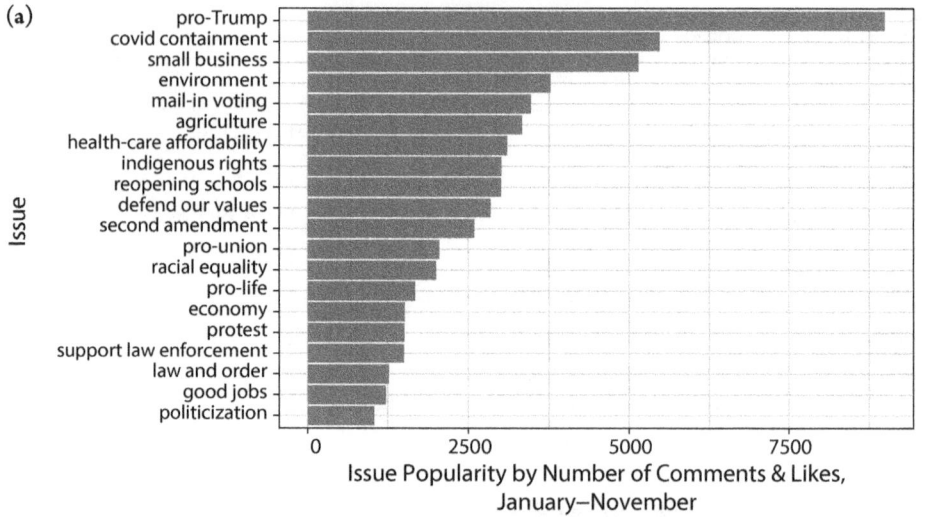

Issue Popularity by Number of Comments & Likes,
January–November

(b)

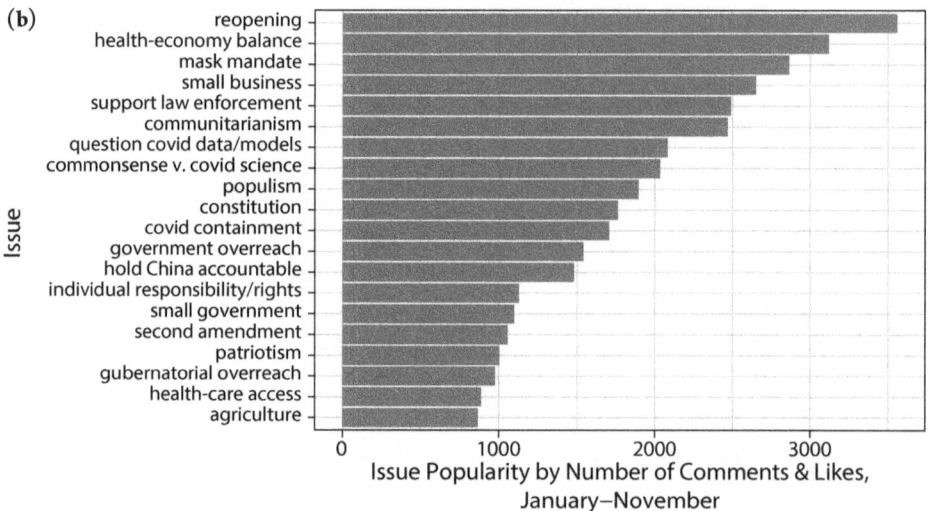

Issue Popularity by Number of Comments & Likes,
January–November

FIGURE A4. Most popular issues on Facebook, by place. (a) Motorville;
(b) Lutherton; (c) Gravesend.

them fashion, posing the "regular people" against political or corporate elites.
This excludes any posts that evoke a kind of rural resentment (Cramer 2016),
as I reserved more specific codes for these: for example, "urban v. rural" indicates a post advocating for governors to treat urban and rural communities
differently during Covid; and "rural way of life" indicates a post that promises

(c)

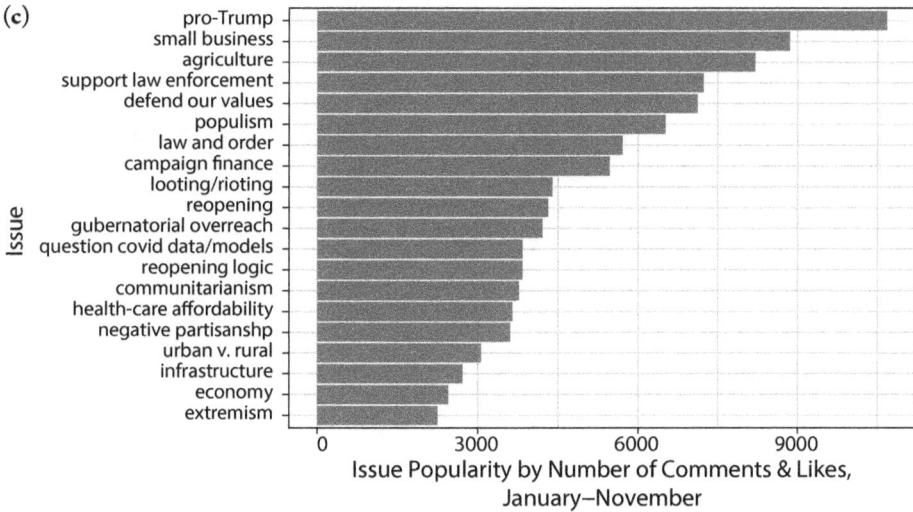

FIGURE A4. (continued)

to defend rural communities from outside forces such as the opposing candidate, Washington, D.C., or the governor. "Gubernatorial overreach" is distinct from "government overreach," and requires that the post refer explicitly to the state's governor—these were particularly common in both Lutherton and Gravesend during Covid-19. "Communitarianism" indicates any post describing local volunteering efforts, applauding nonprofits or churches for community engagement, or otherwise providing an avenue by which residents might learn of collective, private solutions to social problems. There are several posts that include discussions of reopening states' economies during the spring of 2020. Those coded as "reopening" simply advocate for governors to ease or lift stay-at-home orders. Those coded as "reopening logic" question the "arbitrariness" of the closures—a common concern, for example, is why Wal-Mart was able to remain open but mom-and-pop stores were not. Finally, there are several codes that indicate a politician exhorting the public to question the Covid-19 response in some way. The most common form of this is for a post to note how inaccurate the early Covid projections were or to question the way that Covid deaths and cases have been reported. These posts were labeled "question covid data/models." Another set of posts, often by one particular politician in Lutherton, repeatedly called on viewers to apply common sense to Covid mitigation policies. These might, for example, pose a rhetorical question such as: "Ask yourself, what good will a cloth mask do to stop millions of particles smaller than a pin needle from escaping your mouth?" These were coded "commonsense v. covid science."

After coding the posts, I weighted them by the number of comments and likes they received to produce the plots shown in figure A4.

NOTES

Introduction

1. The names of all research sites and participants are pseudonymized throughout the book to protect participants' anonymity. This was a methodological choice that has both costs and benefits. Please see appendix B for further discussion of these trade-offs. In a previous publication (Ternullo 2022b), I referred to Lutherton as Meriville; Motorville as Iverson; and Gravesend as Williston. I have changed the names here to evoke the differences between the cities so that they are easier to recall for readers.

2. Lerer and Epstein 2019.

3. This included 24 residents in Motorville; 30 in Lutherton; and 32 in Gravesend. See table A1 for a summary of the demographic and political characteristics of residents from each field site and table A2 for a timeline of these interviews.

4. See Tuan 1975. As Molotch, Freudenburg, and Paulsen (2000, 794) summarize, organizations "bridge the somewhat ineffable 'betweenness' of people's subjective experiences and the objective realities of locale."

5. See Molotch, Freudenburg, and Paulsen 2000 for an account of the path-dependent process of place formation.

6. Voters occupy "cross-cutting cleavage positions" and become "cross-pressured" when their social group memberships are not all associated with the same party (Lipset 1960). This can, of course, change over time as the parties cultivate the political allegiances of different social groups.

7. On this point, see Wright and Boudet 2012. Voting behavior does not have a one-to-one relationship with partisanship, but aggregate voting across multiple levels of government is a reasonable proxy for the portion of residents who identify with one party or the other.

8. None of the evidence that I present here will contradict Hopkins's or others' arguments about nationalization (see also Moskowitz 2021). Rather, I'll show how—alongside national news consumption—residents continue to learn about their communities in a way that is consequential for their partisanship.

9. Bonikowski 2017.

10. See Jardina 2019.

11. On group-based logics of partisanship, see Kane, Mason, and Wronski 2021. On immigrant partisan identity, see Lee and Hajnal 2011. When it comes to social identity formation, the idea that context can raise the salience of group identity is not new; in fact, it's foundational to both self-categorization theory (Turner et al. 1987) and social psychological studies of social movements, which argue that participation in social movements or collective action intensifies

participants' group identification (De Weerd and Klandermans 1999; Klandermans et al. 2002). However, this relationship is bidirectional: strong group identification predicts the emergence of a "politicized collective identity" or "movement identity," which then further sustains collective identity (Polletta and Jasper 2001; Simon and Klandermans 2001; van Stekelenburg and Klandermans 2013) or can even create collective identities where none existed prior (Minkoff 1997). My argument builds on these accounts but redirects the analytic lens toward people who are *not* involved in the kinds of social movement or identity organizations that we know foster group identity; among these people, what are the mundane social interactions and experiences that make certain group identities more salient than others?

12. Berelson, Lazarsfeld, and McPhee 1954; Campbell et al. 1960; Lazarsfeld, Berelson, and Gaudet 1948.

13. For example, Lee (2002) makes a similar argument in a related domain: public opinion formation. His model of "activated mass opinion" suggests that meso-level dynamics, in this case social movement activism during the civil rights era, are central to understanding how people make sense of the political world. Similarly, political scientists have long examined the relationship between social context and intergroup animosity, political participation, and attitudes toward social programs (e.g., Key 1949; Hopkins 2010; Enos 2017; Mutz 2002; Gay 2001; Michener 2018; Fraga, Moskowitz, and Schneer 2021).

14. Berelson, Lazarsfeld, and McPhee 1954; Lazarsfeld, Berelson, and Gaudet 1948. For more recent studies of the social contexts of political discussion networks and how they shape Americans' voting behavior, see Huckfeldt and Sprague 1987, 1995; Carlson, Abrajano, and García Bedolla 2020.

15. See, e.g., Cook 2020; Edsall 2016.

16. See Rodden 2019.

17. Some, for example, think of the post-stagflation neoliberal economic order or the rise of Reagan Republicanism as a key turning point (see, e.g., Fraser and Gerstle 1989; Rodgers 2011). But when we consider how these changes impacted White, working-class members of the New Deal coalition, the Racial Realignment is central (Petrocik 1981; Huckfeldt and Kohfeld 1989).

18. I rely on county-level data to indicate each city's politics, as that is the lowest scale at which we have historic voting and demographic data. These data are always susceptible to modifiable areal unit problem, so we can't assume the same relationships hold at lower levels of aggregation—i.e., the city (see, in particular, Rodden 2017). Moreover, as both Rodden (2017) and Witovsky (2021) show, the densest and largest towns—even in otherwise "red" counties— are often much more Democratic than the rural parts of the county, in part because town centers tend to be where people of color live. But based on archives describing victors in citywide offices, these county-level statistics provide a reasonable approximation of the voting behavior in each of the cities during this time. Even today, while Motorville, Lutherton, and Gravesend cities are somewhat more Democratic-leaning than their respective counties as a whole, the cities and counties have typically moved in similar directions, except in Motorville where the city has remained much more Democratic than the very rural parts of the county. For this reason, I also interviewed residents who live in the unincorporated areas and small towns outside the cities that are the focal points of analysis.

19. Dixon 2020.

20. These interviews were "semi-structured"—meaning that I followed an interview guide of open-ended questions but also allowed residents to guide the conversation and probed their responses where necessary.

21. See Katz and Lazarsfeld 1955.

22. This proved to be one of the main benefits of snowball sampling in this case (see Small 2009 and Weiss 1994).

23. The first- and fourth-round interviews lasted about an hour and 15 minutes, on average. The second-round interviews were a little over an hour on average, and the third interview was, by design, a short check-in of about 30 minutes as states debated relaxing Covid restrictions in the spring of 2020.

24. See Robison et al. 2018 for a summary of the most frequently used methods in American political behavior research. For some exceptions to this rule, which highlight the utility of in-depth interviewing for studying American political behavior, see Brower and Knight 2022; Cramer 2016; Michener 2018; Rogers 2006. On the strength of interviews as a method for revealing patterns in meaning-making, see Lamont and Swidler 2014; Pugh 2013.

25. As Swidler (2008) writes, this is the core task of the sociologist: to document how the outside world "gets in" to individuals, shaping their beliefs and understandings.

26. See figures 4 and 5 and table 1 for the data sources.

27. See table A3 for a summary of the dates for which I have data from each newspaper.

28. I did this along with the help of several research assistants. In total, we collected data on 3,436 posts. See appendix B for further details on data collection and analysis.

29. As Timmermans and Tavory (2012) note, we can only know what findings are surprising during empirical research if we are in conversation with existing theory in the field—this directs us to focus on what cannot be explained already and to recognize theoretical saturation as the point at which our emerging theory can explain both the dominant strands of the surprising pattern and important sources of deviation (Low 2019).

30. As Paulsen (2004) argues, local accounts are crucial to understanding place distinctiveness, but we also have to interrogate *how* place leads residents to develop those accounts. On the utility of like-case comparison for revealing exactly these dynamics, see Brown-Saracino 2018. On triangulation, see Small 2011.

31. On the utility of multiple interviews for theory building, see Hoang 2018. I was able to transcribe and code all first-round interviews before the second round. I did the same between the third and fourth rounds. I did not have time to do this between the second and third rounds, as I conducted those almost back-to-back: the third-round interviews were an unexpected addition to the research design because of the vociferous debates going on in April and May 2020 about lifting states' "stay-at-home" orders.

32. Gimpel and Schuknecht (2003) refer to the former as a "compositional" approach and the latter as a "contextual" approach.

33. See Huddy 2018; Lee and Hajnal 2011.

34. See Achen and Bartels 2016; Green, Palmquist, and Schickler 2002; Mason and Wronski 2018.

35. See Huddy 2001, 2013. Social identity theory, as developed by Tajfel (1981) and Tajfel and Turner (1979), and later amended by Turner et al. (1987), emerged out of the finding that even the smallest experimental manipulations could create a feeling of in-group attachment among

members and induce feelings of in-group bias and out-group hostility. In routine social settings, social identity emerges when individuals see their social environment as composed of distinct groups and compare among them; their need for positive distinction will drive them to identify with a group that "contributes positively to someone's self-concept"; and group identification will lead to both in-group attachment and out-group differentiation (De Weerd and Klandermans 1999, 1075). With respect to political behavior, social identity theory is, as Huddy (2013) notes, compatible with the Michigan model but provides a more explicit psychological model of how objective group membership translates into subjective group identity and then social identification.

36. Many factors shape the emergence of strong group identification (see Huddy 2013), but symbolic concerns—the sense of a group's social standing vis-à-vis other groups (Tajfel 1981)—and a desire to protect that standing when it is subject to perceived threat (Blumer 1958; Bobo 1999; Bobo and Hutchings 1996) tend to be paramount.

37. Within sociology, De Leon, Desai, and Tuğal (2009) of the "political articulation" school have argued that parties are at least somewhat autonomous from social structure, allowing them to constitute new social groups. Similarly, political scientists in the "UCLA" school (see Bawn et al. 2012; Cohen 2008; Karol 2009) argue that the political valence of social groups, and the meaning of the parties themselves, evolves as social groups advocate for inclusion in a party coalition or press their existing party coalition for change. Both theories highlight the role of parties' strategic efforts in the process of translation from objective social structural divisions to specific versions of group-based parties. These efforts, of course, feed back into the psychological processes of group identification described above (see Huddy 2013). As Kane, Mason, and Wronski (2021) argue, two key preconditions for a groups-based theory of political parties are that citizens know which groups go with which party and that they have feelings toward many social groups, including those to which they do not belong. The former is helped along as party leaders adapt to an increasingly socially and ideologically sorted electorate and can make more straightforward claims about which groups they (do and do not) represent (Claassen et al. 2021; Levendusky 2009; Mason and Wronski 2018).

38. See Hout, Brooks, and Manza 1995.

39. There were decades-long tensions within both parties prior to 1964, as the civil rights movement shifted public opinion and elected several sympathetic legislators to Congress (Lee 2002; Schickler 2016), but nationally, this election marked a turning point. See Carmines and Stimson 1989.

40. McGirr 2015; Schlozman 2015.

41. On union decline in the United States, see Mayer 2004. This led to a series of debates in the 1990s about the "death of class" in American politics (see Clark and Hoffmann-Martinot 1998; Clark and Lipset 1991; Waters and Pakulski 1996), which reached a tentative resolution in a series of studies by sociologists Clem Brooks and Jeff Manza (Brooks and Manza 1997a, 1997b).

42. Lipset 1960.

43. See, e.g., Morgan and Lee 2017.

44. On status threat among the White, working class and support for Trump and other populist candidates, see Mutz 2018; Gidron and Hall 2017. On the role of growing racial threat in exacerbating the link between Whites' racial resentment and anti-statism, see Tesler 2012; Wetts and Willer 2018. On racism, sexism, and anti-immigrant sentiments and support for

Trump, see Schaffner, MacWilliams, and Nteta 2018; Reny, Collingwood, and Valenzuela 2019. See Tesler 2016 on growing racial polarization in the Obama era.

45. As Carnes and Lupu (2021) have pointed out, there was remarkable stability in the voting behavior of the White, working class between 2012 and 2016: this group has, on average, favored Republican presidential candidates since at least the 1980s, increasingly so since the early 2000s.

46. According to this kind of "compositional" explanation for the correspondence between where people live and how they vote, this correlation emerges either because people choose to live in places that match their politics (e.g., Bishop 2009) or because different kinds of people prefer to live in different kinds of places (e.g., urban vs. rural; see Rodden 2019). See Small 2004 for a summary of structuralist approaches to the study of place in sociology.

47. Amid growing attention to how globalization was reshaping the local, sociologists in the early 2000s began reasserting the importance of "place-specific culture" (Griswold and Wright 2004, 1414). See also Gieryn 2000. In these accounts, place has independent effects on its residents—not just on their life outcomes (Sharkey and Faber 2014) but also on the way they act, interact, and form opinions. In this vein, scholars have shown that places shape the emergence of local social movements (Wright and Boudet 2012; Nelson 2021) and that local social movements shape residents' politics (Andrews, Beyerlein, and Tucker Farnum 2016; Wallace, Zepeda-Millán, and Jones-Correa 2014; McVeigh, Cunningham, and Farrell 2014).

48. On union decline and the rise of economic inequality, see Hirsch and Macpherson 2019; Rosenfeld 2014; Western and Rosenfeld 2011. On devolution and marketization, see Marwell 2004; Smith and Lipsky 1993.

49. See Carr and Kefalas 2009. Over a third of U.S. counties, predominantly non-metro ones, are seeing population declines (Johnson 2013).

50. For a review, see Valentino and Hutchings in 2004.

51. See also Metzl 2018.

52. Benford and Snow (2000) describe diagnostic frames as *attributional* because they identify the source of the problem, the "culpable agent" (616).

53. This is exactly what García Bedolla (2005) finds in her study of political identity among Latinx voters in two Los Angeles communities. In general, as Lee and Hajnal (2011) argue, nonpartisanship among Latinx and Asian Americans presents opportunities for both Democrats and Republicans to try to cultivate their political loyalties on the basis of different social identities.

54. See Small 2004 on the constraints of structure in place narratives. Similarly, as Brown-Saracino (2007) writes, neighborhood newcomers often "choose" whom to consider "authentic old-timers" with claims on the place, but they make those choices within certain constraints of actual neighborhood history. See also Parker and Ternullo 2022.

55. Spatial inequalities in nonprofit service provision are important factors in shaping unequal social outcomes (see Allard 2009; Marwell and Gullickson 2013), but as both Pacewicz 2016 and Safford 2009 argue, the relational dimension is key to how cities solve problems.

56. This account is rooted in cognitive-cultural arguments in sociology, which claim that beliefs emerge through routine experiences of problem-solving within a particular institutional environment. See Lizardo and Strand 2010; Martin and Desmond 2010; Strand and Lizardo 2015.

57. Katz and Lazarsfeld 1955.

58. Brown-Saracino 2015; Cheng 2013; Fine 2012.

59. Wong 2010.

60. In the context of social movements, as Benford and Snow (2000) note, mobilizing frames are more likely to be successful when they are "resonant with the personal, everyday experiences of the targets" (621) and when they "resonate with the targets' cultural narrations" (622).

61. See Gieryn 2000; Paulsen 2004.

62. See Kusenbach 2008 for a discussion of places as nested. In studies of American political culture scholars often focus on regional differences (e.g., Elazar 1975; Griswold and Wright 2004; Mellow 2008). But thinking about places as cities means that counties are particularly important for understanding the local context. Counties are the lowest level of political party organization and the sites of administration for many social welfare programs. This is another reason why I interviewed residents who live in the county but not in the central cities.

63. See Pierson 2000 on why path-dependent processes often require external disruptions to change.

64. Lizardo and Strand 2010.

65. As Paulsen (2004) describes methodological approaches for studying place, it typically involves comparing "like places" and triangulating between local accounts and material realities to understand how place informs behavior. For additional empirical approaches following this strategy, see Kaufman and Kaliner 2011; Molotch, Freudenburg, and Paulsen 2000.

66. Achen and Bartels 2016.

67. On psychological traits, see Gerber et al. 2010 and Hetherington and Weiler 2009. On parents' party attachment, see Campbell et al. 1960.

Chapter 1: The Uneven Geography of Heartland Politics: The Local Ramifications of Political Transformation from the New Deal to Trump

1. Page and Walker (1991) refer to this as "agro-industrialization."

2. Bluestone and Harrison 1982.

3. In every decennial census count from 1870 to 1910, German-born immigrants made up more than 75 percent of Lutherton County's foreign-born population but never more than 7 percent of the total population. But there is also evidence that Germanic identity did not end with first-generation immigrants: in the 1906 Census of Religious Bodies (now housed at the Association of Religious Data Archives), nearly 10 percent of Lutherton County's population were members of German-speaking Lutheran denominations that later merged into the Lutheran Church-Missouri Synod. This is despite the fact that by 1910, less than 2 percent of the county's population was actually born in Germany.

4. Although this was a slow process that took place over several years (see Black and Black 2003).

5. Karol 2009; Schlozman 2015.

6. Rosenfeld 2014; Western and Rosenfeld 2011.

7. On the co-optation of labor by the Democratic Party, see Eidlin 2018.

8. As Molotch, Freudenburg, and Paulsen (2000) argue, places become "durably distinct" over time because when actors confront key decision points, they do so by "drawing on the configurations of place that have so durably come down" (817). As they show in the cases of Santa Barbara and Ventura, despite shared *structural possibilities*—i.e., either place could have become much like the other—key differences in how local actors responded to the early development of the oil industry shaped the organizational and physical landscape and created a place

character that made certain kinds of future action more likely. On critical junctures as opportunities for change in path-dependent relationships, see Capoccia 2015 and Pierson 2000.

9. Please see appendix B and table A3 for details on data collection and analysis. I am indebted to researchers at the county historical societies as well as a research assistant from Motorville who spent countless hours in the public library collecting newspaper clippings for me.

10. Mudge 2018.

11. On Social Security's racially exclusionary origins, see Brown 1999 and Katznelson 2005.

12. See Ladd and Hadley 1978.

13. Rosenfeld 2014. As Schlozman (2015) notes, the coalition partnership was not secured until 1944.

14. On the localization of the American labor movement, see Clark 1989. Regional variation is in part due to differences in industrial development and in part because of White southerners' resistance to both working-class and racial mobilization (Friedman 2000).

15. For example, a local organization founded by German immigrants published a socialist newspaper in Motorville for several decades starting in 1910. Moreover, Eugene Debs, the Socialist Party candidate for president, garnered over 10 percent of the vote in Motorville in 1916 and 1920. In Lutherton and Gravesend, the Socialist Party never won more than 3 percent of the vote.

16. See Fink 1983.

17. The count of local labor unions and data on strikes come from a newspaper archive at the Motorville Public Library documenting accounts of organized labor's activities at the end of the nineteenth century. The archive contains articles primarily from two publications, including firsthand accounts of strikes, speeches, etc., as well as editorials about the events.

18. The relationship between unionization and immigration is a complicated one: many unions, particularly those affiliated with the AFL, opposed immigration on the grounds that it created a "reserve army" of workers willing to work for lower wages (Fink 1983). But immigration did fuel the rise of unions in the late nineteenth century even as it sparked ethnoracial conflict (Hannan and Freeman 1987; Olzak 1989).

19. This is despite the AFL's commitment to organizing along craft lines, typically leading to a "job consciousness" rather than a broader class consciousness (Perlman 1966).

20. See Voss 1993.

21. There was vibrant internal debate within the AFL about their organizing approach (Shapiro 1985; Stepan-Norris and Zeitlin 1989). Moreover, many locals were left to choose whether and how to engage in local politics (Schlozman 2015).

22. Montgomery 1987.

23. From an oral history of a Motorville labor leader who was active during the Depression and later. See Lynd 1996 for several case studies of radical and place-based unionization efforts during the 1930s that operated outside of both the AFL and the CIO.

24. By the end of World War II there was a general tempering of political radicalism within the labor movement after Communist Party members were purged from the AFL-CIO (Stepan-Norris and Zeitlin 2003).

25. That said, both Gravesend and Lutherton also had a Knights of Labor assembly and the local newspapers in both Lutherton and Gravesend also document a scattering of strikes in the 1900s, 1910s, and 1920s. But it wasn't until the 1930s that both cities developed and sustained the organizational components of a labor movement.

26. Social movement activity and subnational politics suggest that party leaders were on a slow march toward Racial Realignment during the 1940s and 1950s. See Baylor 2013; Chen 2007; Schickler 2016; Lee 2002.

27. Carmines and Stimson 1989.

28. On the regional and racial implications of the realignment, see Black and Black 2003; Huckfeldt and Kohfeld 1989; Petrocik 1981.

29. On the history of civil rights mobilization and racial oppression in the North, see Woodard and Theoharis 2019. On sundown towns, see Loewen 2005.

30. For an account of Buckley's racial politics, see Terbeek 2021.

31. See, for example, the APSA Committee on Political Parties' 1950 report, "Toward a More Responsible Two-Party System."

32. Within my sample of articles, the *Lutherton Gazette* ran twelve editorials arguing that the country needed to lower taxes, decrease the size of the federal government, or return control to local communities. Two of these were nationally syndicated columns from John Chamberlain and Buckley. Gravesend ran fifteen editorials containing similar content. In contrast, Motorville ran three similar editorials, none of which were by local editors, but also ran one local editorial advocating for greater centralization.

33. See Lewis 2019 and Williams 2016 on the early anti-abortion movement and evangelicals' changing discourse on abortion after *Roe v. Wade*.

34. Kellstedt et al. 1994; Putnam and Campbell 2010.

35. This led to the formation of the National Right to Life in 1968 (Williams 2016).

36. Based on Association of Religion Data Archives (ARDA) statistics.

37. Black and Black 2003.

38. See Putnam and Campbell 2010.

39. This was based on the original clustering analysis I did. See table 1.

40. Clawson and Clawson 1999; Western 1997.

41. See also https://fredblog.stlouisfed.org/2014/04/.

42. Bronfenbrenner and Juravich 2002; Clawson and Clawson 1999. On the effects of right-to-work laws, see Ellwood and Fine 1987.

43. Dixon 2020.

44. See figures A1 and A2.

45. Based on phonebook listings of the largest employers in the county, by decade, dating back to 1950.

46. See Dixon 2020 on the mobilization for public sector unionization rights in Wisconsin.

47. Per the Bureau of Labor Statistics' work stoppages data.

48. See Dixon 2020. As Flavin and Hartney (2015) show, these laws were a particular boon to the political participation of teachers.

49. Chauhan 1979.

50. According to economic development documents from the time.

51. Dixon 2020.

52. See figure 5.

53. Molotch, Freudenburg, and Paulsen 2000.

Chapter 2: Local Organizations and the Shape of Problem-Solving in Motorville, Lutherton, and Gravesend

1. See McQuarrie and Marwell 2009.

2. See Marwell and Morrissey 2020; Pierre 1999, 2005. In some instances, the local state is sidelined entirely from these processes (Levine 2016, 2021).

3. The mix of public and private has deep roots in the history of U.S. social provision and state formation (see Balogh 2009; Clemens 2020; Mayrl and Quinn 2016; Morgan and Campbell 2011). But the contemporary instantiation is the result of historical changes dating back to LBJ's War on Poverty and the Economic Opportunity Act of 1964 (Dunning 2022). See Smith and Lipsky 1993 on the more recent turn toward competition and marketization. For studies that focus on how shifting federal policies have favored different models of partnership between the state (local, state, and federal governments) and civil society in the realms of both social welfare provision and economic development, see Clemens and Guthrie 2010; Levine 2021; Marwell 2007; McQuarrie 2010, 2013; Pacewicz 2016.

4. See also Hoyt and Leroux 2007; Rothrock 2008. William Julius Wilson (1987) famously argued that deindustrialization and segregation had concentrated poverty in inner cities and created a spatial mismatch between jobs and where people lived. As Simes (2021) points out today, this is now characteristic of postindustrial cities outside of major metros, where legacies of segregation allow police to concentrate social control in racialized communities.

5. On the rise of nonstandard employment in nonmetropolitan communities, see Mc-Laughlin and Coleman-Jensen 2008.

6. The result is what political scientist Scott Allard (2009) refers to as the uneven "geography of the social safety net." See also Allard and Small 2013; Safford 2009; Simes 2021. For studies focused specifically on rural and ex-urban areas, see Lobao 2004; Warner 2003; Warner and Hefetz 2003.

7. See "Real Wage Trends, 1979 to 2019."

8. Kaufman 2015.

9. Clawson and Clawson 1999, 113.

10. The largest unions by membership size are the American Federation of Teachers, the United Food and Commercial Workers, the United Steelworkers, and several building trades.

11. Beck 2017.

12. That said, unions' political activism in other cities and states has stood out as a way to generate gains for workers during a time when national labor policies have not been as favorable (see Brady, Baker, and Finnigan 2013; Cummings and Boutcher 2009; Sachs 2011).

13. Based on ARDA data from 2010.

14. See Beyerlein and Hipp 2006; Pattillo-McCoy 1998; Verba, Schlozman, and Brady 1995.

15. Driskell, Lyon, and Embry 2008.

16. As Chaves (2004) points out, this role of church-as-facilitator is fairly typical among U.S. congregations.

17. Based on the Census Bureau's 2017 Survey of State and Local Government Finances and the Urban Institute's IRS Business Master File data on nonprofits.

18. This assumption may not be true in reality: although the city manager system was designed to limit corruption and reduce quid pro quo within city government, there is evidence that some interest groups do better with a manager rather than a mayor (Lubell, Feiock, and De

La Cruz 2009) and that, in general, managers are just as representative of local public opinion as are elected mayors (Tausanovitch and Warshaw 2014).

Chapter 3: How Local Contexts Produce (Anti)-Statism in Motorville and Lutherton

1. There is a long-standing literature on how welfare state institutions shape citizens' normative ideas about how the state should function. See Campbell 2012; Pierson 1992; Staerklé, Likki, and Scheidegger 2012; Steensland 2006.

2. See also Hacker 2002; Mettler 2018; Morgan and Campbell 2011.

3. On the media's racialization of welfare recipients, see Gilens 2000. A long-standing research tradition links White racial resentment to low support for redistributive policies of all kinds. See Bobo and Kluegel 1993; Tesler 2012; Wetts and Willer 2018; White 2007.

4. On how different organizational ties lead to different kinds of public and collective action in both rural and urban communities, see Flora et al. 1997; Lobao, Adua, and Hooks 2014; Morton, Chen, and Morse 2008; Pacewicz 2016; Safford 2009. On diagnostic frames, see Benford and Snow 2000.

5. This argument draws on cultural sociologists' claims that beliefs emerge from repeated experiences within institutional contexts that support those beliefs. See Lizardo 2017; Martin and Desmond 2010; Strand and Lizardo 2015.

6. Tocquevillian approaches to the study of civic associations assume that participation increases political engagement and trust in government, and is good for democracy (Putnam, Leonardi, and Nanetti 1993; Paxton 2007). But see Riley 2005 for a critique.

7. See also Bond et al. 2012.

8. This is based on my coding of the geographic scope and content of local politicians' public Facebook posts. See table A4 for details.

9. This is a fairly typical experience among U.S. churchgoers. See Brewer, Kersh, and Petersen 2003; Chaves 2004.

10. Small 2004.

11. See figure A4.

12. See Sewell 1992 on the "transposability" of cultural schemas.

13. The United States is distinct from most of its advanced industrialized peers in that it provides welfare not on a universal, rights-based principle or solely on the principle of need but often on the principle of deservingness, determining which social groups are worthy of which kinds of social services (Esping-Anderson 1990; Katz 1986).

14. "Wage growth" refers to census data on change in real median family incomes.

15. In contrast to the Louisiana town that Arlie Hochschild (2016) studies.

16. Morgan and Campbell 2011; Mettler 2011.

17. This echoes a long-standing critique of the claim that there is a straightforward link between individual-level participation in civil society organizations and polity-level improvement in democratic institutions (per Putnam, Leonardi, and Nanetti 1993)—this account assumes that organizations teach civic virtues without examining important differences in what people learn within different kinds of organizations and the implications of those lessons for democracy (Seligson 1999; Fung 2003; Skocpol 2003; Riley 2005).

18. Zaller 1992; Lenz 2009. My argument is consistent with other work on contextual factors that shape political opinion "from below" (Lee 2002).

19. On Americans' communitarianism, see Fischer 2008.

20. On boundary work, see Lamont 2000.

Chapter 4: From Place to Partisan Identity in Motorville and Lutherton

1. On the role of ideological entrepreneurs in bringing these issue positions together, see Noel 2013. Scholars offer varying interpretations of the causal relationships between parties and groups: either parties evolve as social groups advocate for inclusion in a party coalition or press their existing party coalition for change (Bawn et al. 2012; Schlozman 2015) or parties shape the formation of social groups themselves (De Leon, Desai, and Tuğal 2009; Desai 2002; Eidlin 2018). In both accounts, "ideology" may not be the driver, but it can play a role in justifying diverse issue bundles within one party.

2. Similarly, social structural divisions and state policies that reify or remake those divisions indicate constraints on individuals' social identity formation: Paschel 2016; Mora 2014; Loveman and Muniz 2007.

3. See Claassen et al. 2021; Mason 2016; Mason and Wronski 2018. In fact, one of the most oft-reproduced findings in American political behavior research is that Americans' issue positions are relatively unconstrained by ideology (Baldassarri and Gelman 2008; Converse 2006; Kinder and Kalmoe 2017) and their voting behavior is relatively unconstrained by the policies that would benefit them financially (Kiewiet and Lewis-Beck 2011; Kinder and Kiewiet 1981).

4. Kane, Mason, and Wronski 2021, 1786; see also Lee and Hajnal 2011.

5. See Hopkins 2018.

6. But for spatial accounts of realignment, see Darmofal 2008; Darmofal and Nardulli 2010; Nardulli 1995.

7. See Lee 2008.

8. See figure A3 for a snapshot of American National Election Studies (ANES) data on union voting from 1948 to 2016.

9. As Wong (2010) describes, community is not necessarily circumscribed by geography, but when a community is circumscribed in place, it means that these everyday social interactions become key to sustaining the community's boundaries (Brown-Saracino 2018; Tavory 2016). These interactions may occasionally involve boundary work, instances where residents define who they are and who their community is *in opposition to* other social groups in order to reassert their own moral worth (Lamont 2000).

10. On resonance, see McDonnell, Bail, and Tavory 2017.

11. Wong 2010.

12. Brown-Saracino 2018.

13. Tavory 2016.

14. As Patrick shared this story after I had visibly switched off the recorder, I explicitly asked his consent to use this information.

15. Based on 2010 ARDA data.

16. When it comes to immigration, many Americans combine opinions that we may think of as oppositional (Hainmueller and Hopkins 2015).

17. See, e.g., Doane and Bonilla-Silva 2013; Jardina 2019; Lewis 2004.

18. On structure and culture in place, see Small 2004.

19. Along with social movement groups and ideological entrepreneurs (Noel 2013; Bawn et al. 2012; Schlozman 2015).

20. Tesler 2016.

21. Lutherton residents are not alone in this, as White evangelicals are one of the most sorted groups in American politics (Mason and Wronski 2018).

22. See, e.g., Halpern-Meekin et al. 2015.

23. See figure A3.

24. See Jardina 2019.

25. Ternullo 2022b.

26. Achen and Bartels 2016, 266.

27. See Achen and Bartels 2016; Lee and Hajnal 2011.

28. Margolis 2018.

Chapter 5: Politics in a Dying Place: Organizational Instability and Postindustrial Populism in Gravesend

1. The shift that took place in Americans' civic engagement since the 1960s (per Putnam 2000) varied across social groups. For White Americans, the universe of voluntary associations shifted after the 1960s: from a world of *local* religious, fraternal, and civic organizations that often crossed occupational and class lines (though less so gender and racial lines) to advocacy groups based in Washington, D.C., that depended on members' donations rather than their participation (Pierson and Skocpol 2007; Skocpol 2003). In contrast, just at the time that Putnam documented a marked decline in civic associationism, marginalized groups were mobilizing politically (Boggs 2001) and community organizations were proliferating in major cities (Lee, McQuarrie, and Walker 2015; Levine 2017; McQuarrie 2013).

2. Americans continue to attend church and participate in charity organizations at relatively high levels in comparison with Western European and OECD nations (see Ammerman 2005 and the World Values Survey's seventh wave, conducted from 2017 to 2020).

3. For example, see Gest 2016; Wuthnow 2018.

4. On the role of growing racial threat in exacerbating the link between Whites' racial resentment and anti-statism, see Tesler 2012; Wetts and Willer 2018.

5. Recent scholarship has shown that Whites' subjective experience of status threat (regardless of actual material changes they experience) is a key part of the explanation for their turn toward Donald Trump in 2016 (Mutz 2018; Bobo 2017) and that those who experience this threat most intensely are those near, but not at, the bottom rungs of the social hierarchy (Gidron and Hall 2017; Kuziemko et al. 2014).

6. A straightforward social capital argument would posit that more individual-level ties to associations (and more associations at the city level) would increase generalized trust and trust in government; and further, that associations connected with other associations are even better at this (Paxton 2002, 2007).

7. See Frymer and Grumbach 2021.

8. On farm consolidation, see MacDonald, Hoppe, and Newton 2018.

9. Per Silva 2019.

10. On Trump's rhetoric, see Lamont, Park, and Ayala-Hurtado 2017. On the relationship between anti-immigrant attitudes and Obama/Trump voting among Whites, see Reny, Collingwood, and Valenzuela 2019.

11. On resonance, see McDonnell, Bail, and Tavory 2017. Populist discourse in American politics is neither a new phenomenon nor one that is limited to right-wing politicians (see Bonikowski and Gidron 2016; Fahey 2021). What has changed, instead, is the *context of reception* for those claims, which appeal particularly to globalization's losers (Bonikowski 2017).

12. See appendix B for details. Posts are "typified" so as not to identify Gravesend.

13. Wetts and Willer 2018; although see Hopkins 2010.

14. I spoke to four former union members in total. The only one who retains a belief that Democrats are the party for unions still lives in social housing built by organized labor decades ago and socializes routinely with retired labor leaders.

15. Teixeira 2022.

16. Frymer and Grumbach 2021; Gidron and Hall 2017.

17. Rosenfeld 2014.

Chapter 6: Local Contexts amid National Crisis: Economic Downturn in Motorville, Lutherton, and Gravesend

1. For summaries of this perspective, see, e.g., Staerklé, Likki, and Scheidegger 2012; Thelen 1999.

2. On critical junctures, see Capoccia 2015; Mahoney 2000. For examples of crises producing change in U.S. welfare state or fiscal policy, see Dauber 2013; Fourcade-Gourinchas and Babb 2002; Somers and Block 2005. Even in such moments of crisis, scholars have found that elected officials do rely on existing organizational materials as a practical means of resolving new challenges (Clemens 2020, chap. 5; Eaton and Weir 2015). As such, while agents of the state are afforded additional leeway to reconfigure institutional arrangements during moments of crisis, they are rarely working with a blank slate (Mayrl and Quinn 2016).

3. See Allcott et al. 2020 and Kushner Gadarian, Goodman, and Pepinsky 2020 for evidence of early partisan polarization in public health behaviors and attitudes about Covid policies.

4. This is consistent with other accounts of the relationship between institutions and beliefs: in unsettled times or moments of crisis, actors "misfire" in new environments that no longer support their habitual actions, creating "belief-situation mismatches" that can produce "a chronic lag and misfiring of dispositions and habits" (Strand and Lizardo 2015, 51). When this occurs, actors may seek to preserve the past, enacting beliefs that anticipate one environment without making the investments to succeed in another. It is only when actors reflectively recognize the change in the external environment that they may consciously search for new models and encounter institutional entrepreneurs who attempt to impose alternative ideologies (Lizardo and Strand 2010). In other words, old habits die hard. In fact, this is also consistent with how political actors responded to the Great Depression (Clemens 2020, chap. 5).

5. Mettler 2011; Morgan and Campbell 2011; Hacker 2002.

6. See Cohen 1990 and Gordon 1994.

7. I had just completed my second round of interviews in Gravesend in March 2020 when stay-at-home orders were imposed. I began calling people in Motorville and Lutherton for the

second-round interviews and incorporated new questions about the pandemic as I did so. I completed these interviews in mid-April and shortly thereafter began a third round of interviews across all three places as states were lifting their stay-at-home orders. This means I have three interviews with residents of Motorville and Lutherton between the stay-at-home orders and the presidential election, and two interviews during that period with most Gravesenders. To make up for this, I reinterviewed four Gravesenders in March and early April 2020.

8. See https://www.hudexchange.info/programs/hdx/pit-hic/.

9. On the design of Old-Age Insurance under the Social Security Act of 1935, see Cates 1983.

10. Mettler 2011.

Chapter 7: The End of Place? How the Nationalization of Politics Shapes Place-Based Partisanship

1. On the "network society," see Castells 2010. For a popular account, see Friedman 2007. See Lichter and Brown 2011 for a discussion of how this is in part erasing distinctions between rural and urban America.

2. See Hindman 2011; Hopkins 2018.

3. On the 2018 election cycle, see Shearer 2018. On the 2020 election cycle, see Thompson 2020.

4. For further evidence that partisanship is driving voting behavior in statewide, Senate, and U.S. House of Representative races, thus "nationalizing" American politics, see Abramowitz and Webster 2015 and Warshaw 2019 for a review. Despite a tendency toward increasing partisanship and ideological behavior in local elections, other factors do still matter a great deal. For evidence on the incumbency advantage at the subnational level, see de Benedictis-Kessner 2018; Ferreira and Gyourko 2009; Trounstine 2011. For research on personal knowledge of local politicians, see Oliver and Ha 2007.

5. On settled times, see Swidler 1986.

6. Although most Americans may not engage in this kind of selective exposure to partisan news sources (see Prior 2013), some of the most polarized do, and this just polarizes them further (Levendusky 2013).

7. See Allcott et al. 2020. Another contingent of interviewees, who lacked a trusted media source and sufficient political knowledge to guide them through these emergent partisan debates, had difficulty forming any opinions at all. See Ternullo 2022b for an in-depth discussion.

8. The contemporary environment offers a wide variety of information sources, including partisan-leaning ones (Jamieson and Cappella 2010), allowing people to select information that conforms to their political predispositions (Taber and Lodge 2006). As noted above, not everyone gathers information this way, but for those who do—as Isabelle and Jeff indicate—the outcome is rapid and intense issue polarization.

Conclusion: The Future of Heartland Politics

1. On linked fate and regional heterogeneity, see Escaleras, Kim, and Wagner 2019. On Republican identity among Latinx voters, see Cadena 2022.

2. See Paschel 2016; Loveman and Muniz 2007; De Leon, Desai, and Tuğal 2009.

3. Low information about American party politics may also coincide with cross-pressured status, particularly among new immigrant groups (Lee and Hajnal 2011).

4. Achen and Bartels 2016; Kane, Mason, and Wronski 2021.

5. On romantic relationships, see Alford et al. 2011; Huber and Malhotra 2017. On marketplace interactions, see McConnell et al. 2018.

6. See also Galvin and Thurston 2017.

7. In general, people with more resources—usually time and money—are more likely to vote (see Brady, Verba, and Schlozman 1995).

8. Ternullo 2022a.

9. See Weise and Corkery 2021.

REFERENCES

Abramowitz, Alan I., and Steven W. Webster. 2015. "All Politics Is National: The Rise of Negative Partisanship and the Nationalization of US House and Senate Elections in the 21st Century." Prepared for presentation at the Annual Meeting of the Midwest Political Science Association, Chicago.

Achen, Christopher H., and Larry M. Bartels. 2016. *Democracy for Realists: Why Elections Do Not Produce Responsive Government*. Princeton: Princeton University Press.

Alford, John R., Peter K. Hatemi, John R. Hibbing, Nicholas G. Martin, and Lindon J. Eaves. 2011. "The Politics of Mate Choice." *Journal of Politics* 73 (2): 362–79.

Allard, Scott W. 2009. *Out of Reach: Place, Poverty, and the New American Welfare State*. New Haven: Yale University Press.

Allard, Scott W., and Mario L. Small. 2013. "Reconsidering the Urban Disadvantaged: The Role of Systems, Institutions, and Organizations." *ANNALS of the American Academy of Political and Social Science* 647 (1): 6–20.

Allcott, Hunt, Levi Boxell, Jacob Conway, Matthew Gentzkow, Michael Thaler, and David Y. Yang. 2020. "Polarization and Public Health: Partisan Differences in Social Distancing during the Coronavirus Pandemic." NBER Working Paper, no. w26946.

American Political Science Association Committee on Political Parties. 1950. *Toward a More Responsible Two-Party System: A Report*. New York: Rinehart.

Ammerman, Nancy Tatom. 2005. *Pillars of Faith: American Congregations and Their Partners*. Berkeley: University of California Press.

Andrews, Kenneth T., Kraig Beyerlein, and Tuneka Tucker Farnum. 2016. "The Legitimacy of Protest: Explaining White Southerners' Attitudes toward the Civil Rights Movement." *Social Forces* 94 (3): 1021–44.

Baldassarri, Delia, and Andrew Gelman. 2008. "Partisans without Constraint: Political Polarization and Trends in American Public Opinion." *American Journal of Sociology* 114 (2): 408–46.

Balogh, Brian. 2009. *A Government Out of Sight: The Mystery of National Authority in Nineteenth-Century America*. Cambridge: Cambridge University Press.

Bawn, Kathleen, Martin Cohen, David Karol, Seth Masket, Hans Noel, and John Zaller. 2012. "A Theory of Political Parties: Groups, Policy Demands and Nominations in American Politics." *Perspectives on Politics* 10 (3): 571–97.

Baylor, Christopher A. 2013. "First to the Party: The Group Origins of the Partisan Transformation on Civil Rights, 1940–1960." *Studies in American Political Development* 27 (2): 111–41.

Beck, Molly. 2017. "Fewer than Half of Wisconsin School Districts Have Certified Teachers Unions." *Wisconsin State Journal*, December 31, 2017. https://madison.com/news/local/govt -and-politics/fewer-than-half-of-wisconsin-school-districts-have-certified-teachers-unions /article_44e4b2e4-3ee5-5dc2-89c4-5219f53e720e.html.

Benford, Robert D., and David A. Snow. 2000. "Framing Processes and Social Movements: An Overview and Assessment." *Annual Review of Sociology* 26: 611–39.

Berelson, Bernard R., Paul F. Lazarsfeld, and William N. McPhee. 1954. *Voting: A Study of Opinion Formation in a Presidential Campaign*. Chicago: University of Chicago Press.

Beyerlein, Kraig, and John R. Hipp. 2006. "From Pews to Participation: The Effect of Congregation Activity and Context on Bridging Civic Engagement." *Social Problems* 53 (1): 97–117.

Bishop, Bill. 2009. *The Big Sort*. New York: Mariner Books.

Black, Earl, and Merle Black. 2003. *The Rise of Southern Republicans*. Cambridge, MA: Harvard University Press.

———. 2007. *Divided America: The Ferocious Power Struggle in American Politics*. New York: Simon and Schuster.

Blight, David W. 2020. "The United States Is Being Taught by Facts and Events." *The Atlantic*, March 25. https://www.theatlantic.com/ideas/archive/2020/03/americans-are -rediscovering-importance-government/608710/.

Bluestone, Barry, and Bennett Harrison. 1982. *The Deindustrialization of America: Plant Closings, Community Abandonment, and the Dismantling of Basic Industry*. New York: Basic Books.

Blumer, Herbert. 1958. "Race Prejudice as a Sense of Group Position." *Pacific Sociological Review* 1 (1): 3–7.

Bobo, Lawrence D. 1999. "Prejudice as Group Position: Microfoundations of a Sociological Approach to Racism and Race Relations." *Journal of Social Issues* 55 (3): 445–72.

———. 2017. "Racism in Trump's America: Reflections on Culture, Sociology, and the 2016 US Presidential Election." *British Journal of Sociology* 68 (S1): S85–104.

Bobo, Lawrence, and Vincent L. Hutchings. 1996. "Perceptions of Racial Group Competition: Extending Blumer's Theory of Group Position to a Multiracial Social Context." *American Sociological Review* 61 (6): 951–72.

Bobo, Lawrence, and James R. Kluegel. 1993. "Opposition to Race-Targeting: Self-Interest, Stratification Ideology, or Racial Attitudes?" *American Sociological Review* 58 (4): 443–64.

Boggs, Carl. 2001. "Social Capital and Political Fantasy: Robert Putnam's 'Bowling Alone.'" *Theory and Society* 30 (2): 281–97.

Bond, Robert M., Christopher J. Fariss, Jason J. Jones, Adam D. I. Kramer, Cameron Marlow, Jaime E. Settle, and James H. Fowler. 2012. "A 61-Million-Person Experiment in Social Influence and Political Mobilization." *Nature* 489 (7415): 295.

Bonikowski, Bart. 2017. "Ethno-Nationalist Populism and the Mobilization of Collective Resentment." *British Journal of Sociology* 68 (November): S181–213.

Bonikowski, Bart, and Noam Gidron. 2016. "The Populist Style in American Politics: Presidential Campaign Discourse, 1952–1996." *Social Forces* 94 (4): 1593–1621.

Brady, David, Regina S. Baker, and Ryan Finnigan. 2013. "When Unionization Disappears: State-Level Unionization and Working Poverty in the United States." *American Sociological Review* 78 (5): 872–96.

Brady, Henry E., Sidney Verba, and Kay Lehman Schlozman. 1995. "Beyond SES: A Resource Model of Political Participation." *American Political Science Review* 89 (2): 271–94.

Brewer, Mark D., Rogan Kersh, and R. Eric Petersen. 2003. "Assessing Conventional Wisdom about Religion and Politics: A Preliminary View from the Pews." *Journal for the Scientific Study of Religion* 42 (1): 125–36.

Bronfenbrenner, Kate, and Tom Juravich. 2002. "It Takes More than House Calls." *Industrial Relations: Labour Markets, Labour Process and Trade Unionism* 2: 400.

Brooks, Clem, and Jeff Manza. 1997a. "The Social and Ideological Bases of Middle-Class Political Realignment in the United States, 1972 to 1992." *American Sociological Review* 62 (2): 191–208.

———. 1997b. "Class Politics and Political Change in the United States, 1952–1992." *Social Forces* 76 (2): 379–408.

Brower, Margaret Teresa, and David J. Knight. 2022. "Young Adults of Color, Urban Divestment and Political Socialization in Neighborhoods." *Politics, Groups, and Identities* 1–20. https://www.tandfonline.com/doi/pdf/10.1080/21565503.2022.2134044.

Brown, Michael K. 1999. *Race, Money, and the American Welfare State*. Ithaca, NY: Cornell University Press.

Brown-Saracino, Japonica. 2007. "Virtuous Marginality: Social Preservationists and the Selection of the Old-Timer." *Theory and Society* 36 (5): 437–68.

———. 2015. "How Places Shape Identity: The Origins of Distinctive LBQ Identities in Four Small U.S. Cities." *American Journal of Sociology* 121 (1): 1–63.

———. 2018. *How Places Make Us: Novel LBQ Identities in Four Small Cities*. Fieldwork Encounters and Discoveries. Chicago: University of Chicago Press.

Cadena, Roger Sargent, Jr. 2022. "Paradoxical Politics? Partisan Politics, Ethnoracial Ideologies, and the Assimilated Consciousnesses of Latinx Republicans." *Sociology of Race and Ethnicity* 9 (3): 295–310.

Campbell, Andrea Louise. 2012. "Policy Makes Mass Politics." *Annual Review of Political Science* 15 (1): 333–51.

Campbell, Angus, Philip E. Converse, Warren E. Miller, and Donald E. Stokes. 1960. *The American Voter*. New York: John Wiley & Sons.

Capoccia, Giovanni. 2015. "Critical Junctures and Institutional Change." In *Advances in Comparative-Historical Analysis*, ed. J. Mahoney and K. Thelen, 147–79. New York: Cambridge University Press.

Carlson, Taylor N., Marisa Abrajano, and Lisa García Bedolla. 2020. *Talking Politics: Political Discussion Networks and the New American Electorate*. New York: Oxford University Press.

Carmines, Edward G., and James A. Stimson. 1989. *Issue Evolution: Race and the Transformation of American Politics*. Princeton: Princeton University Press.

Carnes, Nicholas, and Noam Lupu. 2021. "The White Working Class and the 2016 Election." *Perspectives on Politics* 19 (1): 55–72. https://doi.org/10.1017/S1537592720001267.

Carr, Patrick J., and Maria Kefalas. 2009. *Hollowing out the Middle: The Rural Brain Drain and What It Means for America*. Boston: Beacon Press.

Castells, Manuel. 2010. *The Rise of the Network Society*. 2nd ed. The Information Age: Economy, Society, and Culture. Vol. 1. Chichester, West Sussex: Wiley-Blackwell.

Cates, Jerry R. 1983. *Insuring Inequality: Administrative Leadership in Social Security, 1935–54*. Ann Arbor: University of Michigan Press.

Chauhan, D. S. 1979. "The Political and Legal Issues of Binding Arbitration in Government." *Monthly Labor Review* 102 (9): 35–41.

Chaves, Mark. 2004. *Congregations in America*. Cambridge, MA: Harvard University Press.

Chen, Anthony S. 2007. "The Party of Lincoln and the Politics of State Fair Employment Practices Legislation in the North, 1945–1964." *American Journal of Sociology* 112 (6): 1713–74.

Cheng, Wendy. 2013. "The Changs Next Door to the Diazes: Suburban Racial Formation in Los Angeles's San Gabriel Valley." *Journal of Urban History* 39 (1): 15–35.

Claassen, Ryan L., Paul A. Djupe, Andrew R. Lewis, and Jacob R. Neiheisel. 2021. "Which Party Represents My Group? The Group Foundations of Partisan Choice and Polarization." *Political Behavior* 43 (2): 615–36.

Clark, Gordon L. 1989. *Unions and Communities under Siege: American Communities and the Crisis of Organized Labor*. Cambridge: Cambridge University Press.

Clark, Terry N., and Vincent Hoffmann-Martinot. 1998. *The New Political Culture*. Boulder, CO: Westview Press.

Clark, Terry N., and Seymour Martin Lipset. 1991. "Are Social Classes Dying?" *International Sociology* 6 (4): 397–410.

Clawson, Dan, and Mary Ann Clawson. 1999. "What Has Happened to the US Labor Movement? Union Decline and Renewal." *Annual Review of Sociology* 25 (1): 95–119.

Clemens, Elisabeth S. 2020. *Civic Gifts: Voluntarism and the Making of the American Nation-State*. Chicago: University of Chicago Press.

Clemens, Elisabeth S., and Doug Guthrie, eds. 2010. *Politics and Partnership*. Chicago: University of Chicago Press.

Cohen, Lizabeth. 1990. *Making a New Deal: Industrial Workers in Chicago, 1919–1939*. Cambridge: Cambridge University Press.

Cohen, Marty. 2008. *The Party Decides: Presidential Nominations before and after Reform*. Chicago: University of Chicago Press.

Connell, Robert W. 1972. "Political Socialization in the American Family: The Evidence Re-Examined." *Public Opinion Quarterly* 36 (3): 323–33.

Converse, Philip E. 2006. "The Nature of Belief Systems in Mass Publics (1964)." *Critical Review* 18 (1–3): 1–74.

Cook, Nancy. 2020. "Trump's Culture Wars Worked in 2016. His Aides Worry the World Has Changed." *Politico*, July 9. https://www.politico.com/news/2020/07/09/trump-culture-war-reelection-aides-354072.

Cramer, Katherine J. 2016. *The Politics of Resentment: Rural Consciousness in Wisconsin and the Rise of Scott Walker*. Chicago: University of Chicago Press.

Cummings, Scott L., and Steven A. Boutcher. 2009. "Mobilizing Local Government Law for Low-Wage Workers." *University of Chicago Legal Forum* (1): 187–246.

Darmofal, David. 2008. "The Political Geography of the New Deal Realignment." *American Politics Research* 36 (6): 934–61.

Darmofal, David, and Peter F. Nardulli. 2010. "The Dynamics of Critical Realignments: An Analysis across Time and Space." *Political Behavior* 32 (2): 255–83.

Dauber, Michele Landis. 2013. *The Sympathetic State: Disaster Relief and the Origins of the American Welfare State*. Chicago: University of Chicago Press.

De Benedictis-Kessner, Justin. 2018. "Off-Cycle and out of Office: Election Timing and the Incumbency Advantage." *Journal of Politics* 80 (1): 119–32.

De Benedictis-Kessner, Justin, and Christopher Warshaw. 2020. "Politics in Forgotten Governments: The Partisan Composition of County Legislatures and County Fiscal Policies." *Journal of Politics* 82 (2): 460–75.

De Leon, Cedric, Manali Desai, and Cihan Tuğal. 2009. "Political Articulation: Parties and the Constitution of Cleavages in the United States, India, and Turkey." *Sociological Theory* 27 (3): 193–219.

De Weerd, Marga, and Bert Klandermans. 1999. "Group Identification and Political Protest: Farmers' Protest in the Netherlands." *European Journal of Social Psychology* 29 (8): 1073–95.

Desai, Manali. 2002. "The Relative Autonomy of Party Practices: A Counterfactual Analysis of Left Party Ascendancy in Kerala, India, 1934–1940." *American Journal of Sociology* 108 (3): 616–57.

Dixon, Marc. 2020. *Heartland Blues: Labor Rights in the Industrial Midwest*. New York: Oxford University Press.

Doane, Ashley W., and Eduardo Bonilla-Silva. 2013. "Rethinking Whiteness Studies." In *White Out: The Continuing Significance of Racism*, ed. Ashley W. Doane and Eduardo Bonilla-Silva, 11–26. New York: Routledge.

Driskell, Robyn L., Larry Lyon, and Elizabeth Embry. 2008. "Civic Engagement and Religious Activities: Examining the Influence of Religious Tradition and Participation." *Sociological Spectrum* 28 (5): 578–601.

Dunning, Claire. 2022. *Nonprofit Neighborhoods: An Urban History of Inequality and the American State*. Chicago: University of Chicago Press.

Eaton, Charlie, and Margaret Weir. 2015. "The Power of Coalitions: Advancing the Public in California's Public-Private Welfare State." *Politics & Society* 43 (1): 3–32.

Edsall, Thomas B. 2016. "The Great Trump Reshuffle." *New York Times*, May 4, sec. Opinion. https://www.nytimes.com/2016/05/04/opinion/campaign-stops/the-great-trump -reshuffle.html.

Eidlin, Barry. 2018. *Labor and the Class Idea in the United States and Canada*. Cambridge: Cambridge University Press.

Elazar, Daniel J. 1975. "The American Cultural Matrix." In *The Ecology of American Political Culture: Readings*, ed. Daniel J. Elazar and Joseph Zikmund. New York: Crowell.

Ellwood, David T., and Glenn Fine. 1987. "The Impact of Right-to-Work Laws on Union Organizing." *Journal of Political Economy* 95 (2): 250–73.

Enos, Ryan D. 2017. *The Space between Us: Social Geography and Politics*. Cambridge: Cambridge University Press.

Escaleras, Monica, Dukhong Kim, and Kevin M. Wagner. 2019. "You Are Who You Think You Are: Linked Fate and Vote Choices among Latino Voters." *Politics & Policy* 47 (5): 902–30.

Esping-Anderson, Gosta. 1990. *The Three Worlds of Welfare Capitalism*. Cambridge: Polity.

Fahey, James J. 2021. "Building Populist Discourse: An Analysis of Populist Communication in American Presidential Elections, 1896–2016." *Social Science Quarterly* 102 (4): 1268–88.

Feldman, Stanley, and John Zaller. 1992. "The Political Culture of Ambivalence: Ideological Responses to the Welfare State." *American Journal of Political Science* 36 (1): 268–307.

Ferreira, Fernando, and Joseph Gyourko. 2009. "Do Political Parties Matter? Evidence from US Cities." *Quarterly Journal of Economics* 124 (1): 399–422.

Fine, Gary Alan. 2012. "Group Culture and the Interaction Order: Local Sociology on the Meso-Level." *Annual Review of Sociology* 38: 159–79.

Fink, Leon. 1983. *Workingmen's Democracy: The Knights of Labor and American Politics*. Working Class in American History. Urbana: University of Illinois Press.

Fischer, Claude S. 2008. "Paradoxes of American Individualism." *Sociological Forum* 23 (2): 363–72.

Flavin, Patrick, and Michael T. Hartney. 2015. "When Government Subsidizes Its Own: Collective Bargaining Laws as Agents of Political Mobilization." *American Journal of Political Science* 59 (4): 896–911.

Flora, Jan L., Jeff Sharp, Cornelia Flora, and Bonnie Newlon. 1997. "Entrepreneurial Social Infrastructure and Locally Initiated Economic Development in the Nonmetropolitan United States." *Sociological Quarterly* 38 (4): 623–45.

Fourcade-Gourinchas, Marion, and Sarah L. Babb. 2002. "The Rebirth of the Liberal Creed: Paths to Neoliberalism in Four Countries." *American Journal of Sociology* 108 (3): 533–79.

Fraga, Bernard L., Daniel J. Moskowitz, and Benjamin Schneer. 2021. "Partisan Alignment Increases Voter Turnout: Evidence from Redistricting." *Political Behavior*, February. https://doi.org/10.1007/s11109-021-09685-y.

Frank, Thomas. 2004. *What's the Matter with Kansas? How Conservatives Won the Heart of America*. New York: Henry Holt and Company.

Fraser, Steve, and Gary Gerstle, eds. 1989. *The Rise and Fall of the New Deal Order, 1930–1980*. Princeton: Princeton University Press.

Friedman, Gerald. 2000. "The Political Economy of Early Southern Unionism: Race, Politics, and Labor in the South, 1880–1953." *Journal of Economic History* 60 (2): 384–413.

Friedman, Thomas L. 2007. *The World Is Flat: A Brief History of the Twenty-First Century*. 1st further updated and expanded hardcover ed. New York: Farrar, Straus and Giroux.

Frymer, Paul, and Jacob M. Grumbach. 2021. "Labor Unions and White Racial Politics." *American Journal of Political Science* 65 (1): 225–40.

Fung, Archon. 2003. "Associations and Democracy: Between Theories, Hopes, and Realities." *Annual Review of Sociology* 29 (1): 515–39.

Galvin, Daniel J., and Chloe N. Thurston. 2017. "The Democrats' Misplaced Faith in Policy Feedback." *The Forum* 15 (2): 333–43.

García Bedolla, Lisa. 2005. *Fluid Borders: Latino Power, Identity, and Politics in Los Angeles*. Berkeley: University of California Press.

Gay, Claudine. 2001. "The Effect of Black Congressional Representation on Political Participation." *American Political Science Review* 95 (3): 14.

Gerber, Alan S., Gregory A. Huber, David Doherty, Conor M. Dowling, and Shang E. Ha. 2010. "Personality and Political Attitudes: Relationships across Issue Domains and Political Contexts." *American Political Science Review* 104 (1): 111–33.

Gest, Justin. 2016. *The New Minority: White Working Class Politics in an Age of Immigration and Inequality*. Oxford: Oxford University Press.

Gidron, Noam, and Peter A. Hall. 2017. "The Politics of Social Status: Economic and Cultural Roots of the Populist Right." *British Journal of Sociology* 68 (S1): S57–84.

Gieryn, Thomas F. 2000. "A Space for Place in Sociology." *Annual Review of Sociology* 26 (1): 463–96. https://doi.org/10.1146/annurev.soc.26.1.463.

Gilens, Martin. 2000. *Why Americans Hate Welfare: Race, Media, and the Politics of Antipoverty Policy*. Chicago: University of Chicago Press.

Gimpel, James, and Jason Schuknecht. 2003. *Patchwork Nation: Sectionalism and Political Change in American Politics*. Ann Arbor: University of Michigan Press.

Gordon, Linda. 1994. *Pitied but Not Entitled: Single Mothers and the History of Welfare, 1890–1935*. New York: Free Press.

Green, Donald, Bradley Palmquist, and Eric Schickler. 2002. *Partisan Hearts and Minds: Political Parties and the Social Identities of Voter*. New Haven: Yale University Press.

Griswold, Wendy, and Nathan Wright. 2004. "Cowbirds, Locals, and the Dynamic Endurance of Regionalism." *American Journal of Sociology* 109 (6): 1411–51.

Hacker, Jacob S. 2002. *The Divided Welfare State: The Battle over Public and Private Social Benefits in the United States*. New York: Cambridge University Press.

Hainmueller, Jens, and Daniel J. Hopkins. 2015. "The Hidden American Immigration Consensus: A Conjoint Analysis of Attitudes toward Immigrants." *American Journal of Political Science* 59 (3): 529–48.

Halpern-Meekin, Sarah, Kathryn Edin, Laura Tach, and Jennifer Sykes. 2015. *It's Not Like I'm Poor: How Working Families Make Ends Meet in a Post-Welfare World*. Oakland: University of California Press.

Hannan, Michael T., and John Freeman. 1987. "The Ecology of Organizational Founding: American Labor Unions, 1836–1985." *American Journal of Sociology* 92 (4): 910–43.

Hetherington, Marc J., and Jonathan Weiler. 2009. *Authoritarianism and Polarization in American Politics*. New York: Cambridge University Press.

Hill, Richard Child, and Cynthia Negrey. 1987. "Deindustrialization in the Great Lakes." *Urban Affairs Quarterly* 22 (4): 580–97.

Hindman, Matthew. 2011. "Less of the Same: Local News on the Internet." Washington, DC: FCC. https://apps.fcc.gov/edocs_public/attachmatch/DOC-307476A1.pdf.

Hirsch, Barry T., and David A. Macpherson. 2019. "Union Membership and Coverage Database from the CPS." Unionstats.com.

Hoang, Kimberly Kay. 2018. "Risky Investments: How Local and Foreign Investors Finesse Corruption-Rife Emerging Markets." *American Sociological Review* 83 (4): 657–85.

Hochschild, Arlie. 2016. *Strangers in Their Own Land: Anger and Mourning on the American Right*. New York: The New Press.

Hopkins, Daniel J. 2010. "Politicized Places: Explaining Where and When Immigrants Provoke Local Opposition." *American Political Science Review* 104 (1): 40–60.

———. 2018. *The Increasingly United States: How and Why American Political Behavior Nationalized*. Chicago: University of Chicago Press.

Hout, Michael, Clem Brooks, and Jeff Manza. 1995. "The Democratic Class Struggle in the United States, 1948–1992." *American Sociological Review* 60 (6): 805–28.

Hoyt, Lorlene, and Andre Leroux. 2007. "Voices from Forgotten Cities: Innovative Revitalization Coalitions in America's Older Smaller Cities." PolicyLink. https://www.policylink.org/resources-tools/voices-from-forgotten-cities-innovative-revitalization-coalitions-in-americas-older-small-cities.

Huber, Gregory A., and Neil Malhotra. 2017. "Political Homophily in Social Relationships: Evidence from Online Dating Behavior." *Journal of Politics* 79 (1): 269–83.

Huckfeldt, Robert, and Carol W. Kohfeld. 1989. *Race and the Decline of Class in American Politics*. Urbana: University of Illinois Press.

Huckfeldt, Robert, and John Sprague. 1987. "Networks in Context: The Social Flow of Political Information." *American Political Science Review* 81 (4): 1197–1216.

———. 1995. *Citizens, Politics and Social Communication: Information and Influence in an Election Campaign.* Cambridge: Cambridge University Press.

Huddy, Leonie. 2001. "From Social to Political Identity: A Critical Examination of Social Identity Theory." *Political Psychology* 22 (1): 127–56.

———. 2013. "From Group Identity to Political Cohesion and Commitment." In *Oxford Handbook of Political Psychology*, ed. Leonie Huddy, David O. Sears, and Jack Levy, 737–73. New York: Oxford University Press.

———. 2018. "The Group Foundations of Democratic Political Behavior." *Critical Review* 30 (1–2): 71–86.

Huddy, Leonie, Lilliana Mason, and Lene Aarøe. 2015. "Expressive Partisanship: Campaign Involvement, Political Emotion, and Partisan Identity." *American Political Science Review* 109 (1): 1–17.

Hutchings, Vincent L., and Nicholas A. Valentino. 2004. "The Centrality of Race in American Politics." *Annual Review of Political Science* 7 (1): 383–408.

Jamieson, Kathleen Hall, and Joseph N. Cappella. 2010. *Echo Chamber: Rush Limbaugh and the Conservative Media Establishment.* New York: Oxford University Press.

Jardina, Ashley. 2019. *White Identity Politics.* Cambridge Studies in Public Opinion and Political Psychology. Cambridge: Cambridge University Press.

Jerolmack, Colin, and Alexandra K. Murphy. 2019. "The Ethical Dilemmas and Social Scientific Trade-Offs of Masking in Ethnography." *Sociological Methods & Research* 48 (4): 801–27.

Johnson, Kenneth M. 2013. "Deaths Exceed Births in Record Number of US Counties." *The Carsey School of Public Policy at the Scholars' Repository.* 191. https://scholars.unh.edu/carsey/191.

Kane, John V., Lilliana Mason, and Julie Wronski. 2021. "Who's at the Party? Group Sentiments, Knowledge, and Partisan Identity." *Journal of Politics* 83 (4): 1783–99.

Karol, David. 2009. *Party Position Change in American Politics: Coalition Management.* New York: Cambridge University Press.

Katz, Eliyahu, and Paul F. Lazarsfeld. 1955. *Personal Influence: The Part Played by People in the Flow of Mass Communications.* Foundations of Communications Research. Glencoe, IL: Free Press.

Katz, Michael B. 1986. *In the Shadow of the Poorhouse: A Social History of Welfare in America.* New York: Basic Books.

Katznelson, Ira. 2005. *When Affirmative Action Was White: An Untold History of Racial Inequality in Twentieth-Century America.* New York: Norton.

Kaufman, Dan. 2015. "Scott Walker and the Fate of the Union." *New York Times*, June 12, sec. Magazine. https://www.nytimes.com/2015/06/14/magazine/scott-walker-and-the-fate-of-the-union.html.

Kaufman, Jason, and Matthew E. Kaliner. 2011. "The Re-Accomplishment of Place in Twentieth Century Vermont and New Hampshire: History Repeats Itself, until It Doesn't." *Theory and Society* 40 (2): 119–54. https://doi.org/10.1007/s11186-010-9132-2.

Kellstedt, Lyman A., John C. Green, James L. Guth, and Corwin E. Smidt. 1994. "Religious Voting Blocs in the 1992 Election: The Year of the Evangelical?" *Sociology of Religion* 55 (3): 307–26.

Key, V. O. 1949. *Southern Politics in State and Nation*. New York: Alfred A. Knopf.

Kiewiet, D. Roderick, and Michael S. Lewis-Beck. 2011. "No Man Is an Island: Self-Interest, the Public Interest, and Sociotropic Voting." *Critical Review* 23 (3): 303–19.

Kinder, Donald R., and Nathan P. Kalmoe. 2017. *Neither Liberal nor Conservative: Ideological Innocence in the American Public*. Chicago: University of Chicago Press.

Kinder, Donald R., and D. Roderick Kiewiet. 1981. "Sociotropic Politics: The American Case." *British Journal of Political Science* 11 (2): 129–61.

Klandermans, Bert, Jose Manuel Sabucedo, Mauro Rodriguez, and Marga De Weerd. 2002. "Identity Processes in Collective Action Participation: Farmers' Identity and Farmers' Protest in the Netherlands and Spain." *Political Psychology* 23 (2): 235–51.

Kusenbach, Margarethe. 2008. "A Hierarchy of Urban Communities: Observations on the Nested Character of Place." *City & Community* 7 (3): 225–49.

Kushner Gadarian, Shana, Sara Wallace Goodman, and Thomas B. Pepinsky. 2020. "Partisanship, Health Behavior, and Policy Attitudes in the Early Stages of the COVID-19 Pandemic." SSRN Scholarly Paper ID 3562796. Rochester, NY: Social Science Research Network.

Kuziemko, Ilyana, Ryan W. Buell, Taly Reich, and Michael I. Norton. 2014. "'Last-Place Aversion': Evidence and Redistributive Implications." *Quarterly Journal of Economics* 129 (1): 105–49.

Ladd, Everett Carll, Jr., and Charles D. Hadley. 1978. *Transformations of the American Party System: Political Coalitions from the New Deal to the 1970s*. New York: W. W. Norton.

Lamont, Michèle. 2000. *The Dignity of Working Men: Morality and the Boundaries of Race, Class, and Immigration*. Russell Sage Foundation Books at Harvard University Press. Cambridge, MA: Harvard University Press.

Lamont, Michèle, Bo Yun Park, and Elena Ayala-Hurtado. 2017. "Trump's Electoral Speeches and His Appeal to the American White Working Class." *British Journal of Sociology* 68: S153–80.

Lamont, Michèle, and Ann Swidler. 2014. "Methodological Pluralism and the Possibilities and Limits of Interviewing." *Qualitative Sociology* 37 (2): 153–71.

Lazarsfeld, Paul F., Bernard R. Berelson, and Hazel Gaudet. 1948. *The People's Choice: How the Voter Makes Up His Mind in a Presidential Campaign*. New York: Columbia University Press.

Lee, Caroline W., Michael McQuarrie, and Edward T. Walker. 2015. *Democratizing Inequalities: Dilemmas of the New Public Participation*. New York: New York University Press.

Lee, Taeku. 2002. *Mobilizing Public Opinion: Black Insurgency and Racial Attitudes in the Civil Rights Era*. Chicago: University of Chicago Press.

———. 2008. "Race, Immigration, and the Identity-to-Politics Link." *Annual Review of Political Science* 11 (1): 457–78.

Lee, Taeku, and Zoltan L. Hajnal. 2011. *Why Americans Don't Join the Party: Race, Immigration, and the Failure (of Political Parties) to Engage the Electorate*. Princeton: Princeton University Press.

Lenz, Gabriel S. 2009. "Learning and Opinion Change, Not Priming: Reconsidering the Priming Hypothesis." *American Journal of Political Science* 53 (4): 821–37.

Lerer, Lisa, and Reid J. Epstein. 2019. "These Are the Mistakes Democrats Don't Want to Repeat in 2020." *New York Times*, July 18, sec. U.S. https://www.nytimes.com/2019/07/18/us/politics/2020-candidates-election-2016.html.

Levendusky, Matthew. 2009. *The Partisan Sort: How Liberals Became Democrats and Conservatives Became Republicans*. Chicago: University of Chicago Press.

———. 2013. "Why Do Partisan Media Polarize Viewers?" *American Journal of Political Science* 57 (3): 611–23.

Levine, Jeremy R. 2016. "The Privatization of Political Representation: Community-Based Organizations as Nonelected Neighborhood Representatives." *American Sociological Review* 81 (6): 1251–75.

———. 2017. "The Paradox of Community Power: Cultural Processes and Elite Authority in Participatory Governance." *Social Forces* 95 (3): 1155–79.

———. 2021. *Constructing Community: Urban Governance, Development, and Inequality in Boston*. Princeton: Princeton University Press.

Lewis, Amanda E. 2004. "'What Group?' Studying Whites and Whiteness in the Era of 'Color-Blindness.'" *Sociological Theory* 22 (4): 623–46.

Lewis, Andrew R. 2019. "The Transformation of the Christian Right's Moral Politics." *The Forum* 17 (1): 25–44.

Lichter, Daniel T., and David L. Brown. 2011. "Rural America in an Urban Society: Changing Spatial and Social Boundaries." *Annual Review of Sociology* 37 (1): 565–92.

Lipset, Seymour Martin. 1960. *Political Man: The Social Bases of Politics*. Garden City, NY: Doubleday.

———. 1963. *The First New Nation: The United States in Historical and Comparative Perspective*. New York: Basic Books.

Lizardo, Omar. 2017. "Improving Cultural Analysis: Considering Personal Culture in Its Declarative and Nondeclarative Modes." *American Sociological Review* 82 (1): 88–115.

Lizardo, Omar, and Michael Strand. 2010. "Skills, Toolkits, Contexts and Institutions: Clarifying the Relationship between Different Approaches to Cognition in Cultural Sociology." *Poetics* 38 (2): 205–28.

Lobao, Linda. 2004. "Continuity and Change in Place Stratification: Spatial Inequality and Middle-Range Territorial Units." *Rural Sociology* 69 (1): 1–30.

Lobao, Linda, Lazarus Adua, and Gregory Hooks. 2014. "Privatization, Business Attraction, and Social Services across the United States: Local Governments' Use of Market-Oriented, Neoliberal Policies in the Post-2000 Period." *Social Problems* 61 (4): 644–72.

Loewen, James. 2005. *Sundown Towns: A Hidden Dimension of American Racism*. New York: The New Press.

Loveman, Mara, and Jeronimo O. Muniz. 2007. "How Puerto Rico Became White: Boundary Dynamics and Intercensus Racial Reclassification." *American Sociological Review* 72 (6): 915–39.

Low, Jacqueline. 2019. "A Pragmatic Definition of the Concept of Theoretical Saturation." *Sociological Focus* 52 (2): 131–39. https://doi.org/10.1080/00380237.2018.1544514.

Lubell, Mark, Richard C. Feiock, and Edgar E. Ramirez De La Cruz. 2009. "Local Institutions and the Politics of Urban Growth." *American Journal of Political Science* 53 (3): 649–65.

Lynd, Staughton. 1996. *"We Are All Leaders": The Alternative Unionism of the Early 1930s*. The Working Class in American History. Urbana: University of Illinois Press.

MacDonald, James M., Robert Hoppe, and Doris Newton. 2018. "Three Decades of Consolidation in U.S. Agriculture." Economic Information Bulletin no. 189. Washington, DC: United States Department of Agriculture.

Mahoney, James. 2000. "Path Dependence in Historical Sociology." *Theory and Society* 29 (4): 507–48.

Margolis, Michele F. 2018. *From Politics to the Pews: How Partisanship and the Political Environment Shape Religious Identity*. Chicago: University of Chicago Press.

Margolis, Michele F., and Michael W. Sances. 2017. "Partisan Differences in Nonpartisan Activity: The Case of Charitable Giving." *Political Behavior* 39: 839–64.

Martin, John Levi, and Matthew Desmond. 2010. "Political Position and Social Knowledge 1." *Sociological Forum* 25 (1): 1–26.

Marwell, Nicole P. 2004. "Privatizing the Welfare State: Nonprofit Community-Based Organizations as Political Actors." *American Sociological Review* 69 (2): 265–91.

———. 2007. *Bargaining for Brooklyn: Community Organizations in the Entrepreneurial City*. Chicago: University of Chicago Press.

Marwell, Nicole P., and Aaron Gullickson. 2013. "Inequality in the Spatial Allocation of Social Services: Government Contracts to Nonprofit Organizations in New York City." *Social Service Review* 87 (2): 319–53.

Marwell, Nicole P., and Shannon L. Morrissey. 2020. "Organizations and the Governance of Urban Poverty." *Annual Review of Sociology* 46 (1): 233–50.

Mason, Lilliana. 2016. "A Cross-Cutting Calm: How Social Sorting Drives Affective Polarization." *Public Opinion Quarterly* 80 (S1): 351–77.

Mason, Lilliana, and Julie Wronski. 2018. "One Tribe to Bind Them All: How Our Social Group Attachments Strengthen Partisanship." *Political Psychology* 39 (S1): 257–77. https://doi.org/10.1111/pops.12485.

Mattiuzzi, Elizabeth, and Margaret Weir. 2020. "Governing the New Geography of Poverty in Metropolitan America." *Urban Affairs Review* 56 (4): 1086–1131.

Mayer, Gerald. 2004. "Union Membership Trends in the United States." Washington, DC: Congressional Research Service.

Mayrl, Damon, and Sarah Quinn. 2016. "Defining the State from within: Boundaries, Schemas, and Associational Policymaking." *Sociological Theory* 34 (1): 1–26.

McConnell, Christopher, Yotam Margalit, Neil Malhotra, and Matthew Levendusky. 2018. "The Economic Consequences of Partisanship in a Polarized Era." *American Journal of Political Science* 62 (1): 5–18.

McDonnell, Terence E., Christopher A. Bail, and Iddo Tavory. 2017. "A Theory of Resonance." *Sociological Theory* 35 (1): 1–14.

McGirr, Lisa. 2015. *Suburban Warriors: The Origins of the New American Right*. Princeton: Princeton University Press.

McLaughlin, Diane K., and Alisha J. Coleman-Jensen. 2008. "Nonstandard Employment in the Nonmetropolitan United States." *Rural Sociology* 73 (4): 631–59.

McQuarrie, Michael. 2010. "Nonprofits and the Reconstruction of Urban Governance: Housing Production and Community Development in Cleveland, 1975–2005." In *Politics and Partnership*, ed. Elisabeth S. Clemens and Doug Guthrie, 237–68. Chicago: University of Chicago Press.

———. 2013. "No Contest: Participatory Technologies and the Transformation of Urban Authority." *Public Culture* 25 (1: 69): 143–75.

McQuarrie, Michael, and Nicole P. Marwell. 2009. "The Missing Organizational Dimension in Urban Sociology." *City & Community* 8 (3): 247–68.

McVeigh, Rory, David Cunningham, and Justin Farrell. 2014. "Political Polarization as a Social Movement Outcome: 1960s Klan Activism and Its Enduring Impact on Political Realignment in Southern Counties, 1960 to 2000." *American Sociological Review* 79 (6): 1144–71.

Mellow, Nicole. 2008. *The State of Disunion: Regional Sources of Modern American Partisanship.* Baltimore: Johns Hopkins University Press.

Mettler, Suzanne. 2011. *The Submerged State: How Invisible Government Policies Undermine American Democracy.* Chicago Studies in American Politics. Chicago: University of Chicago Press.

———. 2018. *The Government-Citizen Disconnect.* New York: Russell Sage Foundation.

Metzl, Jonathan. 2018. *Dying of Whiteness.* New York: Basic Books.

Michener, Jamila. 2018. *Fragmented Democracy: Medicaid, Federalism, and Unequal Politics.* New York: Cambridge University Press.

Minkoff, Debra C. 1997. "Producing Social Capital: National Social Movements and Civil Society." *American Behavioral Scientist* 40 (5): 606–19.

Molotch, Harvey, William Freudenburg, and Krista E. Paulsen. 2000. "History Repeats Itself, but How? City Character, Urban Tradition, and the Accomplishment of Place." *American Sociological Review* 65 (6): 791–823.

Montgomery, David. 1987. *The Fall of the House of Labor: The Workplace, the State, and American Labor Activism, 1865–1925.* Cambridge: Cambridge University Press.

Mora, G. Cristina. 2014. *Making Hispanics: How Activists, Bureaucrats, and Media Constructed a New American.* Chicago: University of Chicago Press.

Morgan, Kimberly J., and Andrea Louise Campbell. 2011. *The Delegated Welfare State: Medicare, Markets, and the Governance of Social Policy.* Oxford Studies in Postwar American Political Development. New York: Oxford University Press.

Morgan, Stephen L., and Jiwon Lee. 2017. "Social Class and Party Identification during the Clinton, Bush, and Obama Presidencies." *Sociological Science* 4 (August): 394–423.

Morton, Lois W., Yu-Che Chen, and Ricardo S. Morse. 2008. "Small Town Civic Structure and Interlocal Collaboration for Public Services." *City & Community* 7 (1): 45–60.

Moskowitz, Daniel J. 2021. "Local News, Information, and the Nationalization of U.S. Elections." *American Political Science Review* 115 (1): 114–29.

Mudge, Stephanie L. 2018. *Leftism Reinvented: Western Parties from Socialism to Neoliberalism.* Cambridge, MA: Harvard University Press.

Mutz, Diana C. 2002. "The Consequences of Cross-Cutting Networks for Political Participation." *American Journal of Political Science* 46 (4): 838–55. https://doi.org/10.2307/3088437.

———. 2018. "Status Threat, Not Economic Hardship, Explains the 2016 Presidential Vote." *Proceedings of the National Academy of Sciences* 115 (19): E4330–39.

Nardulli, Peter F. 1995. "The Concept of a Critical Realignment, Electoral Behavior, and Political Change." *American Political Science Review* 89 (1): 10–22.

Nelson, Laura K. 2021. "Cycles of Conflict, a Century of Continuity: The Impact of Persistent Place-Based Political Logics on Social Movement Strategy." *American Journal of Sociology* 127 (1): 1–59.

Noel, Hans. 2013. *Political Ideologies and Political Parties in America.* Cambridge Studies in Public Opinion and Political Psychology. New York: Cambridge University Press.

Oliver, J. Eric, and Shang E. Ha. 2007. "Vote Choice in Suburban Elections." *American Political Science Review* 101 (3): 393–408.

Olzak, Susan. 1989. "Labor Unrest, Immigration, and Ethnic Conflict in Urban America, 1880–1914." *American Journal of Sociology* 94 (6): 1303–33.

Pacewicz, Josh. 2016. *Partisans and Partners: The Politics of the Post-Keynesian Society*. Chicago: University of Chicago Press.

Page, Brian, and Richard Walker. 1991. "From Settlement to Fordism: The Agro-Industrial Revolution in the American Midwest." *Economic Geography* 67 (4): 281–315.

Parker, Jeffrey Nathaniel, and Stephanie Ternullo. 2022. "Gentrifiers Evading Stigma: Social Integrationists in the Neighborhood of the Future." *Social Problems*. https://academic.oup .com/socpro/advance-article-abstract/doi/10.1093/socpro/spac026/6587368.

Paschel, Tianna S. 2016. *Becoming Black Political Subjects: Movements and Ethno-Racial Rights in Colombia and Brazil*. Princeton: Princeton University Press.

Pattillo-McCoy, Mary. 1998. "Church Culture as a Strategy of Action in the Black Community." *American Sociological Review* 63 (6): 767–84.

Paulsen, Krista E. 2004. "Making Character Concrete: Empirical Strategies for Studying Place Distinction." *City & Community* 3 (3): 243–62. https://doi.org/10.1111/j.1535-6841.2004 .00080.x.

Paxton, Pamela. 2002. "Social Capital and Democracy: An Interdependent Relationship." *American Sociological Review* 67 (2): 254–77.

———. 2007. "Association Memberships and Generalized Trust: A Multilevel Model across 31 Countries." *Social Forces* 86 (1): 47–76.

Perlman, Selig. 1966. *A Theory of the Labor Movement*. Reprints of Economic Classics. New York: A. M. Kelley.

Petrocik, John R. 1981. *Party Coalitions: Realignments and the Decline of the New Deal Party System*. Chicago: University of Chicago Press.

Phillips, Kevin. 1969. *The Emerging Republican Majority*. The James Madison Library in American Politics Edition. Princeton: Princeton University Press.

Pierre, Jon. 1999. "Models of Urban Governance: The Institutional Dimension of Urban Politics." *Urban Affairs Review* 34 (3): 372–96.

———. 2005. "Comparative Urban Governance: Uncovering Complex Causalities." *Urban Affairs Review* 40 (4): 446–62.

Pierson, Paul. 1992. "When Effect Becomes Cause: Policy Feedback and Political Change." *World Politics* 45: 595.

———. 2000. "Increasing Returns, Path Dependence, and the Study of Politics." *American Political Science Review* 94 (2): 251–67.

Pierson, Paul, and Theda Skocpol. 2007. *The Transformation of American Politics: Activist Government and the Rise of Conservatism*. Princeton: Princeton University Press.

Polletta, Francesca. 1998. "Contending Stories: Narrative in Social Movements." *Qualitative Sociology* 21 (4): 419–46.

Polletta, Francesca, and James M. Jasper. 2001. "Collective Identity and Social Movements." *Annual Review of Sociology* 27 (1): 283–305. https://doi.org/10.1146/annurev.soc.27.1.283.

Polsby, Nelson W., and Aaron B. Wildavsky. 1988. *Presidential Elections: Contemporary Strategies of American Electoral Politics*. 7th ed. New York: Free Press.

Prior, Markus. 2013. "Media and Political Polarization." *Annual Review of Political Science* 16 (1): 101–27.

Pugh, Allison J. 2013. "What Good Are Interviews for Thinking about Culture? Demystifying Interpretive Analysis." *American Journal of Cultural Sociology* 1 (1): 42–68.

Putnam, Robert D. 2000. *Bowling Alone: The Collapse and Revival of American Community*. New York: Simon and Schuster.

Putnam, Robert, and David Campbell. 2010. *American Grace: How Religion Divides and Unites Us*. New York: Simon and Schuster.

Putnam, Robert D., Robert Leonardi, and Raffaella Y. Nanetti. 1993. *Making Democracy Work: Civic Traditions in Modern Italy*. Princeton: Princeton University Press.

"Real Wage Trends, 1979 to 2019." 2020. Washington, DC: Congressional Research Service.

Reny, Tyler T., Loren Collingwood, and Ali A. Valenzuela. 2019. "Vote Switching in the 2016 Election: How Racial and Immigration Attitudes, Not Economics, Explain Shifts in White Voting." *Public Opinion Quarterly* 83 (1): 91–113. https://doi.org/10.1093/poq/nfz011.

Reyes, Victoria. 2020. "Ethnographic Toolkit: Strategic Positionality and Researchers' Visible and Invisible Tools in Field Research." *Ethnography* 21 (2): 220–40.

Riley, Dylan. 2005. "Civic Associations and Authoritarian Regimes in Interwar Europe: Italy and Spain in Comparative Perspective." *American Sociological Review* 70 (2): 288–310.

Robison, Joshua, Randy T. Stevenson, James N. Druckman, Simon Jackman, Jonathan N. Katz, and Lynn Vavreck. 2018. "An Audit of Political Behavior Research." *SAGE Open* 8 (3): 1–14.

Rodden, Jonathan. 2017. "'Red' America Is an Illusion: Postindustrial Towns Go for Democrats." *Washington Post*, February 14. https://www.washingtonpost.com/news/monkey-cage/wp/2017/02/14/red-america-is-an-illusion-postindustrial-towns-go-for-democrats-heres-the-data/.

———. 2019. *Why Cities Lose: The Deep Roots of the Urban-Rural Political Divide*. New York: Basic Books.

Rodgers, Daniel T. 2011. *Age of Fracture*. Cambridge, MA: Belknap Press of Harvard University Press.

Rogers, Reuel Reuben. 2006. *Afro-Caribbean Immigrants and the Politics of Incorporation: Ethnicity, Exception, or Exit*. Cambridge: Cambridge University Press.

Rosenfeld, Jake. 2014. *What Unions No Longer Do*. Cambridge, MA: Harvard University Press.

Rothrock, Laura Ann. 2008. "Business Improvement Districts: An Effective Revitalization Tool for Massachusetts' Forgotten Cities?" PhD thesis, Massachusetts Institute of Technology.

Sachs, Benjamin I. 2011. "Despite Preemption: Making Labor Law in Cities and States." *Harvard Law Review* 124 (5): 1153–1224.

Safford, Sean. 2009. *Why the Garden Club Couldn't Save Youngstown: The Transformation of the Rust Belt*. Cambridge, MA: Harvard University Press.

Schaffner, Brian F., Matthew MacWilliams, and Tatishe Nteta. 2018. "Understanding White Polarization in the 2016 Vote for President: The Sobering Role of Racism and Sexism." *Political Science Quarterly* 133 (1): 9–34.

Schickler, Eric. 2016. *Racial Realignment: The Transformation of American Liberalism, 1932–1965*. Princeton: Princeton University Press.

Schlozman, Daniel. 2015. *When Movements Anchor Parties: Electoral Alignments in American History*. Princeton Studies in American Politics. Princeton: Princeton University Press.

Seligson, Amber L. 1999. "Civic Association and Democratic Participation in Central America: A Test of the Putnam Thesis." *Comparative Political Studies* 32 (3): 342–62.

Sewell, William H., Jr. 1992. "A Theory of Structure: Duality, Agency, and Transformation." *American Journal of Sociology* 98 (1): 1–29.

Shapiro, Stanley. 1985. "'Hand and Brain': The Farmer-Labor Party of 1920." *Labor History* 26 (3): 405–22.

Sharkey, Patrick, and Jacob W. Faber. 2014. "Where, When, Why, and for Whom Do Residential Contexts Matter? Moving Away from the Dichotomous Understanding of Neighborhood Effects." *Annual Review of Sociology* 40 (1): 559–79.

Shearer, Elisa. 2018. "Social Media Outpaces Print Newspapers in the U.S. as a News Source." *Pew Research Center* (blog). December 10. https://www.pewresearch.org/fact-tank/2018 /12/10/social-media-outpaces-print-newspapers-in-the-u-s-as-a-news-source/.

Silva, Jennifer M. 2019. *We're Still Here: Pain and Politics in the Heart of America*. New York: Oxford University Press.

Simes, Jessica T. 2021. *Punishing Places: The Geography of Mass Imprisonment*. Oakland: University of California Press.

Simon, Bernd, and P. G. Klandermans. 2001. "Toward a Social Psychological Analysis of Politicized Collective Identity: Conceptualization, Antecedents and Consequences." *American Psychologist* 56: 319–31.

Skocpol, Theda. 2003. *Diminished Democracy: From Membership to Management in American Civic Life*. Vol. 8. Julian J. Rothbaum Distinguished Lecture Series. Norman: University of Oklahoma Press.

Small, Mario Luis. 2004. *Villa Victoria: The Transformation of Social Capital in a Boston Barrio*. Chicago: University of Chicago Press.

———. 2009. "How Many Cases Do I Need?' On Science and the Logic of Case Selection in Field-Based Research." *Ethnography* 10 (1): 5–38.

———. 2011. "How to Conduct a Mixed Methods Study: Recent Trends in a Rapidly Growing Literature." *Annual Review of Sociology* 37 (1): 57–86. https://doi.org/10.1146/annurev.soc .012809.102657.

Smith, Steven Rathgeb, and Michael Lipsky. 1993. *Nonprofits for Hire: The Welfare State in the Age of Contracting*. Cambridge, MA: Harvard University Press.

Somers, Margaret R., and Fred Block. 2005. "From Poverty to Perversity: Ideas, Markets, and Institutions over 200 Years of Welfare Debate." *American Sociological Review* 70 (2): 260–87.

Staerklé, Christian, Tiina Likki, and Régis Scheidegger. 2012. "Contested Welfare States: Welfare Attitudes in Europe and Beyond." In *A Normative Approach to Welfare Attitudes*, 82–120. Stanford: Stanford University Press.

Steensland, Brian. 2006. "Cultural Categories and the American Welfare State: The Case of Guaranteed Income Policy." *American Journal of Sociology* 111 (5): 1273–1326.

Steensland, Brian, Lynn D. Robinson, W. Bradford Wilcox, Jerry Z. Park, Mark D. Regnerus, and Robert D. Woodberry. 2000. "The Measure of American Religion: Toward Improving the State of the Art." *Social Forces* 79 (1): 291–318.

Stepan-Norris, Judith, and Maurice Zeitlin. 1989. "'Who Gets the Bird?' Or, How the Communists Won Power and Trust in America's Unions: The Relative Autonomy of Intraclass Political Struggles." *American Sociological Review* 54 (4): 503–23.

———. 2003. *Left Out: Reds and America's Industrial Unions*. Cambridge: Cambridge University Press.

Strand, Michael, and Omar Lizardo. 2015. "Beyond World Images: Belief as Embodied Action in the World." *Sociological Theory* 33 (1): 44–70.

Svallfors, Stefan. 2007. *The Political Sociology of the Welfare State: Institutions, Social Cleavages, and Orientations*. Stanford: Stanford University Press.

Swidler, Ann. 1986. "Culture in Action: Symbols and Strategies." *American Sociological Review* 51 (2): 273–86.

———. 2001. "What Anchors Cultural Practices." in *The Practice Turn in Contemporary Theory.*, ed. Theodore R. Schatzki, Karin Knorr Cetina, and Eike von Savigny, 74–92. London: Routledge.

———. 2008. "Comment on Stephen Vaisey's 'Socrates, Skinner, and Aristotle: Three Ways of Thinking about Culture in Action.'" *Sociological Forum* 23 (2): 614–18.

Taber, Charles S., and Milton Lodge. 2006. "Motivated Skepticism in the Evaluation of Political Beliefs." *American Journal of Political Science* 50 (3): 755–69.

Tajfel, Henri. 1981. *Human Groups and Social Categories: Studies in Social Psychology*. Cambridge: Cambridge University Press.

Tajfel, Henri, and John C. Turner. 1979. "An Integrative Theory of Intergroup Conflict." In *The Social Psychology of Intergroup Relations*, ed. W. G. Austin and S. Worchel, 33–37. Monterey, CA: Brooks/Cole.

Tausanovitch, Chris, and Christopher Warshaw. 2014. "Representation in Municipal Government." *American Political Science Review* 108 (3): 605–41.

Tavory, Iddo. 2016. *Summoned: Identification and Religious Life in a Jewish Neighborhood*. Chicago: University of Chicago Press.

Teixeira, Ruy. 2022. "Democrats' Long Goodbye to the Working Class." *The Atlantic*, November 6. https://www.theatlantic.com/ideas/archive/2022/11/democrats-long-goodbye-to -the-working-class/672016/.

Terbeek, Calvin. 2021. "'Clocks Must Always Be Turned Back': *Brown v. Board of Education* and the Racial Origins of Constitutional Originalism." *American Political Science Review* 115 (3): 821–34.

Ternullo, Stephanie. 2022a. "The Electoral Effects of Social Policy: Expanding Old-Age Assistance, 1932–1940." *Journal of Politics* 84 (1): 226–41.

———. 2022b. "'I'm Not Sure What to Believe': Media Distrust and Opinion Formation during the COVID-19 Pandemic." *American Political Science Review* 116 (3): 1096–1109.

Tesler, Michael. 2012. "The Spillover of Racialization into Health Care: How President Obama Polarized Public Opinion by Racial Attitudes and Race." *American Journal of Political Science* 56 (3): 690–704.

———. 2016. *Post-Racial or Most-Racial?: Race and Politics in the Obama Era*. Chicago: University of Chicago Press.

Thelen, Kathleen. 1999. "Historical Institutionalism in Comparative Politics." *Annual Review of Political Science* 2 (1): 369–404.

Thompson, Alex. 2020. "Trump's Campaign Knocks on a Million Doors a Week; Biden's Knocks on Zero." *Politico*, August 4. https://www.politico.com/news/2020/08/04/trump-joe -biden-campaign-door-knockers-391454.

Timmermans, Stefan, and Iddo Tavory. 2012. "Theory Construction in Qualitative Research: From Grounded Theory to Abductive Analysis." *Sociological Theory* 30 (3): 167–86.

Trounstine, Jessica. 2011. "Evidence of a Local Incumbency Advantage." *Legislative Studies Quarterly* 36 (2): 255–80.

Tuan, Yi-Fu. 1975. "Place: An Experiential Perspective." *Geographical Review* 65 (2): 151–65.

Turner, John C., Michael A. Hogg, Penelope J. Oakes, Stephen D. Reicher, and Margaret S. Wetherell. 1987. *Rediscovering the Social Group: A Self-Categorization Theory*. Cambridge, MA: Basil Blackwell.

van Stekelenburg, Jacquelien, and Bert Klandermans. 2013. "The Social Psychology of Protest." *Current Sociology* 61 (5–6): 886–905.

Verba, Sidney, Kay Lehman Schlozman, and Henry E. Brady. 1995. *Voice and Equality: Civic Voluntarism in American Politics*. Cambridge, MA: Harvard University Press.

Voss, Kim. 1993. *The Making of American Exceptionalism: The Knights of Labor and Class Formation in the Nineteenth Century*. Ithaca: Cornell University Press.

Wallace, Sophia J., Chris Zepeda-Millán, and Michael Jones-Correa. 2014. "Spatial and Temporal Proximity: Examining the Effects of Protests on Political Attitudes." *American Journal of Political Science* 58 (2): 433–48.

Warner, Mildred. 2003. "Competition, Cooperation and Local Governance." In *Challenges for Rural America in the Twenty-First Century*, ed. David L. Brown and Louis E. Swanson. University Park: Penn State University Press.

Warner, Mildred, and Amir Hefetz. 2003. "Rural-Urban Differences in Privatization: Limits to the Competitive State." *Environment and Planning C: Government and Policy* 21 (5): 703–18.

Warshaw, Christopher. 2019. "Local Elections and Representation in the United States." *Annual Review of Political Science* 22 (1): 461–79.

Waters, Malcolm, and Jan Pakulski. 1996. *The Death of Class*. Thousand Oaks, CA: Sage.

Weise, Karen, and Michael Corkery. 2021. "Amazon Workers Vote Down Union Drive at Alabama Warehouse." *New York Times*, April 9, sec. Technology. https://www.nytimes.com/2021/04/09/technology/amazon-defeats-union.html.

Weiss, Robert Stuart. 1994. *Learning from Strangers: The Art and Method of Qualitative Interview Studies*. New York: Free Press.

Western, Bruce. 1997. *Between Class and Market: Postwar Unionization in the Capitalist Democracies*. Princeton: Princeton University Press.

Western, Bruce, and Jake Rosenfeld. 2011. "Unions, Norms, and the Rise in US Wage Inequality." *American Sociological Review* 76 (4): 513–37.

Wetts, Rachel, and Robb Willer. 2018. "Privilege on the Precipice: Perceived Racial Status Threats Lead White Americans to Oppose Welfare Programs." *Social Forces* 97 (2): 793–822.

White, Ismail K. 2007. "When Race Matters and When It Doesn't: Racial Group Differences in Response to Racial Cues." *American Political Science Review* 101 (2): 339–54.

Williams, Daniel K. 2016. *Defenders of the Unborn: The Pro-Life Movement before Roe v. Wade*. Oxford: Oxford University Press.

Wilson, William J. 1987. *The Truly Disadvantaged: The Inner City, the Underclass, and Public Policy*. Chicago: University of Chicago Press.

Witovsky, Benny. 2021. "National Politics, Local Fissures: A Closer Look at the Rural-Urban Divide." Presented at the American Sociological Association Annual Meeting.

Wong, Cara. 2010. *Boundaries of Obligation in American Politics: Geographic, National, and Racial Communities*. Cambridge: Cambridge University Press.

Woodard, Komozi, and Jeanne Theoharis. 2019. *The Strange Careers of the Jim Crow North: Segregation and Struggle outside of the South.* New York: New York University Press.

Wright, Rachel A., and Hilary Schaffer Boudet. 2012. "To Act or Not to Act: Context, Capability, and Community Response to Environmental Risk." *American Journal of Sociology* 118 (3): 728–77.

Wuthnow, Robert. 2018. *The Left Behind: Decline and Rage in Rural America.* Princeton: Princeton University Press.

Zaller, John. 1992. *The Nature and Origins of Mass Opinion.* Cambridge: Cambridge University Press.

INDEX

Note: *italic* pages refer to figures and tables

A NOTE ON THE TYPE

This book has been composed in Arno, an Old-style serif typeface in the classic Venetian tradition, designed by Robert Slimbach at Adobe.

GPSR Authorized Representative: Easy Access System Europe - Mustamäe tee 50, 10621 Tallinn, Estonia, gpsr.requests@easproject.com

www.ingramcontent.com/pod-product-compliance
Lightning Source LLC
Chambersburg PA
CBHW020843270326
41928CB00006B/521